Effective Marketing

McGRAW-HILL LIBRARY OF

Second Edition

BUSINESS MANAGEMENT

Effective

Marketing

McGRAW-HILL BOOK COMPANY, INC.

New York Toronto London 1949

EFFECTIVE MARKETING

v

THE MAPLE PRESS COMPANY, YORK, PA.

CONTENTS

v

EFFECTIVE MARKETING

I

The Seven Marketing Principles

T. O. M. Sopwith's "Endeavour" was probably the fastest and best equipped of the long line of distinguished British yachts ever to challenge for the America's cup. Yet she lacked one of the most important sails a modern yacht can carry—a Genoa jib! She had to borrow one from the "Yankee," and, before the series was over, have one made here in the United States.

It was an astonishing omission, one of those unexplainable mental lapses the newspapers write about; and yet these omissions of essentials in every phase of human activity are almost the rule rather than the exception. They are responsible for most failures. They trap criminals. They wreck trains on land and ships at sea. They change the course of history.

In marketing, too, the lack of a "Genoa jib" all too frequently turns success into failure. To market a product profitably, certain major objectives must be clearly defined. To attain these objectives, basic marketing principles, functional in character, must be followed as faithfully as the experienced mariner follows the chart of his course. Neglect or failure to understand the importance of these principles and their interdependence will seriously handicap or completely wreck anyone who attempts to sail to victory in the marketing race.

The business world never stands still. From year to year and generation to generation new inventions, new fads, new fancies, new ideas, and the impact of world-wide disturbances take their toll of established custom. Constant change is the law of life, as any museum will attest. Big boy dinosaur was great in his day, but he has long since been the victim of his own wheel base. He demonstrated the utter futility and uselessness of mere size, and then he went away!

Similarly, our museum of business is filled with warnings to the wise—relics of vanished industries and bygone business methods that failed to adjust themselves to shifting environment. There we find the whipsocket manufacturer who did not hear the horn of the approaching automobile; the retail storekeeper who went down before the advance of the enlightened merchandising methods of the chains— and all the rest of that unhappy crew of business mariners, betrayed on their marketing voyage by unheeded tides of new inventions, unforeseen fashions, shifting conditions, changing buying tastes.

One of the most important of the changes in the business world is the shift from the early emphasis placed on production to a growing recognition of the need for more efficient distribution. The case of the corner grocer illustrates the point. Originally he was a "storekeeper" and he was just that—the keeper of a place where goods were stored. Today the alert retailer finds it necessary to take a broader view of his place in the marketing picture. To survive in the face of the new competition, the former storekeeper must now adopt the methods of his more progressive competitors, accept new concepts of his economic relationships, and become a real merchant.

SELL TO SURVIVE

The kaleidoscopic changes which characterize modern business have not altered the fact that the ability to sell profitably is the cornerstone of any sound venture that hopes to survive and progress in a profit-and-loss economy.

Laborsaving devices and the availability of large blocks of capital have made possible such a flood of goods that every known market is being combed over and new markets are eagerly sought. Products must be sold. More and more energy must be devoted to the task. All this sales activity is used to speed the flow of products from the factory, the warehouse, and the retail store into the customer's hands.

This increased sales effort, originally limited to a relatively few lines, is speeding up selling in all lines so that the merchandiser finds himself a member of a crowd. Furthermore, if the crowd begins to run, he has to run also, or be trampled on or left behind.

It is an inescapable conclusion that every industry must market its goods more efficiently if it is to survive. The American public has money to spend, more money than have the buyers in any other market, but there are a thousand and one amusing, flattering, thrilling products crying for the consumer's attention and his pocketbook. Naturally the consumer buys first from those concerns that sell him best. And then, after he has paid for the new car and the wife's new dress and the golf club membership and the vacation trip, if there is any money left, the consumer may spend it for the less exciting products of the less aggressive merchandisers.

ORGANIZED COMMON SENSE

Efficient distribution is vital to every business. And the principles of effective marketing, which underly efficient distribution, are not so very different whether one is selling sun lamps or sun glasses, straw hats or roofing, automobiles or atomizers.

What are these marketing principles? When you analyze them as put into operation by the most successful corporations, you find they are actually the large-scale, systematic application of ordinary horse sense—for the science of marketing is nothing but organized, trained common sense!

The most successful marketing organizations set up these major objectives, at which they consistently aim and which they never overlook:

> To sell at a profit
> To sell more goods to present customers
> To sell goods to new customers
> To develop new markets and expand old ones
> To improve present products and develop new products

The executives of the successful, going business, large or small, give their thought, time, and energy every working day to the attainment of these major marketing objectives. All five are vitally important and interrelated. No one of these objectives can be long ignored or even temporarily neglected if maximum marketing success is to be achieved.

These objectives are clear and simple. Any businessman understands them and their implications. It has remained for modern business leaders to work out methods for their accomplishment whereby minimum expenditures of money and time assure maximum returns of sales and profits.

It is in the analysis of these principles of effective marketing, thus developed and put into use, that the progressive merchandiser finds the most valuable ground for planning and application.

There is nothing in these marketing methods not easily available to any sales organization and there is no sales organization, no matter how small, which cannot profit by their use.

PLAN FOR SALES

When you see a football team march steadily down the field toward the goal, you can be sure that behind it is a well-organized plan to win. The quarterback doesn't call his plays hit or miss; he plans his attack. He calls one play to set the stage for the second; the second to lead into the third—until the ball is over the line. And his plan always permits him to be an opportunist and take advantage of the unforeseen breaks in the game to score a quick touchdown.

Marketing is no different from football or any other kind of competition. Careful, well-laid plans invariably precede the winning plays in the profitable marketing of a product or service.

Sound planning is essential to marketing success.

In a complex procedure including so many ramifications as modern merchandising, it is sheer necessity. Sound planning leads to a clarification of the factors involved and their classification under logical groupings. It correlates all the details so that the final objective, the production of sales at a profit, is more easily attainable.

Marketing operations, for the purpose of simplification and the planning of activities, are grouped under the following major headings:

1. Getting the Product Right
2. Organizing for Selling
3. Knowing Your Market
4. Understanding the Customer's Viewpoint
5. Keeping Ahead of the Parade
6. Planning and Working Your Plan
7. Promotion Programs

GETTING THE PRODUCT RIGHT

The first step in the building of a sound marketing program is the availability and value of a good, salable product or service. No marketing operation can hope to build a permanent success unless the product or service sold satisfies a definite need and performs a desired service satisfactorily.

The basic objective of all marketing and advertising activity is the interpretation of the inherent values in a product rather than an attempt to build values into the product which do not exist. The strongest sales statement and the best advertising is to tell something about the product that is of real interest to the buyer, which he can prove for himself.

For sound commercial progress it is also essential that the product or service sold be priced equitably so that its sale is a profitable one to everyone concerned—the manufacturer, the seller, the workers, and the consumers.

Boiled down into a simple marketing principle, these facts might be expressed as follows:

> *Effective marketing is based on getting the product right, keeping it so, and pricing it equitably.*

ORGANIZING FOR SELLING

The second step in the development of an effective marketing program is the creation of an organization designed primarily to smooth the way for and make profitable selling possible. All the varied departments of the business—manufacturing, finance, accounting, credit, warehousing, purchasing, traffic, and sales—are geared together to accomplish the organization's major activity, the sale of goods.

This is simple, even elementary. Yet there are far too many business organizations badly crippled in their sales efficiency by faulty organization of their important pre-selling or post-selling business functions. The great need is for proper perspective—to see how important each function is and to give it corresponding attention, no more and no less than it deserves. It is easy to allow personal whims or prejudice or the pressure of relatively unimportant details to interfere with this clear view. All too frequently we are too close to our jobs to see the broad problem clearly, with resultant disorganization and inefficiency.

The progressive marketer concentrates all his energies, bending them to the all-important task of getting goods sold. He has a well-balanced supporting organization, designed to lighten the load of the sales force and smooth the way for efficient selling by coordinated effort.

We are led, then, to this logical end, which we may accept as the second principle:

> *Effective marketing requires an organization so coordinated that maximum attention is devoted to the all-important task of selling goods.*

KNOWING YOUR MARKET

A third cornerstone of effective marketing is investigation. To market profitably the seller must be in possession of all the important facts about his market. Large organizations apply various terms to this function, such as research, market analysis, field surveys, and pre-testing. Expressed in common-sense terms, the function of investigation is learning what goods can be sold, where sold at a profit, and how best to sell them.

Unless the seller is in possession of current and adequate market knowledge about his product and his competitor's and about the wants and needs of his own customers, he will not succeed in discovering his most profitable markets, either present or potential.

There are thousands of examples, all leading to the conclusion:

Knowing your market means making it easier for your prospects to become customers. Those who make it easier get more business.

UNDERSTANDING THE CUSTOMER'S VIEWPOINT

Modern marketing is epitomized in the statement, "Selling is not so much a matter of goods, but a matter of people," as opposed to the older philosophy, "The public be damned!"

This newer attitude is one of adaptation to the consumer's wants, based upon a study of his needs, desires, and idiosyncrasies.

People buy ideas when they buy products. The sale is actually made in the mind of the buyer; the thing he buys is the utility and service he expects to receive from the product. Therefore, consumers are not so concerned with what the manufacturer puts into the product as they are interested in what they can get out of the product in terms of usefulness, satisfied desires, increased happiness, and the gratification of human wants and needs.

Adapting the approach to the customer's point of view requires insight, vision, and a sympathetic understanding of human nature in the mass. Knowledge of these factors is the power that eliminates useless sales effort spent bucking well-entrenched sales resistance and permits greater sales returns by selling around known sales objections instead of against them.

The spirit of this fourth cornerstone of effective marketing we may express in these words:

Understand the customer's viewpoint. Study human nature so that your sales program keeps step with the demand of the buying public.

KEEPING AHEAD OF THE PARADE

Keeping pace with the modern business parade requires a shrewd anticipation of the direction the parade will take in accordance with the wishes of its Grand Marshal, the Consumer.

In marketing operations, as on target ranges, one must shoot at well-defined targets, and the aim must be constantly shifted to keep moving targets in range. Consequently, the alert marketer keeps pace with changing conditions of the public's attitude toward his product and his sales policies. He is abreast of and understands the implications involved in broad movements and attitudes which bear directly upon his product's acceptance or which give prophetic insight into new and profitable markets in the process of formation. He is eager and willing to make changes that will keep him ahead of the parade.

The fifth principle is:

Effective marketing requires a far-sighted anticipation of market trends and changing conditions, and a willingness to meet the changed situations.

PLANNING AND WORKING YOUR PLAN

The most successful military campaigns are invariably preceded by careful long-range planning and the possession of adequate facts about the enemy's strength and resources. They are further characterized by a close coordination and welding together of the activities of the transportation, supply, infantry, aviation, artillery, and mechanized units of the army.

In like manner, marketing procedure in its most successful accomplishments is always preceded by careful planning, motivated by a close coordination of all the factors involved, and further characterized by the careful attention given to the basic functional principles herewith outlined.

The whole matter of planning may be summarized thus:

Effective marketing demands careful planning, the correlation of varied activities, and the vision and courage to put the plan into action.

PROMOTION PROGRAMS

While investigation will reveal the market, profitable cultivation of the market requires the selection and use of the best selling tools. Sales promotion is needed to precede, augment, accelerate, smooth the way for, and follow personal sales activity. Few business organizations, if any, can afford to maintain a sales force adequate to reach all of their customers and logical prospects. Sales promotion broadens, enlarges, and multiplies the selling force.

Sales promotion includes all aids to personal sales activity. It is an active and effective division of sales management, a characteristic feature of modern selling, embracing

1. The use of intelligence and originality in selecting and devising the best selling tools, and
2. Alert, energetic, and consistent use of these sales tools.

Sales promotion, whether accomplished by consumer or trade advertising, radio, direct mail, display, publicity, dealer training, or miscellaneous creative sales activities, is primarily concerned with producing sales at a profit by properly interpreting the merits of the product to consumers in language they understand.

As "Poor Richard's Almanac" noted, "Little strokes fell great oaks." Unfortunately many small companies fail to realize the significance of that proverb. They pay too little attention to their promotion because they feel that they cannot compete in this respect with larger, more established organizations. This, of course, is entirely erroneous. Few companies ever start out with sizable advertising schedules or large booklets and brochures. Instead, they invariably use one or more carefully selected magazines, newspapers, possibly a local radio station and a combination of smaller, inexpensive printed pieces that are well conceived.

A little budget may necessitate spending more time in preparation. It may mean testing the market in a few territories instead of nationally. It may require a series of promotional folders sent out periodically rather than a single large presentation.

Size, bulk, and color do not always determine the effectiveness of a mail campaign. A good sound theme, a well-executed format, and a properly timed continuity on a small scale usually produce good results for the small company or individual business proprietor.

Our seventh and final principle of effective marketing is:

Cultivate your market and promote sales aggressively by carefully selecting and using the best tools.

SEVEN SALES STEPS

A systematic and common-sense résumé of the philosophy and the principles of effective marketing reaches the logical conclusion that to sell profitably you must follow these seven steps:

1. You must get your product right, keep it so, and price it equitably.
2. You must build your organization to devote maximum effort to sales.
3. You must, by market investigation, learn where, to whom, and how best to sell.
4. You must adapt yourself to the customer's point of view.
5. You must look ahead, anticipate, and prepare for new profitable markets.

6. You must plan carefully and have the vision and courage to work your plan.

7. You must promote sales aggressively by selecting and using the best selling tools.

There is nothing mysterious, exclusive, or original in the principles of effective marketing. No individual or corporation has a monopoly on their use. Any individual retailer or business concern can employ them. Every successful marketing organization, irrespective of its size, does employ them.

This book is largely devoted to showing how these principles are being used by modern merchandisers. It is interesting to note the many variations of productive marketing work in which the soundness of the principles is so effectively demonstrated. The successful marketer may find, too, that his own sales activities are in complete accord with them.

❖ ❖ Big businesses are not always big because of their size. The degree of bigness depends largely on the success of expert minds in planning and coordinating their complex marketing efforts, which intertwine and interweave all other business functions. Whatever the size of your business you can do big business the "big business way" by applying these seven basic principles of marketing success:

1. Get and keep your product right. Price it to produce an equitable profit.

2. Concentrate your energies on the ultimate job of selling goods.

3. Know what goods can be sold, when and where sold at a profit, and how best to sell them.

4. Understand the customer's point of view. Sell him as he wants to be sold.

5. Look ahead for changes in your market. Prepare for new and profitable sources of sales.

6. Adopt sound, stable sales plans and policies. Then work your plans.

7. Use the modern sales tools best suited to promote the sale of your products. Go after business aggressively and keep eternally after it.

❖ ❖ ❖ ❖

II

Getting the Product Right

"Bene mihi, bene vobis," said my guest at the club, raising his glass in a toast.

"What, in good plain English, does that mean?" I asked.

"That happens to be one of the earliest known toasts of recorded history. It was used by the soldiers of the first Roman legions. It means, literally, 'good for me, good for you!'"

"Good for me, good for you" might well be emblazoned on the shield of the modern marketer. Under this banner and following this precept, he makes his product a worthy, useful contribution to society; he supplies the highest quality attainable at the lowest possible price. His product is priced properly so that its sale is profitable and it renders real value to everyone concerned—the manufacturer, the seller, the workers, and the ultimate consumer.

Without relaxing his efforts to improve manufacturing techniques and thus to produce better products at lowered costs, without diminishing his unceasing program of research, without turning his back on new developments, the modern executive is turning his best thoughts and efforts to making the sale of his products a more efficient, more nearly scientific procedure.

Good for me, good for you.

If more men are to be employed in gainful work, more goods must be produced. If more goods are to be produced, they must satisfy known human wants so that they can be sold. Thus sales make jobs. Business is not merely a matter of competitors stealing sales from one another. No business stands alone. Every business has mutual interests with others.

"Sales create sales. The profits of one man quickly find their way to another businessman's cash register," said Mr. James G. Blaine, president of The Marine Midland Trust Company. "Men prosper as their neighbors prosper."

The truth of this statement becomes all the more apparent when one's thinking is divorced from the complexities of large-scale operations and the proportion is reduced to its lowest common denominator —a small town—a motorcar dealer—a clothier and a farmer.

The car dealer sells a car. After paying his salesmen and mechanics and his overhead, he has a net profit.

The local clothier is a salesman, too. He sells the car dealer a new suit of clothes. After meeting his pay roll and overhead, he has a net profit—a surplus to spend with some other businessman.

The farmer, who is not a party to either of the two transactions, now has an increased market for his foodstuffs. The two businessmen, all their employees, everyone with whom the profits from the two sales are spent—and their employees—the workmen who made the suit and the motorcar—the miner who mined the coal that produced heat and light for the two stores—the railway employees who transported the suit, and the motorcar, and the coal—all have had their buying power affected by those two sales. You speed the wheels of business for everyone, including yourself, when you make a purchase, for every sale actually carries with it a chain of effects upon employment so long as to be untraceable; the prosperity of a community or a nation depends almost entirely upon the speed with which goods and services are exchanged within that community.

Everyone, in the final analysis, has something to sell. The banker sells the resources and facilities of his institution; the school teacher sells her training and ability; the boy who mows the lawn sells his energy and initiative; the attorney sells his briefs and precedents; the farmer sells his knowledge of soils and seasons and his labor; and the factory worker sells his skill and craftsmanship. Prosperity is dependent upon the rate of exchange between these and thousands of other groups—upon the speed with which each is able to sell its wares to the others.

This attitude is not a matter of wistful wishing, nor a Pollyannish conception of economics, but rather one of intelligent, enlightened self-interest. Marketing operations need not be, and are not, conducted on a basis of sentiment or emotion in order that they may be mutually profitable.

It is frequently true that laudable sentiments and worthy emotions are an unconscious attempt to comply with sound economics. The golden rule, despite man-made laws to the contrary and numerous attempts to take short cuts, still remains the best basis on which to build a lasting business success.

Effective marketing is based on getting and keeping the product and price right.

THE RIGHT PRODUCT

The conception of the basis for a sound marketing operation just expressed is relatively new. The earlier reasoning assumed that marketing began where production left off; in other words, the manufacturer made his product in the light of his own experience, judgment, or wishes, and then turned it over to the sales department to market.

In too many instances it was found that the product could not be sold profitably in spite of the well-meaning and, in many cases, expert efforts of high-priced and efficient sales and advertising departments. Gradually, then, manufacturers realized that a product, if it is to survive, must serve a real need and give genuine value, from the purchaser's point of view, and that sales efforts and advertising alone cannot make or long sustain an artificial market.

As an outgrowth of this newer, more realistic philosophy, few market organizations today attempt to sell their product until they are certain that it is so designed as to be salable and that it meets a real or latent, but readily aroused, demand from the consumer's standpoint.

At first, this newer point of view found expression primarily in the designing of more attractive packages and the improvement of shipping containers. Important as these points are in the salability of a product, they do not dig deep enough into the problem of producing sustained volume at a profit.

Now, in the more progressive business organizations, the sales and advertising departments are continually active in and frequently originate the preliminary work of product planning and designing. Research, production, sales, and advertising coordinate their efforts and knowledge to produce products that can be sold and that will meet real human wants, the basis of all sustained and profitable product appeal.

SATISFYING A REAL NEED

Why do people buy goods? The right answer to this question is fundamental to an understanding of sound marketing practice.

People buy goods because they serve an obvious, logical need or because the ownership of the goods will satisfy a craving, a desire, or a want.

Under the first of these classifications falls the purchase of a tire by a motorist, a tool by a machinist, or raw materials to be used in the operation of a business.

Under the second you find the sportsman who may spend a hundred dollars for a set of golf clubs, a woman who will buy a scarf that catches her fancy, an art collector who purchases a piece of tapestry that appeals to his highly developed aesthetic sense.

Psychologists in colleges and practical psychologists engaged in marketing agree that the basis of all product appeal is the ability of the product to satisfy human wants. These wants may be numerous as to kind and of varied urgency and persistence. However, relatively few desires determine the majority of purchases by consumers, and familiarity with these especially powerful forms serves the needs of most marketers.

These are termed *primary wants* because the things wanted are desired for their own sake. The want is immediate, and goods and services are usually required to satisfy the want. Probably 85 per cent or more of all purchases by consumers may be traced to the operation of one or more of these basic, primary human motives:

> *Self-preservation* in the form of food, drink, or shelter.
> *Comfort* in the form of recreation or relaxation.
> *Approval* in the form of social approval from others.
> *Self-satisfaction* in the form of mastering obstacles, gaining superiority over others, aiding the welfare of loved ones, or escaping from pain or danger.
> *Companionship* with persons of the opposite sex.

Many products or services serve human beings indirectly rather than directly. Consumers recognize indirect qualities as desirable, and the importance of these "derived" wants should not be overlooked in the marketing operation. Some of the secondary "derived" wants are the desires for quality, efficiency, style, beauty, health, economy, education, or convenience.

That these appeals, whether primary or secondary in nature, are strong, powerful influences is readily apparent when one analyzes honest product claims that afford one or more of these satisfactions. The practical way in which this is done is suggested by advertisement headlines such as:

> "Protect your home and loved ones from the dangers of fire."
> "Rest and relax here by the sea."
> "Come where it's cool and comfortable all summer."
> "Why the boss praised Jones."
> "French in 10 easy lessons."
> "Your wife need never work."
> "Ease pain and headache, now, in a few minutes."
> "Use the powder movie stars recommend."
> "Men admire soft, lovely hair."

It should be emphasized that both the "primary" and the "derived" wants enumerated here represent but a few of the many human wants known to practical psychologists. In the study of specific products the marketer will undoubtedly find other product appeals that are equally as important as those here reviewed. The important thing is to search out these primary appeals latent in the product and use them as a basis for the marketing presentation and sales strategy.

> *Effective selling is the presentation of the inherent truth about a product, in an interesting fashion.*

KEEPING THE PRODUCT RIGHT

It is not enough to start with a product that serves a real human need and renders value for the price charged. The product, obviously, must be technically sound. If mechanical, it must work properly. If it is an article to be consumed, such as a prepared food or a drug, the formula must be correct, the product beneficial. If the product is of the type where the application procedure plays an important part in the service it renders, as does the workmanship used in transforming roofing shingles into a roof, this procedure must be simplified and made clear to the user. Climatic or other conditions that will affect the shipping, storing, or use of the product must be properly controlled.

The product must meet these requirements and in addition be continuously improved to meet changing tastes, new requirements, scientific advancement, the dictates of style and fashion, and public opinion.

E. I. du Pont de Nemours & Company has stated in an annual report that 40 per cent of the company's business for that year came from products unknown ten years before! While dramatic, this is not an unusual situation.

In an effort to keep pace with changing consumer demands and reduce the gamble in business, modern marketers use various methods to augment their judgment as producers. One of the most popular of these methods is the survey of the public's opinion, prejudices, likes, and dislikes. Sometimes these

Where Product Ideas Come From

The man who thought that the same kind of canvas used for shoe linings would make a nice nonstarched collar for men made at least a million dollars out of the idea.

Van Heusen, who revolutionized the collar business, was a shoe-machinery salesman. The man who invented the celluloid photograph negative was a minister.

Why didn't some wagon or buggy manufacturer invent the automobile instead of leaving the job to a lawyer in Rochester, a bicycle maker in Cleveland, and a stationary engineer in Detroit?

The answer is simple. Revolutionary ideas nearly always come from outside the industry because those in it so frequently think in grooves.

A forward step in the field of lighting was the new Mazda 60-watt lamp equipped with its high-efficiency filament. This latest product development gave users 27 times as much light for their lamp dollar as the first 60-watt tungsten bulbs were able to produce. It is significant that this product improvement was developed within the modern laboratories of this great industry.

studies are made before the product is offered for sale, even before it is made.

It should be noted, however, that the results of these market tests are merely opinions and are not to be taken as conclusive. But they are extremely helpful and afford an indication of the reception a product or product improvement is likely to receive. Also they give an insight into the actual or potential demand for the product.

Another variation of this method is to interview present buyers to determine what people are going to want. An outstanding example of the successful use of this method is found in the consumer research studies carried on continuously by the General Motors Corporation to gauge the movement toward new styles and tastes in automobile design.

This research has a curious objective. It is to keep the General Motors Corporation from making the kind of cars that people don't want. To do this job, the researchers find out the kind of cars that people do want. Over the years millions of dollars are spent asking millions of people what they like and do not like in automobiles. The answers disclose some very significant facts about who bought cars—and how! For instance, certain surveys reveal:

1. About eight million families, or one-third of the total, buy their cars new.
2. The new-car buyer starts to think about his purchase nine weeks before he buys, seven weeks before he starts shopping.
3. He considers three cars, usually gets demonstrations in only two.

4. And since most cars made today are good cars and good values, the buyer's decision usually rests on three or four minor features—such as the door handles, large speedometer face, tone of the horn, wide rear seat. And there are 128 such minor features which may determine the decision, so that the salesman has only a 10,688,000 to 1 chance of guessing the right four unless he is forewarned with the facts from these studies.

Details of market-research studies, how they are operated, what questions to ask, and other facts are given in Chapter IV of this book.

TEST CAMPAIGNS

Another accepted method of making certain that a new product or a product improvement is salable is by trial in a preliminary market. Thus a manufacturer of soaps, desiring to add a men's shaving cream to his line, actually sold the new product in carefully selected local markets for a year before introducing it nationally. A specialty manufacturer with an improved product tried it out first with twenty representative dealers scattered across the country before reaching the decision that it could be offered generally.

A variation of this plan for keeping the product right is found in the company-owned retail outlet, or so-called "laboratory store." These outlets, operated by large organizations primarily for product-testing purposes, maintain direct contact with the buying public. Data so assembled are frequently of great value not only in product planning, but in assisting in the determination of the sales and advertising strategy.

A food manufacturer, selling a nationally known line of products, has a well-conceived program for keeping his product right. The company maintains a fully equipped research laboratory, an open mind for accepting new ideas, and a program for stimulating their production. Testing is going on continuously. This testing is first conducted in the laboratory, until the maker is convinced that the product is practical, not only in the laboratory but in the factory.

The product is then tested among the company's executive group to determine whether or not it should be promoted at the time. If the decision is to go ahead aggressively, samples of the product, with a questionnaire, are sent to thousands of consumers with the request that they try the product in their kitchens under normal, everyday conditions.

Frequently three out of four of these "consumer jurors" reply. If the majority of the votes are favorable, the product is then further tested, under the actual marketing conditions, in representative markets. Simultaneous tests are made of advertising and sales appeals to determine how best to promote the product. If the new product shows that it will sell well in these representative test markets, the manufacturer is then ready to spread its distribution. The research and testing period is over; the problem from now on is a sales problem.

If the product fails to sell as anticipated, the manufacturer goes back over his entire data to discover what is wrong and to make improvements that will speed sales. If these do not produce results, the product is dropped, but its failure has had little effect upon the general prestige of the company because its use has not been widespread.

Sometimes laboratory tests are conducted outside the laboratory itself. An automobile manufacturer takes a new car or truck, runs it about the country, keeps accurate cost records of its oil and gas consumption, and proves to himself just how his product stands up under normal operating conditions.

Independent and impartial testing laboratories, for the testing of consumer goods, have been established by Consumers' Research, Inc., and other organized groups of consumers. Marketers can learn much by studying the methods and criticisms of these organizations.

PROPER PRICING

Not only must the product be right and kept so, but it must be equitably priced to produce reasonable profits, if it is to serve as the base upon which a permanently successful business is built.

A proper price does not imply abnormal profit. But since the basic objective of all business operating in a profit-and-loss economy is the production of profit, the product must be sold at a profit if the business is to continue to pay dividends to its stockholders and wages to its employees.

As a boy, the writer remembers the derisive "Get a horse!" shouted to the rich automobile owner as he puffed by in his White Steamer for the Sunday ride.

"Get Out and Get Under" would still be a popular song hit, as it was then, if the automobile industry had not made its first machines to sell at a profit. Automobiles would still be the playthings of the idle rich; dirt roads would be the usual highways instead of the exception, had not this progressive industry produced profits that made its own development and the closely linked development of our national economy possible.

Practically every great industry in this country proves the fact that social benefits accrue from profits —for profits are actually a surplus over and above that which we require for our bare existence and minimum needs. These profits, in the form of goods, money, or time, are the basis for the progress made in our civilization.

The term "profits" may be in disrepute in the minds of some pseudo economists or wild-eyed reformists, but, properly understood, it is to everyone's selfish interests to make certain that all our transactions are conducted on bases that are profitable to all concerned. Since this is as true as the fundamental laws of mechanics, Newton's law of gravitation, and Galileo's law of inertia, it follows that for sound commercial progress it is essential that the product sold be priced properly so that its sale is a profitable one to everyone concerned—the maker, the seller, the worker, and the consumer.

CUSTOMERS SET THE PRICES

Who, finally, sets the price of goods? You do, and I do. We are all inclined to assume that the man who makes the goods sets the prices on them. But that is only one of those half-truths. It is true that a manufacturer states his price, but if that price is higher than people will pay, the manufacturer will not be able to sell at that price, or will be forced to lower the price.

Ordinarily, businessmen compute the cost of manufacturing efficiently, then add a reasonable profit, and announce the total as the price for the goods. If the price is based on efficient manufacture, and if conditions are normal, the manufacturer will be able to sell a good volume of orders at that price. Of course, there are always competitors who will sell at a cut price, but, under normal conditions, good manufacturers don't pay much attention to competitors who cut prices.

However, manufacturers must pay attention to customer reactions to prices because customers are the people who finally determine the price of goods. Manufacturers pay very little attention to the complaints of those customers who are chronic price buyers because manufacturers cannot make concessions to a few exceptional traders and must stick to the price if it is based on efficient manufacture and reasonable profit. But when a large proportion of the trade refuses to place orders, manufacturers must pay attention and must do something about it.

In 1935 and 1936, the cattle-raising states suffered from droughts. Grazing lands dried up, grasses shriveled and died, thousands of head of cattle starved. Consequently the supply of cattle for the 1937 demand was inadequate, and, inevitably, the price of cattle was quite high.

The cattle raisers could not be blamed for asking high prices for steers under the circumstances. They had lost many of their herds, through no fault of theirs, and the only way that they could escape serious financial losses was to charge high prices for the steers that were left.

The packing houses had to get beef for their customers and had to pay the high prices or else do without beef. So they paid and priced their beef accordingly. People simply refused to pay the 1937 price for beef. They bought lamb, chicken, pork, cod, and haddock, and left the packers holding their beef and holding the bag. Thus the packers, through no fault of their own, were caught in a tough position. They had a lot of money tied up in beef and they had to sell the beef to free the money for other purchases, so they reduced the price of beef until it was low enough to attract buyers.

Thus the packing houses announced the price of beef in 1937, but they did not *set* the price. The customers set the price which they would pay, and the packers had to accept the price. In doing that the packers lost a lot of money, but if they had not sold the beef they would have lost a lot more money.

Actually the price of goods is established in much the same manner that prices are set at an old-fashioned auction sale. The buyers decide how much they will pay and that is all the seller can get.

The American Method of Pricing

Highlights from a speech by Ernest R. Breech, Executive Vice-President, Ford Motor Company, before the Tenth Annual Meeting of The American Marketing Association:

"In this connection, if I were asked to suggest an American pricing policy for today and for the future, I think I would suggest that we base any such policy on two elements—

"First, we should strive always to direct our pricing toward the encouragement of volume—toward greater output. I know that there are some situations in which a volume market is not practicable—or even desirable—but maximum production leading toward lower costs and prices is the proven American method. It has revolutionized the whole standard of living of our people. Here, I think, the big companies have an opportunity and a responsibility to show leadership. The biggest enterprises often are in a much better position to take action which goes with this policy.

"Second, as an element of basic policy I would suggest that we take the long-range view in all matters of pricing, that we consider not simply our present markets but our long-term future markets. This is not only good insurance upon the life of any individual enterprise, but it is in line with our obligation to give as much stability as we can to our industrial economy.

"Both of these elements have one thing in common. They recognize the fact that the American consumer is the boss. Only what is good for him can, in the long run, be good for us.

"However you might define the American pricing system, it is not a lazy man's system. For the American consumer is a hard taskmaster. Trying to find out just what people want, estimating what they may be able to pay at any given time to satisfy those needs and desires, designing, manufacturing, and delivering to millions of people scattered all over the map, persuading them to buy when you are ready to sell—this whole formula is always a great and thrilling contest full of risks and rewarding satisfactions. It is a system which has helped to build a great nation of vigorous, skillful, independent people, and it brings out the best in men. I would not trade the American system—no matter how you might define it—for all the other systems in the world."

If the seller demands more, the buyers will not buy. If his costs will not permit him to sell at the price offered, the seller must find a way to lower his costs or go out of business.

THE FALLACY OF PRICE CUTTING

This message was once flashed on the screen in a newsreel:

> Kansas baker outwits rival in bread price war. Competitor drops price to 1 cent a loaf. Baker advertises, offering free pennies to customers to purchase rival's bread.

Naturally, the audience howled. Many, no doubt, gave the matter no second thought. Others considered the one baker clever and mentally applauded his astuteness in putting it over on his rival.

The far-reaching tragedy behind this anecdote, humorous in itself, is one of the most insidious plagues of our present marketing setup. In its simplest terms, the reasoning accountable for this stupid blunder runs about like this from the consumer's point of view: "If I, either knowingly or unknowingly, can obtain more than my money's worth by buying products, service, or labor cheap, I am smart and profit thereby."

The manufacturer reasons this way: "To get more of this market, or to hold off competition in this market, I'll cut my prices and buy my way in or back. There are too many firms in this industry. Later I'll raise prices and make money."

The good customer of the manufacturer reasons thus: "I'm a big account. I will put on the pressure and get a price cut. If A doesn't grant it, B will and A knows he will. They will be glad to get my business to save overhead."

The retail dealer figures it out along these lines: "I can get more of Bill's trade into my place of business if I offer a lower price. I'll cut prices temporarily, get 'em in the habit of dealing with me, and then gradually get my prices back where they belong. The increased volume will more than pay for the temporary loss."

Needless to say, Bill reasons about the same way. Both retailers then proceed to lose money until one is ruined, or good common sense reasserts itself.

There is no doubt but that an outstanding need of business management is a clear conception of the fact that profits make for progress and that there can be no profits or progress unless products are priced for profit. This lack of understanding of the fundamental economic law is at the bottom of many of the difficulties faced by business. That this is a serious problem is attested by the fact that less than 4 per cent of our manufacturing industries carry on for more than thirty years without some form of financial reorganization, spelling loss to the owners of the business.

Such a startling and incongruous fact in a business world whose avowed objective is the producing of profits is an indication of the generally inadequate profit objective established in the minds of those responsible for profit attainment. The marketer, building a program of successful operations, will do well to make certain his product is not only salable, not only acceptable to present consumers, not only adaptable to changing needs, but above all, that the product marketed pays him and his dealers and his consumers profit in value given and received.

"IS MANAGEMENT AGAINST LOW PRICES?"

The compelling headline (above) of an advertisement by N. W. Ayer & Son, Inc., and the text quoted below clearly emphasize that low prices, consistent with legitimate profits, are the goal of enlightened management.

Into the selling price of shoes, refrigerators, farm equipment, radios, light bulbs go all the costs of running a business.

Wages. Raw materials. Rent. Machinery. Insurance. Depreciation. Maintenance and repairs. Taxes. Interest on dollars loaned by the bank.

And included also are profits—compensation for the risks of doing business.

But all these do not write the price tag.

The public writes it.

For no product, however desirable, can be sold for long at too high a price.

There is nothing mysterious about this. If a manufacturer—or a dealer—charges too much, here is what happens:

The article will be priced out of the market. Goods will pile up, and the business slow to a halt.

Competition itself will force a change. Other manufacturers and dealers will offer the product at a price the public can afford.

Low prices are always the goal of intelligent management. The whole history of American industry is a search for techniques to bring prices down. Only prices that customers can pay will attract the customers that make a business pay.

The mechanical refrigerator is one example of management's ability to bring prices down. In 1921, when the refrigerator was introduced, the average price was $550. Twenty years later, right before the war, the average price was $152.

BUILDING COMPETITIVE
ADVANTAGES

Mr. Marvin Bower, Partner, McKinsey & Company, Management Consultants, made these apt comments in a talk before the Boston Conference on Distribution:

To persuade people takes time. Once a machine is delivered, the operator can be put to work quickly. But the dealer can resist persuasion for a long time—so can customers. It takes little time to *issue* an order but a lot of time to get an order—time to persuade people over whom there is no direct control. Money cannot buy time, and time is the priceless ingredient in building distribution effectiveness.

The great danger in the current complacency about distribution lies in overlooking this simple fundamental of time. When the shift from sellers' to buyers' market takes place, even an all-out effort to step up distribution effectiveness will not greatly reduce the time required to attain it.

As most companies must soon enter the competitive arena in earnest, it behooves them to develop real competitive advantages for their products. For when supply of products offers a choice, purchasing agents and consumers are inexorably shrewd in their appraisal of competitive strengths and weaknesses.

In building competitive strengths the distribution executive should ask himself this question: Why should the customer buy my product rather than that of a competitor? If he digs deeply in developing a searching answer to this question, he will find that the reason for the customer buying one product rather than another will be one or a combination of the following factors:

1. *Product performance:* Because of design, quality, usefulness or some other characteristic, the product does a better job for the user.
2. *Customer service:* Convenience of purchase, maintenance policy, or some other aspect of service makes the product more attractive than the competitor's.
3. *Brand acceptance:* Reputation of the company for quality and a brand name established through advertising and service give the customer confidence to buy.
4. *Price:* This is a derived competitive factor. The stronger the other competitive factors, the greater is the value to the customer and, therefore, the higher price he will pay. On the other hand, weaknesses in the other competitive factors require lower price in order to establish competitive advantage.

Every reason why a customer buys one product rather than another is some aspect of these four fundamentals. It is significant to note that *price* is the only one of these competitive fundamentals that can be changed quickly to give a competitive advantage. Superior product performance takes time to develop. Product weaknesses must be determined and through market research and experimentation new strengths built in. Customer-service weaknesses call for slow rebuilding. And time is the very essence of establishing brand acceptance.

Therefore, if any manufacturer does not start soon enough to develop competitive advantages in the form of superior product performance, customer service, or brand acceptance, he will have to rely primarily on price as a competitive weapon. And price is usually an ineffectual competitive weapon because it can be so easily and quickly matched by any competitor.

Hence, if it is not already too late, the program for developing competitive advantage is clear. Some superiority in product performance, customer service, or brand acceptance must be established or the company will have to enter the competitive arena with the single weapon of price.

To ACHIEVE permanent marketing success, your product or service must render genuine value for the price charged; it must be kept right; it must be continuously improved to meet changing conditions.

Your business cannot survive unless you sell your product at a profit. Give careful attention to proper pricing to assure profits.

The customer always sets the price; he determines how much he will pay and that is all the seller can get.

Price cutting is an economic fallacy. Its destructive force curtails progress and sound marketing development.

Customers buy primarily because of product performance, customer service, brand acceptance, or price. Weakness of the first three factors requires a lower price to establish a competitive advantage.

❖ ❖ ❖ ❖

$\mathcal{A}$ Product Problem

A NATIONAL manufacturer of ladies' rubber footwear (galoshes) has decided to introduce color and styling into his line. By doing so he expects to move forward and lengthen his selling season and also sell more rubber footwear per customer as milady becomes conscious of her need for several pairs of galoshes in various colors to harmonize with her winter ensemble. He also wishes (1) to take galoshes out of the snow-storm-emergency type of purchase, (2) to make women more aware of his distinctive line, and (3) to educate consumers to specify his brand of galoshes when buying.

Leading style and color experts in Paris and the United States have decided on a line of galoshes introducing seven new color effects. Members of his own manufacturing and sales staffs are agreed on these colors and styles.

Has this manufacturer taken all necessary steps to reduce the hazards in this business venture? Is he now ready to begin production of these galoshes? Is he in a position to decide on his advertising plans which will be largely based on the news value of the improvements made in the product?

Assume you are the president of this company. What would you decide to do? After you have reduced your policy to writing—and not before then—turn to page 475 and see how this manufacturer handled this problem.

III

Organizing for Selling

COUNTLESS readers of the Mark Twain classic have chuckled over Tom Sawyer's astuteness in organizing the boys of the neighborhood to whitewash the back fence so that when the job was completed, to his aunt's amazement and satisfaction, Tom might go fishing. While Mark Twain did not reveal Tom's future to his followers, the chances are good that had Tom, in adult life, become a marketer, he would have been a superior one, because he early gave promise of skill in organizing effort and in using it to accomplish a major objective.

In similar fashion, the marketer must organize and coordinate the complex features of his business so that maximum attention may be devoted to the major task of selling goods.

The progressive marketer focuses his energies and applies them to the paramount task of getting the product sold. All departments of the business are geared together to accomplish the organization's basic activity, the profitable sale of goods.

This sounds simple and elementary. Like so many other truisms, it is simple and easily comprehensible, and it makes sense to most men. However, like many other basic truths, the difference arises in its application. Some marketers and some businesses apply this formula to their great advantage, while others do so to their confusion and loss of business and, eventually, to their ruin.

This question of organizing for selling is a complex one. Review the list of functions herein summarized, the result of *Mill and Factory's* study of the operations of the General Motors Corporation.

Management coordinates the essential materials and services listed here in the production of an automobile:

Factory labor	Legal requirements
Capital	Raw materials
Tools	Raw minerals
Plants	Raw chemicals
Power	Rail transportation
Machinery	Water transportation
Telephone	Raw farm products
Telegraph	Taxes
Lumber	Research
Oil and gas	Inventions
Refined metals	Semi-finished parts
Refined farm products	Finished parts

Management, in so doing, performs these essential functions of industry:

Design	Wage payment
Production planning	Assembling
Plant engineering	Accounting
Purchasing	Shipment
Finance	Collection
Materials handling	Wholesale dealer sales
Inspection and testing	Consumer sales promotion
Parts manufacture	Consumer sales and finance
Labor supervision	Final delivery
	Return to investors

Someone must do the organizing.

In a procedure involving so many intricate divisions and subdivisions as modern merchandising, proper organization is a necessity. Good organization clarifies objectives, correlates details, permits maximum attention to major jobs and concentration on these major, never-forgotten business objectives:

To sell at a profit
To sell more goods to present customers
To sell goods to new customers
To develop new markets
To aid in product improvement and development

TWO MEN'S JOBS

The efficient organization of a business to assure maximum selling returns is usually the responsibility of two men, the president and the vice-president in charge of sales. They must make certain that the goods produced by the factory are sold at a profit. If they do not lick the sales problem with the forces at their command, the business will ultimately disappear. "Without customers, we don't eat," may be an inelegant way of expressing a basic truth that is inexorable in its workings.

The president, as the operating executive of the business, takes his authority from the stockholders and is subject only to their representatives, the board of directors. His primary responsibility is to produce profits in the form of net earnings with the capital available. His major duties are to see all the parts of the business in proper perspective and to adjust the relationship between the various departments to assure the best results. In so doing, he must delegate important responsibilities for carrying out broad policies and objectives of the business to major departmental heads such as production, finance, and sales.

The vice-president in charge of sales, in the average business, has considerable influence in helping to shape the basic policies of the business. Complete control and operation of the sales program is ordinarily placed in his hands; his major function, stated most simply, is to produce a suitable volume of profitable sales under the conditions imposed on him by his products, the markets he serves, and the broad policies of his company.

A DAY WITH THE S.M.

Sit for a day in the office of a typical sales manager. Watch him work. At the end of the day, ask and answer for yourself the question, "Does effective marketing require organizing effort so coordinated that maximum attention may be devoted to the major task of selling goods?" During nine working hours, the sales manager, whose guest you are, gives some attention to each of the following:

> *Salesmen:* Their training, supervision, and dismissal, either in person or through his division, district, or branch sales managers.
>
> *Sales Program:* The formulation of the broad program and its daily administration are among his chief duties.
>
> *Sales Promotion:* These activities, handled by the sales-promotion and advertising depart-

ments, and the advertising agency, are under his general control or direction.

Direct Selling: The negotiation of important contracts are handled personally, as are contacts with important customers and salesmen. "There is no substitute for the Boss or the appearance of the Boss."

Departmental Activities: The supervision of his staff and general sales-department routine is his direct responsibility.

Coordination of Effort: The coordination of effort between the sales, research, and production departments is in his hands.

Sales Strategy: Sales presentations, tactics, and procedure for special situations for which the ordinary sales program does not make adequate provision also demand his attention. So do decisions regarding exceptions to established policies with respect to prices, discounts, terms, advertising, assistance, or general service.

Sales Stimulation: The supplying of salesmen and customers with products data, market facts, and suggested creative sales activities to maintain morale and build sales in local markets is a daily task.

Industry and Other Outside Contacts: Meetings or discussions with others in the industry, with trade associations and governmental agencies, to find solutions to common problems.

Sales Objectives: The classification of major sales objectives and the formulation of answers that will help turn prospects' excuses into selling points are put into usable form and released to salesmen and dealers.

Legal Requirements: New problems of price control, sales taxes, and changing distribution receive consideration, in addition to the old stand-bys, such as protection of valuable ideas, sales contracts, price schedules, agreements with salesmen, trade-mark infringements, and study of competitors' contracts. The interpretation of new and pending legislation, Federal as well as state, in each of the states in which his company engages in business is another important duty.

Service Policies: Contacts with the credit department to facilitate sales, with the traffic department to expedite shipments, and with the sample department to speed sample requisitions also receive attention.

POOR DEALER ORGANIZATION FATAL

In considering this principle of organizing for selling in relation to small business concerns and retail outlets, investigation reveals a surprising variation in efficiency.

Some shrewd dealers, usually the successful ones in their community, have put together a smoothly operating business machine, centered on the object of selling. Every other function of the business is subordinated to that end. While they purchase carefully and wisely, these dealers do not let themselves become merely purchasing agents or discount hunters. They realize that profits are not made primarily on close buying, but that the road to sizable profits is based on volume and turnover of their capital: the faster their money works, the more profit it collects.

They work out and install a good system of record keeping, but by so doing, they do not become accountants. The financing details of their business are not overlooked, but these dealers never forget that they are merchandisers first, last, and always. All the wheels of their business—purchasing, warehousing, accounting, credit, delivery, location, financing, or other pre-selling or post-selling business functions—are geared together to turn the final wheel—sales.

On the other hand, the retail dealer who is just barely keeping his head above water is usually trying to get along with a business machine that creaks at every turn, that is either too light for its job or so top-heavy and cumbersome that it cannot move.

Every day retailers are failing because they do not know their costs of doing business, yet some retailers have so much system that they have time for nothing else. Some dealers are so intent on saving money by extra-careful purchasing that they upset all the rest of their business to save a few dollars. Others know little or nothing about the cost of handling, delivery, or warehousing of the various lines they handle. Many put too much sales effort behind unprofitable or short-profit items. Some tie up their capital in credit so that not enough is available to maintain an adequate stock of goods.

The great need is for proper perspective, to determine the importance of each function and to give it the attention it deserves. That is true organization, and it is just as important to success in a big business as in a small one.

One of the soundest statements the writer ever heard was made by a prominent banker. It went about as follows:

> "*I have rarely observed or known of a business problem that couldn't be solved by a satisfactory increase in sales volume.*"

COMMON SALES FALLACIES

The sales manager's or owner's major function is to produce a suitable volume of profitable sales. That is a legitimate objective, but like every virtue, if pursued to excess, it becomes a vice.

A man, for example, may help himself over an emotional crisis by the use of a narcotic. If he comes to depend on such stimulants to help him out too frequently, he is almost certain to wind up on the shelf or under the sod at an early age. Similarly, a business, abnormally stimulated, if pressed too hard for immediate volume or volume secured at too great a cost, under stress and strain, may finally lie down or crack up altogether.

There is only one way to regard a business if you are sincerely concerned with its welfare and would like to have it continue its useful career after you have ceased to be its active director. That is through a long-range point of view. You must do nothing today to gain excess volume of sales or to cut expenses to the bone that will take its inevitable costly toll out of the business next week, next month, or next year.

Visit almost any large concern in the United States today and you will find in its research departments and laboratories developments which anticipate needs of three, five, ten years hence. But visit the sales managers of these same concerns and only in rare instances will you find sales planning of a far-sighted kind. All eyes are focused on this month's quota. How does it compare with last year? With the previous month? What can be done to "put the heat on," to build sales during these last few days of the current month?

This situation, far more usual than rare, is the common enemy of American business. Long-range planning and long-range viewpoints are just as necessary and as valuable in sales work as in research or production activities.

Everyone knows stories about actors, prize fighters, and other public figures who are, after a night out, worked on by doctors, handlers, or managers so that they may be put into shape to carry on their assignments. Every sensible man realizes that the lift is temporary and that the person concerned, while appearing to succeed, is actually failing.

Some businesses are like that. They are promoting the sales of their products against the adverse tide of public opinion. They seem to be going ahead despite the fact that disaster has already overtaken them and they are marked for failure. They may be getting business, but at too great a cost in loss of prestige, in price cuts, or in other ways.

A Salute to Wives

THERE is a whole new untouched field for direct-mail and selling development in the secondary approach to the wives and families of salesmen. Some companies have successfully sounded out the possibilities—many have not.

Authorities have stated that in the process of making sales the product enters into the transaction to the extent of only 15 per cent, and that 85 per cent of the sales transaction comprises other factors and elements aside from the utility of the product itself.

Undoubtedly the greatest of these other factors and elements is *enthusiasm*. Truly, "nothing great was ever achieved without enthusiasm." And enthusiasm, like charity, begins at the center of influence—the home.

The interest of the whole family is undoubtedly a powerful influence that can be harnessed by the manufacturer. A subtle but definite appeal to the home circle will help speed sales. Most wives want to help their husbands succeed. Make it easier for them to help their men folks sell more of your goods. Take the wives into your confidence. Acquaint them with your plans for their husbands' business success. They will help you and their husbands succeed.

Other business organizations are gradually but surely slipping back. At first their loss in volume or profits or accounts may be so slight as to be hardly noticeable. They are not working hard enough at selling. They fail to appreciate the soundness of the marketing law aptly phrased by Kenneth M. Goode: "Every sales organization, to hold its own every year, must actually solicit its own weight in customers."

If a sales organization has 5,000 active customers on its books, it must make a bid for business with 5,000 new customers. This is based on the assumption that many sales organizations each year lose one-third of their old customers and that solicitation of prospective customers will average about one-third successful. Thus the new customers and the lost customers are made to balance. These figures will vary considerably from industry to industry, but the principle is fundamentally right and one that no marketer can afford to overlook.

SALES TRAINING SPEEDS SALES

While enjoying a round of golf, two sales executives discussed a rival's activities.

"Why is it, Tim," asked the first, "that although Bill spends no more on advertising than we do, has no larger sales force, and sells a product that has no real competitive advantages over ours, he outsells us each year?"

His companion weighed the question thoughtfully.

"Jim," he said, "the only reason I can give is that Bill has a longer drive; he seems to go one step farther than you or I do. His men not only push their products to the trade but actually promise to and do help dealers sell the goods. That gives them a doubly effective story that the trade welcomes; and Bill's organization doesn't consider this dealer sales training a flash in the pan; instead they keep everlastingly at it. And they wisely concentrate about 90 per cent of their training effort on service selling—the kind done day by day—and about 10 per cent on teaching their men to do the occasional job of creative selling."

"That system makes sense," replied the first golfer, "for in some ways this dealer-sales-training effort must be very much like golf. You have to keep at it, day after day, to get and keep in the low eighties."

This conversation hits the nub of an important sales activity which all too frequently is overlooked —the matter of selling a product and at the same time helping the dealer to sell. Tim's wise summing up of the situation seems to emphasize the fact that sales training is not a one-flash proposition but rather a continuous activity that should be extended over a long period of time.

Selling is conviction made lucid. The best trained dealers and dealers' salesmen will sell the most of the manufacturer's goods. Help them sell more!

The effective training of manufacturers' or dealers' salesmen is based on five fundamentals:

1. Gather the basic facts from the field by an unbiased investigation so that a clear

understanding may be reached concerning the sales problems actually confronting salesmen in their daily activities.

2. Organize this material, presenting sales situations and the best sales practices in understandable and interesting fashion. Do not worry about giving too many details. Leave nothing to chance!

3. Dramatize the sales-training material in a program of meetings, by film presentations, or in printed releases so that the student salesman may logically solve the problems presented at stated intervals and realize that orderly progress is being achieved.

4. Continue the sales-training program long enough so that the salesmen become trained in developing habits of the proper selling practices.

5. Get the sales-training plan used.

LICKING PERSONAL DEVILS

Sales training, aside from its basic value in equipping salesmen with facts, performs a significant psychological function in helping dealers and dealers' salesmen in overcoming occasional despondent moods.

"Almost every salesman, whether he knows it or not," states a Plymouth sales-training manual, "has a little 'personal devil' that perches on his shoulder and whispers words of discouragement into his ear. Successful salesmen have them, too, but they have learned not to pay much attention to them. If you really like to sell, you'll brush that devil off your shoulder and go on to success."

This "devil" is *negative thinking*, the guidepost to discouragement and failure. *Positive thinking*, the outstanding characteristic of the effective salesman, is stimulated by constructive sales training that enables salesmen to present the truth in an interesting fashion because they are armed with facts, not theories.

Salesmen need facts. Facts about the product, facts about sales policies, facts to use in overcoming sales objections. And they must rely on the manufacturer to supply them with authentic and complete factual information. There is no other dependable source. The best way to present these facts is through a systematic program of sales education.

TECHNICAL KNOWLEDGE ESSENTIAL

The Lacy Sales Institute has found, from years of contact with sales organizations, that about 25 per cent of the salesmen produce about 75 per cent of the sales and that this relatively small group of stalwarts who are to be found at the top of almost all sales organizations sell an average of nine times as much as the average run-of-the-mill salesmen.

These top-flight salemen, these studies reveal, have one distinguishing characteristic—their greater technical knowledge of the products they are selling. The average salesman and the mediocre salesman may have just as much personality and may work just as hard as the star producers, but they lack technical knowledge of the products or services they are selling.

Technical knowledge about products is usually

most effective when summarized in printed manual form, so presented that the facts are quickly understood by the lay mind. Technical knowledge can be quickly and dramatically imported to salesmen by movies and slide films. The Army and Navy found during the Second World War that trainees absorbed technical information about 50 per cent faster and retained it approximately 30 per cent longer when it was first presented to them by visual educational methods. Such training, provided trainees get permanent reference books for future reference, assures maximum results.

Mr. Sidney Carter has aptly stated that a salesman should possess these qualities:

> "The *curiosity* of a cat.
> The *tenacity* of a bulldog.
> The *determination* of a taxicab driver.
> The *diplomacy* of a wayward husband.
> The *patience* of a self-sacrificing wife.
> The *enthusiasm* of a flapper.
> The *friendliness* of a child.
> The *good humor* of an idiot.
> The *simplicity* of a jackass.
> The *assurance* of a college boy.
> The *tireless energy* of a bill collector."

Other qualities may be desirable, but give a man these, plus *facts* learned through sales training, and you have an unbeatable combination.

The extent to which sales training is used by modern merchandisers is illustrated by this résumé from a sales-training manual issued to dealers selling automobile batteries. Note the detailed instructions given to the salemen and the ingenious "reason why" for the sales answers.

BETTER BATTERY SALESMANSHIP

In any given sale, one or two points which particularly appeal to this customer are going to get the business. You want to find out, as soon as possible, what they are; and play up to them.

To discover what battery service a particular customer thinks most important, *get him talking*. First, look over his car to see:

What kind it is, the make and model
How old it is
How many cylinders it has
The kind and size of his present battery
Electrical accessories: radio, extra lights, horns

What you see gives you an idea of the kind of battery he *ought* to have, and at the same time paves the way to talking about the service his battery should give him. When the customer comes in without his car, you'll have to ask him about these points.

It takes but a moment to look over the customer's car; and even while you're doing it, you can start a conversation about the equipment or the operation of the machine that will break the ice:

"You have a lot of mileage on here for a new car; you must use it a great deal, don't you?"
"A spotlight is a great convenience for night driving, isn't it? Do you drive quite a lot at night?"
"Do you enjoy your radio? Use it much?"
"Do you do much night parking with your lights on?"
"Does your car start easily?"

The customer's replies to such questions show you how his mind is working. The things he talks a lot about or talks about enthusiastically are the ones of greatest interest to him. There's your cue. Seize on those points and explain the importance of the battery in getting these things he wants from his car.

Suppose he tells you that his motor doesn't start as quickly as it once did. You can reply:

> "You have a fine motor in this car, but what you get out of it depends on the battery. An ordinary one won't do the trick. It takes a powerful, lively battery to spin your motor quickly and give you the most efficient service."

Suppose he does a lot of night driving:

> "Then you appreciate the importance of a battery you can depend on to give you plenty of light."

Such brief remarks that take only a moment or so open the customer's eyes, probably for the first time, to the fact that getting what he wants from his car depends on having the right size and kind of battery in it. They make him realize that there are batteries—and batteries.

And while you are about it, it's a good idea to speak, though not too emphatically, of the danger and discomfort of unexpected battery failure. Perhaps something like this:

> "It's important to take stock of what you need from your battery because that's the only way to be sure of getting dependable service. You know, your battery must handle all your electrical accessories—radio, double tail lights, double horns (or whatever the case may be), and still have power for its main job of starting your car and keeping it going.
> "You don't want to take any chances on having your battery go dead when you want to get away in a hurry some cold morning, or on its lying down on you some night on a lonely road, miles from help. That's why I've asked about how you use your car—so that I can suggest the most efficient, most economical battery for your particular needs."

This kind of brief preliminary talk takes far less time to deliver than is used here in explaining it. And it is necessary, even when the customer asks for a battery, in order to get him into the right frame of mind to accept your recommendation of the battery he should have.

TRAINING RETAIL-STORE EMPLOYEES

A national manufacturer who sells tires through company-owned outlets trains retail-store employees continuously by periodic meetings which are presided over by company executives; by the use of sound slide films; and by printed sales manuals. Each sales-training session is concluded by a written test and each salesman's paper is carefully graded and the results reviewed with him by the store manager.

The scope of this sales-training program is reflected in this topical outline.

> Your progress with this company depends on *your capacity for progress.*
>
> Better sales mean better jobs for you. Your company is behind you with constant leadership, product improvement, aggressive advertising, and sales promotion.
>
> Study the fundamental retail policy: merchandise, service, credit extension. Offer suggestive selling policy.
>
> Make yourself a valued employee. The company expects of you: good appearance, promptness, courtesy, cheerfulness, alertness, sales-mindedness, observation, economy, interest in self-improvement.

To build a steady trade, your part is to spot the new customer and sell him. Suggest credit terms: how to get new 30-day accounts. Suggest budget terms. Capitalize on free service, given gladly. Sell the customer on your service. Prevent complaints. Learn how to handle and report complaints.

Learn what the customer wants: freedom from worry, safety, economy, comfort. Be prepared to talk results that interest the customer and increase his pleasure and satisfaction.

Recognize opportunities for sales. Every customer needs something else; watch for it when he places his order, when he is getting free service, when he watches his car being lubricated, when he leaves his car. Point out urgent needs first.

Establish in advance a policy on handling objections. Find a point of agreement; direct attention to results; look upon objections as questions, don't take them too seriously. When the customer is pressed for time, show something to arouse interest. When you can't prevent objections to price, be prepared to handle such objections adequately.

Help your customer to buy. Learn to recognize "signals to close": (1) the assumed-decision method, (2) the minor-point method, and (3) the choice method. Take the lead in closing sales.

CREATIVE SELLING

The newspapers in a certain Middle Western city once included a series of comments on the activities of the local chamber of commerce and motor club in urging the building of a new local viaduct and main traffic highway. There were the usual petitions, mass meetings, public hearings before the city council. A continuous, vigorous agitation was maintained over a period of months.

In every press notice there appeared the name of one man among those leading the fight. He spoke at meetings before the local civic clubs; he was on the chamber's traffic committee; he wrote open letters to the newspapers. Whenever anything was done to further the project, he was always in it. When the bond issue is finally voted and the job gets under way, he will undoubtedly be found supplying the stone, sand, gravel, cement, and other materials.

For this man is none other than a young and progressive building-supply dealer, developing business by one of the means that holds great promise of reward.

This method is known as creative selling. Most successful dealers, local merchants, and star salesmen are using this method every day in the week. With them, it has become a logical part of their selling activities.

The greatest opportunity any local dealer or merchant has for increasing his business is to get out among the people of his community, find out what they are thinking about and what they might need. Armed with this knowledge, he then sets in motion all the forces at his command and all the additional forces he can create in order to supply the community's needs.

Much of the success of the local housing drives held in various communities under the Federal Housing Administration sponsorship in its early days was due to the recognition of the importance of creative selling of this type. Prominent and alert lumber and building-materials dealers became the spearhead around which everyone in the community interested in better living conditions rallied to promote housing activity. City officials, realtors, civic associations, women's clubs, public utilities, contractors, builders, architects, newspaper editors, bankers, all banded together to help promote better housing, which meant more sales of the products sold by the lumber and building-materials distributor.

In this same industry, many aggressive dealers have developed another type of creative selling to a high degree. Realizing that people buy homes and not raw materials in the form of lumber or shingles, these dealers have equipped themselves to serve as Home Headquarters. Here, in their places of business, prospective home owners can get competent advice and information on land values, plan services, free estimates, samples of materials, and printed information about products. Needless to say, these dealers, because of this helpful service, are in a favored position actually to sell the materials used in the homes built by these prospects.

Creative selling, in any local market, to be most profitable must be preceded by a careful analysis of the needs of the public in relation to the product to be sold. This analysis completed, the creative seller then equips himself with convincing sales arguments that will appeal to human desires and civic pride. He proves the need of the product from the standpoint of such matters as the health, safety, and profit to the individual and the community.

Having marshaled the sales arguments, the organizer of creative-sales activity then secures the support of as many leading institutions, organizations, and individuals as are necessary to the success of the venture. These include the civic clubs, public officials, influential citizens, dealers in allied lines, bankers, industrialists, labor leaders, newspapers, and other trade groups peculiar to the individual activity, product, or market.

In getting the creative sales story across, every available method is utilized: personal calls, letters, newspaper articles or editorials, personal speakers at club meetings or conventions, and, last but not least, the persistent cultivation of all people whose influence will help.

THE ART OF SALESMANSHIP

Salesmanship as we know it now in its highly organized form was not needed in the days of old when man cared for his own needs, raised his own food, felled trees for lumber to build his home, and wove his own clothing. Gradually, when it was learned that one member of society excelled in a specific line, specialists were developed in various kinds of work. One man became a little better than his neighbors in making firearms; another was more efficient in making shoes. The producer of firearms offered to make a fowling piece for the cobbler in exchange for a new pair of shoes. Thus surplus production of one man was traded for the surplus output of another.

The more fowling pieces the one man made, the less interest he took in other kinds of work. Finally the time came when all his neighbors had been furnished with firearms and he was through supplying the demand in his community. But he wanted to keep on with his work. He looked around the country, traveled a bit, became a salesman, and found a settlement where no one had good firearms. He solicited orders for guns and supplied this demand, which pleased everyone. The new community was happy to welcome the firearms man, who brought them better weapons than the amateurish affairs they had made. And the firearms man, by continuing to make guns, was developing a trade, which he nourished with orders by becoming a salesman himself or hiring others to act in that capacity.

CREATES AND SATISFIES DESIRES

Now the salesman occupies an important position in our national life. To him has been given a part of the work of raising the standard of living in the United States to a point above that of any other nation. His vigor, his foresight, and his earnest zeal have stirred new enthusiasm for products made by others, and a new wish to own them.

This stimulating of the desire to own has not been

the single objective of the American salesman. At the same time, he has offered help in getting the means whereby these newly born wishes to own more goods may be satisfied.

By creating a volume demand for certain products, he has lowered their production cost to a point that brings them within the reach of the average man of modest income.

Woolen goods are an example. Today the average American household owns more fine woolen blankets and warm woolen clothing than royalty had four hundred years ago. Why? Because, in bygone centuries, there had not been created a sufficient demand for woolen goods to turn the attention of man to their economical production.

The salesman further provides the means for satisfying the demands he creates by furnishing the employment which gives a market for products of factory and farm. By selling Connecticut calico in Utah, he provides a market for Utah fruit in Connecticut. The automobile sold in Nebraska provides employment in Michigan for the workman who consumes the products of Nebraska's farms.

Look at the electric refrigerator. The people whose employment is affected by the sale of a refrigerator are: the salesman who sold it, the truck operator who moved it from factory to owner, the railway employee whose salary is dependent on the movement of freight, and the workers in the manufacturer's factory and offices.

The sale also affects indirectly those who furnish the material that goes into the refrigerator—the miners of tin, iron, and copper; the makers of porcelain, steel, copper tubing, and copper wire; the chemists who supply the refrigerant; the makers of the glass products from which insulating materials are formed; the workers in rubber plants; the lumberjacks who felled the trees; and the sawmill operators who prepared the lumber for crates. When a refrigerator salesman closes a sale, he sets in motion a long procession of effects touching the lives of thousands of other persons.

WHAT SALESMANSHIP DOES

Our prosperity and modern civilization, our American standard of living are dependent largely upon the rate with which we are able to exchange goods and services. This prosperity has never been achieved easily; in fact, the only formula is hard work. A great amount of that hard work, in the form of selling pressure, has been required to put our living standard where it is today.

Think of the amount of sales pressure required to persuade Americans to use electric lights instead of kerosene lamps, to abandon the horse and buggy for the automobile. Most of the good things of life were sold to us: we didn't buy them.

Suppose, for example, there were no life insurance agents.

Do you think many people would own life insurance? If there were no salesmen, how many more of the widows and children bereft each year of their natural protectors would be left unprovided for?

What Is Salesmanship?

"Salesmanship is the art of helping your customer to get more out of life or to do a better job in his business through the use of your product."—Don G. Mitchell, President, Sylvania Electric Products, Inc., New York City.

"Salesmanship is the ability to induce others to accept your point of view."—Norman A. Cahn, Charis Corp., Allentown, Pennsylvania.

"Salesmanship is the ability to understand the customer's problems and to show him how the purchase of your goods and services will solve some of them."—Howard Hammitt, Southern New England Sales Manager, Bastian Bros. Co., Rochester, New York.

"Salesmanship is the act or art of demonstrating to a prospective user that the services rendered to that user by the product which you are selling is of greater value to them than the dollars represented in its sales price."—George S. Jones, Jr., Vice-President, Servel, Inc., Evansville, Indiana.

"Salesmanship is conversation and demonstration . . . Salesmanship is simply the process by which the distribution problem is solved . . . Salesmanship is simply 'organized persuasion.'"—W. E. Holler, General Sales Manager, Chevrolet Motor Division, General Motors Corp.

"Selling is a process by which a conviction is transferred from the mind of the salesman to the mind of the prospect."—Paul G. Hoffman, President, The Studebaker Corp., and Chairman of the Board of Trustees, Committee for Economic Development.

"Salesmanship is the act of helping someone buy something he wants or needs."—H. C. Nelson, Railway Express Agency, Inc., New York City.

"Salesmanship is a special skill which enables the possessor to convince others that they want what he wants them to want."—H. M. Johnson, Vice-President in Charge of Sales, Nuodex Products Co., Inc., Elizabeth, New Jersey.

While most people admit that life insurance is the easiest means by which a man can protect his family, life insurance is sold, not bought! It is the exception, not the rule, for a man who should be carrying life insurance to seek it. Some one has to hunt him up and show him his duty, and sell him the protection he requires for his individual needs.

There is a great deal of glib talk about supply and demand, but many observers overlook the obvious fact that the consumers did not, really, and do not demand the things that are good for them. They have to be sold. We also often hear of the seriousness of a buyers' strike. But a buyers' strike is as nothing in the way of national calamity as would be a sellers' strike in the United States.

Suppose every salesman were to lose his enthusiasm and throw away his samples; suppose every sales manager were to resign; every advertising and promotion man lose his faith? Suppose, for example, those dogged pluggers for insurance decided not to "come in again"? Suppose all those brisk evangels of all the good things called it a day and quit the country cold?

Then there would be a depression. It is not too much to say that there would be a collapse of civilization. Standards of living would tumble. Obsolescence would rule. Stagnation would take the place of turnover; unemployment and frozen assets would be the order of the day. This is no overstatement. Salesmanship means just that to progress. The public must have sales pressure upon it if it is to move ahead. We should still be riding over cobblestones with ironbound wheels if it had not been for the energetic salesman of Detroit and Akron.

Everything we eat, everything we wear, everything we work with in office or plant, everything we enjoy for sport or recreation has had to be sold to us. And any salesman will tell you that it is not an easy job to shake the buying public out of its native lethargy and caution and arouse the purchaser to take what is an ice-water plunge when he buys.

Selling is a force. It is a personal force; a social force. It is, in fact, a universal force. Properly organized and coordinated selling is a force that starts with a definite purpose and ends in its fulfillment, in the delivery of lasting values that produce benefits for all concerned.

The Bumblebee Cannot Fly . . .

ACCORDING to theory of aerodynamics and as may be readily demonstrated through laboratory tests and wind-tunnel experiments, the Bumblebee is unable to fly. This is because the size, weight, and shape of his body, in relation to the total wingspread, make flying impossible.

But . . . the Bumblebee, being ignorant of these profound scientific truths, goes ahead and flies anyway—and manages to make a little honey every day!

❖ ❖ SYSTEMATIZE your business so that major attention is devoted to the selling job. Take these steps:

1. Coordinate all pre-selling and post-selling operations.

2. Organize all departments of the business so that nothing can interfere with the selling activity.

3. Set up clearly defined sales objectives.

4. Arrange for proper sales training of your own salesmen, your distributors' sales representatives, and the retail sales personnel. If you help your dealers sell better, you will build good will and sell more goods.

5. Provide all your sales representatives with facts about your product. No guesswork as to the merits of your product!

6. Strive for increased volume by utilizing all the existing agencies in the community to help create situations where sales will result.

An Organization Problem

A MANUFACTURER of cement, selling a nationally advertised product, wants additional volume. He knows that his distributors follow the general trade practice of splitting orders for cement among several sources of supply. Furthermore his cement has no particular product advantage over that offered for sale by his leading competitors.

An intensive investigation among dealers and a study of trade practices reveals that relatively few dealers are making a normal sales profit, not only on cement but also on the other items they handle. Dealer credit losses are abnormally high; few dealers figure delivery costs properly; accurate sales and cost records are the exception rather than the rule in the conduct of the dealer's business.

What bearing, if any, do these trade facts have on the manufacturer's desire to sell more cement? Can this information be used as the platform for a sales plan to build profitable volume? If so, how?

The way this manufacturer solved his problem is set forth on page 476.

IV

To Market! To Market!

THE most active spot in New York City night life is not The Great White Way, the supper clubs in the Fifties, or the resorts in uptown Harlem; it's the Washington Market in lower Manhattan.

From midnight to daybreak, every night in the week except Saturday, the streets around the market are jammed with trucks, vans, carts, wagons, and drays, most of which have traveled hundreds of miles that day, loaded to bursting with produce from New Jersey, Maryland, Pennsylvania, Long Island, or Connecticut. Others have come from the great freight terminals and steamship piers with the products of farms and orchards from states bordering on the Pacific Ocean.

On the sidewalks outside the commission houses that cover this area, boxes and bales, crates, bags, and baskets of fruits and vegetables are piled, leaving only a narrow space between where men toil, shout, give orders, and take commands.

Here are found celery from Utah, figs from Texas, oranges from California, loganberries from Washington, potatoes from Idaho, pears from Oregon, peaches from Colorado, eggplant from Virginia, alligator pears from Florida, melons from North Carolina, and varied products from other states and Canada and

74

Central and South America. The humble onions, carrots, cauliflower, lettuce, corn, asparagus, leeks, and spinach are also on display as thousands of men work madly to sell and buy and truck away these tons of foodstuff that will feed millions of people within the next twenty-four hours in more than twenty thousand restaurants and hundreds of thousands of homes in the metropolitan New York area.

As the goods produced by the mills and factories of the country, the farm products and those of mine, quarry, forest, fishing, hunting, and oil well pour forth, the greater part goes first to individuals and groups who have no more interest in consuming them than do the original producers. This group is called by various names—traders, jobbers, wholesalers, distributors, retailers, dealers, and, as a broad group classification, "middlemen." The field of human activity engaged in handling this vast flow of commodities, in conveying goods to the market place for 150,000,000 consumers, normally occupies the thought, ingenuity, physical labor, and wealth of about three-fifths as many persons as are customarily engaged in the production of the goods.

Further investigation reveals other important services in the marketing procedure required to place goods in the hands of the people who will use them Briefly sketched, these include the mechanical, creative, and electrical services such as transportation, communication, printing; the financial services of banking and insurance; and the merchandising services of credit, installation, and repair.

When totaled, the cost of all the many and complex business activities involved in the flow of goods and services from producers to consumers—activities termed "marketing" by economists—equals a sizable portion of the total income of the United States, in some years estimated to be slightly less than one-half of the national income. These marketing activities interweave all other types of business operations; they concern every individual business, large or small.

WHY A MIDDLEMAN

Is the average citizen likely to gain the not uncommon notion that these middlemen, engaged in the marketing of goods, these intermediaries between those who originally produce wealth and those who consume it, are exploiting the consumer, the producer, or both? If so, he is not unlike many who regard the middleman as an economic parasite to be tolerated, but whose presence in an economic utopia would be eliminated.

True enough, the distributor obtains goods for less money than the ultimate consumer pays him. But the consumer, all too frequently, is not cognizant of the services that have been performed in making the goods available when and where he wants them, a series of functions which, without the middleman, he himself would have to undertake. If each consumer did perform these services, assuming he was able to, he would find it more expensive in time, effort, and actual money than the amount he now pays the middleman.

The consumer is not merely paying for the goods

he obtains; he is also paying the middleman for the risk he assumes in his purchases and the labor of transporting and handling the goods and holding them in storage until the time the consumer chooses to exchange his money for them.

Unfortunately there is no itemized price tag on goods that shows the exact cost of the "behind-the-scenes" services rendered by the middleman, in addition to the original cost of producing the goods. Thus the New York City housewife purchasing, in her corner grocery store, pears from Oregon or celery from Utah, which arrived there via the Washington Market, may not realize that these foods were kept fresh for months in mammoth warehouses and that the crisp, firm quality she demands is hers to select from only because, previously, scientists spent large sums of money in mastering nature's preservative, cold.

The buyer may also overlook the fact that these foods were then rushed across the continent by fast freight in specially equipped refrigerator cars; and that even such a minor item as the toll charges for the telegraph and telephone services used to flash weather forecasts, prices, orders, and the news of crops across thousands of miles represents another sizable expenditure of money.

These services and the many others used in modern distribution cost money and involve real business risks, and for them the frequently criticized middleman is fairly entitled to the profit he receives.

The middleman came into being because he was originally a necessity, and he stays because he continues to be one. From the earliest times when he carried on his back the wares of stay-at-home producers and eked out his livelihood as an itinerant peddler, he has been helpful in elevating mankind from a primitive, poverty-striken economy, in which each family group or tribe produced all the goods required for its limited needs.

This sometimes-despised middleman is not only the marketer of goods, but his most consequential function is to locate the ultimate consumer who needs and wants the goods he has to sell. He is, at the same time, the agent for the farmer, the grower, the manufacturer. In many cases he is also their warehouseman and almost always their salesman.

Without the middleman's economic and social contributions our present-day society of diversified occupations could not exist because those who produce goods usually have not the money, the knowledge, or the time to distribute and sell the fruits of their labor.

NOT A PERFECT SYSTEM

The system of distribution in which the modern middleman works is subject to periodic criticism. Pitiless publicity is turned on him; isolated cases are cited as damning evidence that the costs of getting goods from those who originally produce them to those who consume them are excessive.

Some of this criticism is justified. Much of it is unfair and based on false premises or half-baked economic theories.

Modern merchandising is by no means perfect, as

everyone knows. Most intelligent marketers admit that the presence of inefficiency, shortsightedness, and needless competition are costly to everyone concerned. There is still elaborate promotion for the worthless or over-priced product. There is still exaggeration, half-truth, and even untruth used to sell goods that perform no real service or deliver no genuine value. Some marketers fail to realize that the soundest merchandising program is the one based on the premise that nothing is ever said about a product which the user cannot prove for himself.

Conscientious, sincere, and intelligent groups of marketers, advertising experts, producers, and consumers are seriously studying these problems, trying to correct them for the general good of all.

Meanwhile, the average consumer, despite occasional grumblings, demonstrates his faith in modern merchandising by his overwhelming preference for goods distributed on a nationwide basis and backed by modern promotion, including advertising.

There are a number of reasons why the consumer takes this stand. None of these springs from an inborn love of the national manufacturer. All can be traced back to that most powerful of all human motives—enlightened, intelligent self-interest.

CONSUMER SURE OF QUALITY

One of the principal reasons for this preference is that a product marketed on a national basis, backed by modern sales promotion, is actually put on trial before the critical eyes of the buying public. The glaring white light of nation-wide product publicity is a great purifier, working both ways, hastening the acceptance of a worthy product or the rapid demise of an inferior one that does not warrant public approval by repeat purchases.

Not only must the modern marketer produce a product of high standards but he must maintain these standards uniformly. If he is to continue to receive public favor, he must constantly improve his product. He cannot stand still; he must continuously offer the public something new, something better.

While the nationally promoted and distributed product is under this pitiless scrutiny, so are similar products of rival manufacturers. This the buyer in the market place, be it the corner grocery, drugstore, department store, or automobile salon, sees what the producer has to offer, compares his offering with that of his competitors—and judges its values for himself. Because of this, the manufacturer, if he is to survive, must market a product of merit that delivers genuine value to the user.

The nationally marketed product gives the consumer the constant quality he has been educated to expect, or he discontinues his patronage. Thus the housewife, buying a nationally distributed coffee, knows exactly the quality standard she may expect from this coffee, if it has already met with her favor. Loose coffee, purchased as did our grandmothers, might be good one time, fair the next, even poor or adulterated on occasion, depending upon the shipments received by the corner grocer.

Orators deliver long speeches and writers bring forth thick volumes about truth in salesmanship and truth in advertising. From a realistic standpoint, the question is an academic one, for the buying public does insist on truth in both salesmanship and advertising and will not continue to buy products grossly misrepresented. The marketer who fails to see the wisdom of truth in both his selling and advertising is shortsighted indeed and doomed to a brief existence as an important factor in his market.

CONSUMER GETS MORE FOR LESS

The fact that modern merchandising technique reduces the cost to the ultimate consumer is undeniable. From 1925 to 1940 the retail price of automobiles, which in 1907 were rich men's toys, was reduced from $31.50 per horsepower to $8.50—a reduction of 73 per cent. Today a much superior one sells for even less, yet labor costs and overhead have mounted steadily and new and more expensive materials are used in producing the modern motor car. How, then, can the cost be less? The answer is that modern marketing has produced sales volume; sales volume has produced greater mass production; greater mass production has lessened the cost to make each individual automobile, and the buyer gets more for less money.

Ever-lower prices are always the objective of intelligent management. The whole history of American industry is a continuous search for techniques to lower prices. In fact only prices that customers can pay attract the customers that make business pay.

In 1910 you paid $25 for a tire that would run about 2,500 miles—a cost of a cent a mile. Today you get a better, safer tire at about one-twentieth of a cent a mile. Pre-selling, through low-cost advertising, as well as improved production methods, are largely responsible for this development.

The same situation prevails with regard to electric refrigerators, radios, oil burners, cameras, vacuum cleaners, shoes, building materials, clothing, long-distance telephone rates—almost every modern commodity or service that comes to mind.

The 25-watt electric bulb in 1908 cost 85 cents. Today more than 116 million are sold each year at an average price of 12 cents. A cellulose acetate yarn, in 1925, cost $2.90 per pound. Production is now greatly increased—and the price is 67 cents per pound.

There is nothing mysterious about any of this. High prices limit a market. Low prices expand a market. A business grows because the number of its customers grows.

Paradoxically, the misinformed consumer offers a noisy objection to the advertising aspect of modern marketing because of the heavy costs involved, but here again facts disprove an erroneous contention. The advertising cost is small when checked against the cost per unit of the nationally advertised product. With each bottle of Coca-Cola, for instance, you pay less than one-fiftieth of a cent for advertising.

Advertising aids distribution by persuading the local dealer to stock the goods he wants, yet, compared with other distributing costs, it is small enough to be disregarded. Advertising, in fact, is the least expensive avenue of approach to the consumer. Do you realize that a full-page black-and-white advertisement in the weekly magazine of the largest circulation (5,400,000), costing the advertiser $15,225, places his message before an audience of approximately 22,500,-000 readers, so that the cost per reader per message is less than one-sixteenth of a cent?

PROVIDING NEWS FOR CONSUMERS

Advertising performs a tangible service by giving information vital to the buying public—where certain articles are sold, their retail price, and when special bargains are offered. Watch what happens in the average home when the newspapers and magazines arrive. Advertisements are read carefully; shopping lists are compiled. Truly advertising is news.

Advertising is the speediest and most direct way of telling the public about inventions and discoveries, an important phase of our highly specialized system of distribution. While these innovations would, of course, come into use without advertising, few people today would be enjoying them. Furthermore, the demand aroused in the consumer by advertising makes it profitable for the inventor and manufacturer to develop and introduce new products.

Indirectly advertising has been of benefit by its influence on cultural life. The growth of the radio, which contributes so freely to our enjoyment, was made possible almost entirely through the support of national and local advertisers. So, too, will the growth of television be accelerated by such support. Newspapers and periodicals are supported chiefly through returns from the same source. Advertising brings the fiction and fact articles of the magazines into the home at but a fraction of the cost to the subscriber of the actual cost of publishing, printing, and mailing. In every way advertising has helped give us a more profound mental growth and outlook.

Modern marketing has brought within grasp of the consumer comforts and luxuries that would not otherwise be attainable. It has saved lives by its effect on the national health through selling better refrigeration and promoting the sanitary-packaged and canned foods, in contrast to the unsanitary open-cracker-barrel methods formerly used.

It has lengthened the span of life and made our American health standards the envy of the world through the farsighted vision of some of the leading insurance companies, who for years have sponsored educational programs in the interest of public welfare.

By relieving mankind, and particularly women, from household drudgery, today's marketing methods have paid dividends beyond all measure of money in leisure and cultural pursuits.

Modern marketing has done this by carrying word of the new products into the household, by developing their quality, and by inducing the customer to buy so that costs were eventually brought within reach of the majority.

WEALTH IS HAPPINESS

Modern marketing was defined earlier as "a service based on organized, trained common sense." And the available facts about marketing are, in reality, just a few elementary truths, proving once again that there's nothing new under the sun.

The difference in results achieved, and they are extreme, are a matter of the skill used in interpreting and applying the seven rules of marketing under which the known facts may be classified for purposes of reflection, planning, and application.

Modern marketing produces wealth for those who understand its technique. And wealth is not only computed in dollars and cents; in its best sense, wealth connotes happiness. Our human happiness, to a large extent, is dependent on our standard of living, which on the American continent has reached heights undreamed of by our forefathers. Much of this standard building is the contribution of the American businessman—the modern marketer.

❖ ❖ **T**HE modern marketer, critics notwithstanding, performs a useful social and economic function. He renders these basic services for the consumer:

1. He buys the goods from the producer, investing his money or credit in the transaction.

2. He transports the goods to a place where the consumer may conveniently shop for them.

3. He holds the goods in storage until the consumer chooses to pay his money for them.

4. He takes a business risk in all these operations.

Since there is no itemized price tag on the goods to show the exact cost of the services just named, many misinformed customers carry the belief the middleman is exploiting the consumer, the producer, or both.

This attitude is contrary to facts.

V

Knowing Your Market

EVERY business has two sides: the inside and the outside. The head of a business, provided he has a good accounting department, usually knows all he needs to know about the inside. He has a clear and balanced picture of his own operations. But how about the outside of the business—the people who can make or break him—his customers, his dealers, his competitors? Of these important factors his knowledge may be wide, but it seldom is as definite, as accurate, or as timely as is his knowledge of the inside factors of his business.

This question is no academic matter. It is a major problem, for experts estimate that in some years businessmen in the United States waste the staggering sum of ten or more billion dollars by inefficient marketing. This waste is due primarily to a lack of definite market facts, currently applicable to the rapidly shifting changes in today's buying trends.

Obviously, then, a cornerstone for less costly and more effective marketing is based on a thorough investigation of the market and the possession, by the merchandiser, of all the important facts about his market. This conception of market research is not confined to the mere gathering of facts, for statistical data, graphs, and charts, as such, are of little value. They require proper interpretation by the competent merchandiser; they serve as the basis for a plan of sales action that enables the marketer to sell around known sales resistance and to produce sales returns that more than justify the costs of the compilation of the market data.

Viewed in this light, market studies are not an added sales expense; they are instead a form of "sales insurance," available at premiums ridiculously low in proportion to the large amount of money that might otherwise be wasted in guesswork. Various terms have been applied to this modern merchandising development by large organizations, such as market analysis, research, field surveys, and consumer-reaction studies.

> *Market research is finding out what goods can be sold: where sold at a profit; and when and how best to sell them.*

The importance of this phase of marketing is illustrated by the story of a historic naval battle familiar to every American school child.

In the famous sea fight of the War of 1812, the American frigate "Constitution" gained an overwhelming victory over the British "Guerrière." It wasn't because the "Constitution" was better handled by her men, for no braver seamen ever walked a frigate's deck than went down with the "Guerrière." What caused the British sea fighters to be so hopelessly outclassed was their clinging to the old-fashioned belief that all you needed to hit the enemy was "judgment." The "Constitution," for

Shift the aim constantly to keep moving targets in range.

the first time in naval history, had *sights* on her cannon—the "Guerrière" had none!

In marketing activity, as in naval battles, you must have "sights"; you must shoot at well-defined targets, and you must shift the aim constantly to keep moving targets in range. When stripped of the technical verbiage so many marketing experts use in attempting to explain the simple and obvious, that is all market research implies.

COSTLY BUSINESS MISTAKES

For many years, a casual rule-of-thumb approach was the customary method of studying a market; the seller, as in the case of the British sea fighters in 1812, relied on judgment—judgment as to how, and where, and to whom his product could be sold. At times this judgment was correct and profits were great. But all too frequently, some market factor of paramount importance was overlooked and losses resulted.

In recent times a number of products have been put on the market only to encounter unexpected set-backs that usually could have been prevented by careful analysis. The instance cited below, taken from many available, serves also to emphasize a related marketing fundamental; namely, that a product to survive must serve a real need and that advertising alone cannot make or sustain a market.

A cigar manufacturer spent a large sum of money pushing a thin panatela type of cigar in Harlem, New York City's negro section, with slight success, despite the known fact that large quantities of cigars are smoked by its residents. Market investigation

All Abyssinians

SOME years ago an enterprising publisher hugely entertained the advertising profession by running an advertisement headed:

"There Are Ten Million People in Abyssinia. All Abyssinians!"

The sense of that entertaining advertising message was: Numbers Do Not Make a Market—Actual Prospects Do.

For instance, according to "America's Needs and Resources," issued by The Twentieth Century Fund, past experience shows that as family incomes rise, a smaller proportion of the increased income goes for necessities and a larger proportion goes for luxuries and durable goods.

In 1909, nearly three dollars out of every four that consumers spent was for food, clothing, and shelter. At higher income levels in 1950, these necessities will account for little more than three out of five dollars, and for slightly less in 1960.

On the other hand, the proportion of income spent for household operation and equipment, transportation, recreation, and medical care will rise. But expenditures for private education, religion, and private social welfare will decline.

With high-level economic activity in 1950, urban per capita cash income will reach around $1,220—almost twice that estimated for the rural nonfarm population and almost three times estimated per capita farm income. A third of urban consumer units will be above the $3,000 level in 1950, but only 13 per cent of the rural nonfarm and 11 per cent of the farm units will be above that level.

Another interesting development that marketers will watch closely is the preponderance of war veterans in our population for the first time in our history. According to the Veterans Administration, veterans and their families will comprise 43 per cent of the country's population by 1952.

While continuing to grow numerically for some time thereafter, this group, according to Veterans Administration computations, will decline in percentage after 1952. By 1957, it will represent 41 per cent of the population.

These estimates indicate that veterans and their immediate families, now numbering 46,000,000, or about 32 per cent of the population, would grow to 62,300,000 by 1952 and 62,500,000 by 1957.

then revealed the fact that negro men preferred a thick, large cigar; the smoking of a thin panatela type was considered effeminate!

FOUR TYPES OF MARKET STUDIES

There are four principal types of market studies that will give any businessman as direct, balanced, and trustworthy a picture of the outside activities of his business as he already has of the inside, because these market studies, too, are based on a thoroughgoing assemblage of significant facts. Such studies may be briefly outlined as follows:

1. *A sales analysis*, showing a concern's own sales by products and by customers, gives market facts as reflected by that concern's own operations. This type of study is a part of inside accounting and is now regular practice in a substantial number of businesses. It is mainly useful in the control of inventory and of direct sales costs. The familiar discovery that, say, 70 per cent of the business is done with 12 per cent of the outlets or on 15 per cent of the products is one of the results of such a study. The gathering of additional outside facts is often necessary in order to point a sound way of using this discovery.

2. *A consumer survey* gathers facts to show (*a*) who the typical consumer of a given type of product or service is: his or her annual income, age, sex, family, etc.; (*b*) what products or services in the field investigated the consumer has bought, and when, where, and under what conditions they were bought; and (*c*) what habits of the consumer affect the purchase and use of products or services in the field investigated.

This type of study helps to guide product design and advertising appeal and helps to determine the most favorable place, time, and terms for the ultimate sale. This is the most vital study of all, for it shows what people want and how they want to buy it. Even well-informed guesses made by those who have been in a business for years are often proved to be in error on this subject. In these days, when a careful scrutiny of lines is being made to determine which can safely be dropped and which are the most promising for future attention, surveys of this type are particularly helpful.

3. *A distribution survey* gathers facts to show through what channels, in what volume, and at what expense the products in a given field pass from producer to consumer. This type of study helps to control both direct and indirect sales costs. It is sometimes found, for example, that a uniform distribution policy is unnecessary; that some territories are less expensively covered by manufacturer's agents, others by jobbers, and still others direct. In other instances facts indicate that a readjustment or concentration of distribution may lower the price to the consumer and increase volume without affecting the manufacturer's price in the same degree.

4. *An appraisal of competitive position* adds to the facts learned about competitors' business in the two types of study just outlined the salient facts about competitive resources and policies. Thus, a judgment may be formed concerning the most effective competitive course to be followed. Since the effort of most business is to establish some characteristic quality or

other advantage for its product, thus introducing some degree of monopoly, this type of study, made for a business which has no patent or natural monopoly, shows how a semi-monopoly may be created by developing distinctive characteristics.

There are many other forms of market study, but these four probably are the most common, and in many cases the most useful.

Because market studies are new to many businesses, and because making them offers many chances for errors of judgment in the selection of facts, it is usually advisable that when they are undertaken for the first time they should be handled by those skilled in this work. When the place of market studies in a business is fully demonstrated, however, they become a regular part of its activity.

THE KIND OF FACTS NEEDED

To market a product profitably on a national basis, the manufacturer of almost any product sold to a mass market needs dependable, up-to-date answers to a number of basic questions. A few of the more important of these, stated in general terms, are:

1. Is the product right? How can it be improved? What new or additional features would customers or prospects like to see incorporated in it?
2. Is the product priced right? Could we get additional profitable volume if prices were lowered? Do we suffer any disadvantage from prices of competitive products?

3. Is the product packaged properly? Could service or style features be built into the product or packages?

4. Is the product distributed through the proper trade channels? Do distributors make sufficient profits to warrant their pushing our products? Are there any defects in service to customers by the trade that handicap sales? Would sales be increased if we altered our distribution setup and sold through other outlets?

5. Could the selling season be lengthened if we emphasized new values to the trade and consumers? If so, how?

6. Is our line of products too long? If so, what slow-selling items should be eliminated? How much effort should be concentrated on the popular items?

7. Do we have a "leader" in our line which helps the sale of other items? If not, would it be advisable to create one?

8. What are the facts about our present customers? To whom are we now selling profitably?

   a. Where do they live?
   b. Why do they buy?
   c. When, how much, and how often do they buy?
   d. Where do they buy?
   e. What price do they pay?
   f. Why do they not buy in larger quantities?

g. What age, sex, and educational, social, economic, and occupational factors influence our present customers?

h. What brands of competitive products are also bought? Why?

i. Is the need for our product clearly defined? Only vaguely present? Or dormant?

9. What are the facts about our potential market?

a. Are there other people to whom we might profitably sell?

(1) Why do they not buy now?

(2) How could they be influenced to buy?

b. What methods are necessary to induce them to buy from us?

(1) What sales promotion might be used to appeal to them?

(2) Are there special obstacles which make selling to them unprofitable or impossible?

10. What about our competition? Is it gaining on us? If so, why? What effects are competitors' sales and advertising activities having on our profits? On our prestige with the trade and with customers?

11. What other products or lines could be sold profitably through the present distribution channels? Would such a policy of expansion be advisable? What effect

would it have on our present trade relations?

12. Should the line of products be further diversified to alleviate seasonal or style factors or severe market slumps due to the effects of other factors?

13. What defects exist in the present selling strategy? Are our salesmen underpaid? Are territories too large or too small? Are we building potential volume in new markets so as to maintain our competitive standing in the national market now and in the future?

14. What long-range market trends as to products, sales policies, and customers' preferences are discernible? What changes are needed to keep pace?

15. Is the sales-promotion program (national advertising, radio, direct mail, etc.) really understood by the trade, our sales force, and consumers? Is it being actively merchandised to the trade by our salesmen? What can be learned in advance of the release of our promotional campaigns by pre-testing so as to assure maximum results?

INFORMATION ABOUT COMPETITORS' PRODUCTS

The extent to which market facts are required and used is reflected in the questions listed here, which formed the basis for a national market investigation

sponsored by leading food, drug, and cosmetic manufacturers so that each of the three might determine,
basically, the competitive standing of their product;
learn more about what competitive brands consumers
were shifting to and why; and in the final analysis
decide how much sales effort certain market areas
should receive.

HOW DOES MY PRODUCT STAND?

Answers to questions like these help manufacturers decide
where and how to sell:

> What is the rank of the leading products in your field,
> including your own?
>
> What percentage of the families using your type of
> product use your brand?
>
> What is the percentage distribution of the users of your
> brand by income groups?
>
> What is the percentage distribution of the users of your
> brand by age groups?
>
> What is the percentage distribution of the users of your
> brand by type of family groups?
>
> What percentage of the users of your brand are home
> owners?
>
> Is the preference for your product increasing or de-
> creasing?
>
> From which competing brands have you been gaining?
> For what reasons?
>
> To which brands have you been losing?
> For what reasons?
>
> Among which income groups have you been gaining?
>
> Among which age groups have you been gaining?
>
> Have your gains been among families with increasing or
> decreasing incomes?
>
> What is the relative stability of demand for your brand
> as against other brands in the same class?

What percentage of those replying listen to your radio programs?

How many of these listeners use your product?

What percentage of these listeners have recently changed to your product?

What guarantee of quality do the users of your product value most?

How important is the doctor's or dentist's influence? The dealer's?

In what type of store do they prefer to buy your product?

What newspaper or combination of newspapers do they read regularly?

What magazines do they read regularly?

What percentage of replies mention your product advertising as an example of truthful or untruthful advertising?

What percentage of replies register complaint against the quality of your product?

SOURCES OF INFORMATION

Where is the merchandiser to find the answers to these and literally hundreds of other questions to enable him to get his share of the consumer's dollar; to market his product efficiently; and to base his marketing operations on facts, not guesswork?

There are two main sources of information: first, existing records and data; and second, facts secured by original investigations. Both are of value; neither should be overlooked. Each should be used to complement the other, and each provides a valuable countercheck against the conclusions drawn from the other. Sound business practice dictates the correlation of all existing data and their review before starting to gather new facts.

99

The chief sources of published data on markets have been indicated by Dr. H. K. Nixon, of the School of Business of Columbia University, to be:

Government publications, such as reports of the Bureau of Home Economics, the Department of Agriculture, the Department of Commerce, the Department of Labor, the Department of State, the Department of the Treasury, the Federal Reserve Board, the Federal Trade Commission. Various departments of the several states also issue useful reports.

Commercial directories and registers. Thomas's "Register of American Manufacturers" is typical.

Market studies by publishers and other media owners, such as "Operations Sales Planning in Nine Great Markets," issued by the Hearst Advertising Service; "A Comparative Study of Magazines—Who Reads Them and Why," sponsored by The McCall Corporation; and the Advertising Research Foundation's "Continuing Study of Newspaper Reading Habits."

Reports published by advertising agencies. For example, "Population and Its Distribution," published by the J. Walter Thompson Company.

Reports of commercial research organizations. For example, "Polk's National Business Census," published by R. L. Polk and Company.

Reports of trade and industrial associations. "An Analysis of the Occupations and Incomes of Subscribers and Buyers of Magazines," published by the American Association of Advertising Agencies, is one of the best examples of this type of information.

Reports of research departments of universities and foundations. "A Study of the Supply and Distribution Areas of the Chicago Grain Market," published by the Bureau of Business and Economic Research, University of Chicago, is an outstanding example. So is The Twentieth Century Fund's "America's Needs and Resources."

Reports of individual companies. For example, "Keytown Telephone Sales Map," published by the American Telephone and Telegraph Company.

"This outline barely suggests the voluminous literature on the subject of marketing," states Dr. Nixon, in "Principles of Advertising." "In addition to the sources mentioned, the advertiser may consult books on his own industry and product, articles in the trade papers, catalogues, encyclopedias, and various compilations such as the 'Reader's Guide to Periodical Literature,' the 'Industrial Arts Index,' the 'New York Times Index,' and the 'Printers' Ink Index.'

"To become familiar with any considerable portion of the published information is a task for the specialist in market study. The individual advertiser, however, can profitably consult the available material in connection with his marketing program. Any organized approach to advertising demands at least a working knowledge of the data available in existing reports."

Merchandisers may find valuable answers to their market research problems by a careful analysis of their own sales records. One manufacturer discovered that 90 per cent of his volume was represented by the sales of only sixteen out of eighty-seven items in his line and that the actual cost of samples for fourteen of his slowest moving items was greater than the dollar gross sales volume of these soon-discarded items. For local market areas, chambers of commerce and other civic groups frequently have useful data for any legitimate purpose.

NEW FACTS FROM MARKET STUDIES

Despite the great mass of market information already available, in many cases it is necessary to undertake market studies to gain new facts. These projects may be handled by:

1. The Questionnaire Method
2. The Observation Method
3. The Correlation Method

All three types of market analysis may be used in arriving at a composite, up-to-the-minute, factual picture of the market in relation to the questions of paramount interest.

The questionnaire method is widely used to secure new market facts from consumers, dealers, wholesalers, and any others who may be able to supply useful facts. Advertising agencies and publishers of national magazines, certain large companies (notably General Motors and Procter & Gamble), and a few national organizations have trained investigators in their employ who conduct market researches by the questionnaire method.

The procedure ranges from a very informal questioning to encourage a free flow of comment to the use of systematic types of the formal questionnaire, wherein specific questions are asked calling for positive or negative answers or for the answering of prepared questions from a listing in the questionnaire form supplied by the research sponsor.

"What is your opinion of the new Buick car?" is an example of the type of informal questionnaire.

"Did you see the Buick advertisement in today's *News-Gazette?*" is the kind of question which requires a positive or negative reply. "What make of car do you now own? What make of car will you buy next?" are examples of prepared questions listed in a formal questionnaire form.

Any of these types of questions may be presented either in personal interviews, by mail, or by telephone. The personal-interview method is to be most relied upon for the soundness of its returns, since by this method trained investigators can secure more trustworthy information regarding each individual on the list and can frequently supplement the questions by observations that have a direct relationship to the questions asked.

Mail questionnaires are apt to be misleading unless it can be demonstrated that the returns received are truly representative of the group as a whole. Telephone questionnaires are useful, but here again great pains must be taken to make certain the people reached are representative of the total group.

THE OBSERVATION METHOD

A second plan of obtaining facts about markets is the observation method.

Typical of the market studies made by this method are the "bathroom and pantry" counts, whereby the investigator lists the brands and quantities of merchandise found on the bathroom and pantry shelves of a number of representative homes in certain key cities. Such a count, although somewhat laborious and costly, gives a clear picture of the actual buying habits and brand preferences of the families interviewed.

This system is particularly effective if the manufacturer wishes to gain information about his product's acceptance in relation to family income; the competitive standing of his product; what brands consumers are shifting to and why; the acceptance of various products in different income groups; the results obtained by recent extensive promotional campaigns; and data reflecting today's buying habits as to kind of outlet, cash or credit buying, advertising media which pulls, and, in some instances, buying expectancy for the coming month or year.

Such market investigators secure and collate precise, accurate data concerning actual existing conditions at the time the market study was made. When these studies are repeated at regular intervals, under identical or similar conditions as to scope and territory, they reveal trends that permit the marketer to anticipate future market requirements with reasonable accuracy. It should be observed, however, that such studies merely record today's facts and, unless repeated frequently, are not to be relied upon for continued market guidance.

Two other kinds of market studies, freely used, are also conducted by the observation method. One concerns itself primarily with style-trend reports, gathered in centers of fashion in the United States and

Europe, whereby styles of clothing and accessories worn by women are recorded.

Another type, used most prominently by chain stores, oil companies, and outdoor advertisers generally, is handled through traffic counts, in which the actual number of people or automobiles passing a certain location are carefully counted at various hours of the day and at certain seasons of the year to determine the relative value of a site for a retail store, a filling station, or an outdoor billboard display.

THE CORRELATION METHOD

This form of market investigation is solely statistical and analytical. It gains its wide recognition as a reliable market measurement because the demand and acceptance for a product is understood to be related (correlated) to other facts already known.

A manufacturer contemplating the introduction of a new type of heater for automobiles, reasonably priced, could quickly determine an approximation of the potential market in northern states by securing the available lists of automobile registrations. He then probably would conduct a test sales campaign in several market areas, thereby deciding how closely actual sales met anticipated sales. This index could be projected against the market as a whole and a reasonable demand, or lack of demand, for his product be thus ascertained.

A number of existing factors are available and are used as possible indexes of purchasing power in relation to various types of products. Some or all of the following are generally referred to and weighted one against the other to give an accurate picture of existing or potential markets:

Automobile registrations
Bank and savings deposits
Crop values by types
Degree of illiteracy
Homes wired for electricity
Income-tax returns
Magazine circulation
Manufactured products as to value and types
Native white population
Number of families
Number of retail outlets
Number of wage earners and wages paid
Percentage of homes owned and homes rented
Racial characteristics
Radio sets owned
Telephone subscribers
Total population and population per square mile
Urban versus rural population by trading areas

It should be understood that what is usually considered a favorable general index may be downright misleading to merchandisers of certain types of products whose actual or anticipated sales have no sensible relationship to the factors employed. Thus the sales of a product such as low-priced catsup will be erroneously anticipated if correlated with income-tax returns, since low-priced condiments in general are used by low-income families to flavor cheap meat products; high-income groups buy less catsup per family.

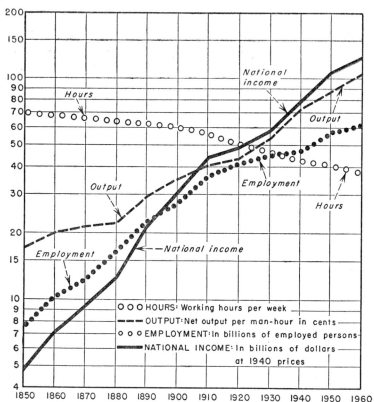

United States economic trends from 1850 to 1960. From a study of "America's Needs and Resources," undertaken by the Twentieth Century Fund. Based on statistics covering the past hundred years, it projects the probable trends of the American economy more than a decade into the future.

Similarly, the anticipated sale of cigars and the amount of sales activity the market deserves may be improperly correlated with the percentage and income classification of the negro population in Harlem, since custom gives prestige to the cigar smoker in this negro community.

Situations such as these, which cannot be determined solely by statistical studies, have resulted in the formation of specialized market yardsticks designed to evaluate the demands for certain products. The marketer of building materials usually relies on a combination of the five factors of income-tax returns, automobile registrations, percentage of white families, number of one- and two-dwelling houses, and number of homes owned versus number rented as a composite signpost to indicate the worth of a specific market area.

CHECK THE RESULTS

In weighing the results of market studies and arriving at conclusions from the facts they reveal, it is advisable to ask these pertinent questions outlined in "Questions to Ask in Appraising Market and Advertising Research," published by the American Association of Advertising Agencies, New York.

> Who made the survey?
> Does the title indicate exactly the scope of the survey?
> Does the report contain all pertinent data as to how, when, and where the survey was made?
> Is the sample sufficient?
> Have data collected in one city or section been used to draw conclusions for the country as a whole?

Are percentages figured for groups or classes that contain too small a number of instances?

Are percentages of increase figured on ample bases?

Was information obtained by mailed questionnaires?

Is causal relationship attributed to one single factor, when other contributing factors are present?

If questionnaires were used, were the questions such as to give fair and adequate answers?

Was information gathered of such a nature that the memories of the people interviewed might have resulted in inaccuracies as to fact?

Can type of information obtained (either by interview or by mail) be relied on as accurate?

Have any original or unique statistical devices been employed?

Are charts misleading?

WHAT A MARKET STUDY REVEALS

The extent, scope, and timeliness of the information that can be secured from a market survey are indicated by the published conclusions of a portion of the findings of a survey on home building and home improvements. The significant information regarding roofing, itemized here, is of unquestioned value in helping to answer the perennial question of where, how, and to whom to sell.

Where Homeowners Would Go for Quotations:

Question: If you decide to re-roof your home, where would you go for information and bids?

Hardware store?.......... Architect?..............
Lumber yard?............ Contractor?.............
Builder?................ Any other?..............
Carpenter?..............

Dealing with OPA

IN the later phases of OPA it was noted by the meat-packing industry that a large part of the meat business of the country, beef production particularly, was being diverted to the black market and other irregular outlets, as reported by the National Association of Public Relations Counsel, Inc. It also appeared that meat retail prices in general reflected this abnormal situation.

Because of these conditions the packing industry and others of similar mind pointed out through the newspapers and other media that the situation was almost out of hand and that the time had come for Congress to end the OPA setup.

The spokesman for OPA, however, stoutly insisted that its regulations were effective and that the black-market argument represented a distortion of the facts.

The accuracy of its observations thus challenged, the packers countered by retaining an independent research organization of unimpeachable standing and assigned it the task of checking conditions as they actually existed in a dozen leading cities.

This first-hand study, which extended over several weeks, showed that actual conditions were even worse than had been claimed by the opponents of OPA. Widely and dramatically publicized, these findings brought about a sharp reversal of public opinion and within a surprisingly short time OPA's activities were officially ended. Other factors, of course, contributed to this action, but the results of this research and their widespread dissemination were undoubtedly largely responsible for the change in public attitudes.

Time has vindicated the wisdom of those who moved thus effectively. The incident, of course, points to the ancient moral that truth is mighty and will prevail, when so presented that he who runs may read—government agencies notwithstanding.

	Replies Received, Average per 100 Families
Lumber yard	22
Contractor	21
Carpenter	12
Builder	16
Hardware store	7
Roofing company	5
Architect	2
No answer	15
	100

Type of Roofing Preferred:

Question: If you re-roof your home, which type of roofing would you use?

Asphalt shingles?.........   Asbestos shingles?........

Copper?...............   Wood shingles?..........

Slate?..................   Tile?...................

	Replies Received, Average per 100 Families
Asphalt shingles	33
Asbestos shingles	22
Wood shingles	10
Tile	3
Tar and gravel	2
Slate	2
B. C. red cedar	2
Steel shingles	1
Copper	1
No answer	26
	102

Explanation: Some named more than one type of roofing.

Reasons for Choice of Roofing:

Question: Why would you choose that type of roofing?

Appearance?............ Fire-resistance............

Durability?............. Economy?..............

Any other reason?........

	Replies Received, Average per 100 Families
Fire-resistance?........................	40
Durability............................	40
Economy.............................	28
Appearance...........................	26
Customary use in community............	3
Suitability............................	1
Insulating properties..................	1
Easier to replace in part...............	1
Necessary for flat roof.................	1
Personal preference....................	1
No answer............................	27
	169

Explanation: Many listed several reasons.

LOCAL MARKET SURVEYS SPEED SALES

Not all surveys are made on a national or sectional basis. More and more local surveys are being made by local merchants, because today's merchandiser needs facts, whether his market is Montgomery County, Ohio, the city of Des Moines, Iowa, or the entire forty-eight states. Here's how some progressive building-material dealers use market surveys to develop business in Anytown, U.S.A.

1. *Personal study by the dealer or by some one in his organization.* Some dealers examine

the community street by street and house by house. A trip through the residential section is sure to disclose new opportunities. This house needs a new roof, that one will have to be painted soon. Mr. R. should have a concrete driveway instead of a cinder one. Dr. S.'s doorsteps are in pretty bad shape. Jim B. ought to be interested in re-siding his home. Mr. M. should be a good prospect for a home-insulation job.

On careful examination, hundreds of examples of this sort present themselves. The follow-up by direct sales effort, closely geared in with this information, usually produces sales that justify the expenditure of time and money in collecting these facts.

2. *Surveys*. Other dealers make door-to-door calls. A simple statement—"We are making a construction survey in Jonesville. Are you planning any building, remodeling, repairing, painting, or roofing?"—generally brings a friendly answer. The information obtained in this way contains definite sales leads. Dealers often use their regular employees for this work and find that such spare-time effort is very satisfactory. Dealers with ice departments have their drivers make inquiries at every stop. Others hire people expressly for the purpose. Women canvassers have been used with varying

success, depending on how fortunate the dealer has been in selecting them. College or high-school students have done this work very satisfactorily in the summer months. Many dealers make their surveys by telephone. One of the office girls calls every subscriber in the telephone book and asks the same questions as in the door-to-door calls. The idea that it is a survey rather than a sales talk makes prospective customers willing to answer. Surveys such as these usually develop enough business to warrant conducting them at least once a year.

A successful basis of paying for this work is by a small salary and a commission on all business that develops in a certain fixed time, usually three to six months.

Where regular surveys are not conducted, some dealers train their organizations to be alert for leads, and offer rewards for good prospects turned in. One of the largest dealers in the country has a bonus system of rewarding employees. Each salesman gathers the building news in his own territory and reports all prospects. For every job sold he receives a certain number of points. But if a job that he has not previously reported is awarded in his territory, a certain number of points is deducted from his bonus record and potential earnings.

THE PSYCHOLOGICAL BAROMETER [1]

The Psychological Barometer is a periodic poll of public opinion and buying habits originated in March, 1932, by Dr. Henry C. Link, of The Psychological Corporation. Though it antedates the *Fortune* and Gallup polls, it is less well known because it is made for companies instead of for publications. It is conducted six times a year, with either 5,000 or 10,000 personal interviews in each survey. Each survey is made with an accurate nationwide sample of the urban population. Since 1932 there have been 92 Barometer surveys, totaling 595,000 personal interviews.

It is called the Psychological Barometer because it measures trends or changes in people's habits, in respect to both buying and thinking. For example, one Barometer shows, from a series of 38 surveys, the changes of people's habits in respect to a certain brand of dentifrice, while another shows the changes in respect to types of dentifrices, whether paste, powder, or some other form. The basic information for these results is obtained by questions such as: What brand of toothpaste or dentifrice did you buy last? Is it a paste . . . powder . . . liquid . . . or other type . . . ?

People versus Sales. The results of such questions do not measure sales, either in dollars or in units; they measure people, or the proportion of personal units

---

[1] The analysis of this method of studying people and their buying habits was prepared by Henry C. Link, Vice-President, The Psychological Corporation, New York.

who are buying or using a given brand. The Psychological Barometer measures the extent to which units of people or households are being influenced toward or away from a particular brand or a particular belief or opinion. Therefore, it is a measure of advertising and other sales influences. Naturally, as more people are influenced to buy a certain brand, its sales are likely to increase. Therefore, there is a fairly close correspondence between the Barometer results and sales indexes.

Advertising Influences. Since the first survey in March, 1932, these Barometers have continued to measure specific sales influences. One of these is the effect of an advertising theme on people's minds. "Look for the date on the can" was the basic advertising theme of Chase & Sanborn coffee. To test its effects, the following question was used:

What brand of coffee advertises, "Look for the date on the can"?

Answers	Per cent				
	Sept., 1932	Dec., 1932	Jan., 1933	May, 1935	March, 1936
Chase & Sanborn..........	68	75	74	78	80
Other brands.............	8	8	9	8	5
Don't know..............	24	17	17	14	15

This test, called the *triple associates test*,[1] has been extensively used in the Barometer surveys to measure the success with which an advertising campaign is

[1] Link, H. C.: A New Method of Testing Advertising Effectiveness, *Harvard Business Review*, **11**, 165–177, 1933.

impressing its product on people's minds. Many other influences, including radio programs, stores or other type of distribution, general publicity, even attendance at the World's Fair, are also measured.

The first public-opinion trends were measured in respect to the N.R.A. with this question:[1]

From what you have seen of the National Recovery Act in your neighborhood, do you believe it is working well?

Answers	Per cent					
	Oct., 1933	Nov., 1933	Jan., 1934	April, 1934	Sept., 1934	Jan., 1935
Yes..................	48	41	55	50	38	38
No..................	27	30	22	23	26	33
Uncertain.............	25	29	23	27	36	29
Total interviews......	1,932	2,386	3,076	5,167	4,000	3,710

One of the more recent public-opinion series is represented by the question:

After this war (or, now that the war is over) do you think that we will make a peace settlement that will last or do you think that we will have another world war in twenty-five years or so?

Answers	Per cent					
	Feb., 1943	Oct., 1944	Apr., 1945	Oct., 1945	Apr., 1946	Oct., 1946
Will have another war.........	43	54	51	59	62	74
Will make a lasting peace......	47	28	33	28	24	18
Don't know................	10	18	16	13	14	8

[1] Link, H. C.: A New Method for Testing Advertising, *Journal of Applied Psychology*, **18**, 1–26, 1934.

(If another war) Who do you think will be our next enemy?

ANSWERS BY THOSE WHO SAID THERE WOULD BE ANOTHER WAR

Country named	Per cent				
	Oct., 1944	Apr., 1945	Oct., 1945	Apr., 1946	Oct., 1946
Russia..................	29	27	37	45	56
Germany................	9	6	2	2	2
Japan...................	5	3	5	1	1
England................	4	4	3	4	3
China..................	1	1	1	1	1
Don't know.............	6	10	11	9	11
Total................	54	51	59	62	74

Many of the public-opinion results have been published in the *Journal of Applied Psychology* and elsewhere.[1]

Measuring Attitudes. The favorable and unfavorable attitudes toward nationally known companies have been measured through these Barometer surveys regularly since 1937. Thus one graph shows a ten-year record of the changing favorable attitudes toward eight of the country's leading corporations. This attitude Barometer is used by these companies as a means of measuring their progress in public esteem, and as a means of evaluating the effects of radio programs and other large-scale public-information campaigns.

From one of the early Barometer surveys, an analysis was made to determine how many interviews

[1] Link, H. C., The Psychological Barometer of Public Attitudes, *Journal of Applied Psychology*, **31**, 129-139, Apr., 1947.

are necessary for results of a certain accuracy.[1] This was probably the first empirical demonstration of the applicability of the established laws of chance to market data. It made it possible to substitute mathematical predictions for the old trial-and-error method of determining when the size of the interview sample reached a certain stability.

A more complete description of the Psychological Barometer is given by Dr. A. D. Freiberg, director of the Market Division of The Psychological Corporation, in "How to Conduct Consumer and Opinion Research"[2] and "Psychological Brand Barometer."

MARKET RESEARCH A VITAL NEED

Market research on a national or local basis is a development that every firm doing business today must take cognizance of some time during its career if it hopes to achieve the ultimate in sales. Realizing the value of market data today, progressive concerns are willing and ready to spend sums of money for this type of activity, which would have seemed out of the question a few years ago.

Merchandising executives are applying a searching attitude to sales operations, seeking, as one sure means of improving profits, to spot profitless volume. Many are finding that one of the keys to profit protection is selling effort concentrated in the profitable markets for their products.

---

[1] Link, H. C.: How Many Interviews Are Necessary for Results of a Certain Accuracy, *Journal of Applied Psychology*, **21**, 1–17 Feb., 1937.

[2] Blankenship, A. B., Ed.: "How to Conduct Consumer and Opinion Research," Harper & Brothers, 1946.

Merchandisers know that the cost of distributing goods is, in many instances, already two to ten times the cost of making them—and rising rapidly. And yet, despite the fact that the use of market research is increasing, United States industry is not yet spending the monies annually for market facts that past experience would seem to warrant.

> *One sure way to cut distribution costs is to know your market better so that you may sell more efficiently. In such a program market research plays an important part. Do not overlook its value.*

✤ ✤ **K**NOW your market. Get all available facts that will make possible more efficient selling. Market research will give the answers, reduce the gamble, minimize guesswork. The four best sources of market facts are:

1. A sales analysis, based on inside records of a concern's own sales.

2. A consumer survey, which assembles facts about who the customer is, what similar products he has bought, and what consumer buying habits influence his purchases.

3. A distribution survey, which shows how products are distributed to customers and at what cost, thereby aiding in the control of selling costs.

4. An analysis of competitive position study, which adds facts about competitors' resources and policies.

✤ ✤ ✤ ✤

A Market Research Problem

THE XYZ Company manufactures a cellulose-acetate product which transmits the healthful ultraviolet rays of the sun. The product, sold commercially, resembles common window screening in appearance. It has been used successfully in hospitals, in place of ordinary window glass. Patients have been cured of rickets when exposed to the sun's ultraviolet rays transmitted through this cellulose-acetate screening.

The sales manager of the XYZ Company raises fine chickens as a hobby. One day he read in a poultry magazine that the high mortality rate of young chickens and the low egg-producing characteristics of hens was due primarily to the lack of proper sunshine in brooders and henhouses.

What market investigations should the XYZ Company undertake before it attempts to formulate a sales policy to sell its product to the poultry trade? The steps which the XYZ Company took are reviewed on page 476.

VI

Why the Public Buys

No actuality of modern times presented a greater opportunity to the observer of human nature in the mass than did the crowds at Chicago's Century of Progress.

In collaboration with J. Parker Van Zandt, Vice-President of American Aviation, then an executive of the fair management, the writer conducted extensive researches on the grounds to determine why some exhibitors succeeded while many more failed, and to get answers to such questions as these:

> What are the dominant types of appeals which the buying public is listening to, acting on, or rejecting? What are the relative merits of these appeals? Their most effective combinations? How can they best be employed on the printed page, in radio, in stores, windows, and elsewhere? How can merchandisers in every field employ these principles more effectively, to speed consumer response and accelerate the turnover of the distribution dollar?

For months an intensive study was conducted based on official records, data assembled by exhibitors, information collected by exhibit supervisors in charge of the various buildings and areas, questionnaires, and personal day-by-day observation and checking. No such comprehensive study was undertaken by others.

The more than forty million visitors formed, without realizing it, the most important and interesting exhibit of all. Their reactions and preferences made of the fair a vast human-nature laboratory—the chance of a lifetime for the trained market analyst to study people in the aggregate.

No claim is made to having discovered, for the first time, strange unsuspected traits of human nature that a good merchandiser did not know existed. What these results do is to supply a fresh method by which principles of modern merchandising may be lifted out of the realm of opinion into matters of demonstrable fact. Using the findings as a yardstick of consumer interests, it is possible to re-orient the relative importance of basic human-nature traits and the modern ways to arouse them; to relegate certain hoary merchandising myths to well-deserved oblivion; and to re-emphasize the growing importance of others.

MILLIONS OF GOLDFISH

There were, in effect, nearly forty million goldfish within a vast bowl, in which their reactions and interests were unconsciously daily on view. We did not demand of the forty million visitors that they be their own psychologists, that they interpret their actions or explain to an interviewer why they preferred one exhibit to another or how and why they chose to spend their limited time when there were so many things to see and do. This survey differs in this fundamental respect from the ordinary research of consumer responses. The findings are findings of fact—free of the element of opinion or self-interpretation—based on the casual, unconscious, and yet final and authoritative preferences of a group equivalent to one-sixth the population of the country, the greatest representative cross section of the American public gathered together up to that time.

What did most people select? Where did the lightning of the people's choice strike? And why?

MARIONETTES ON THE SALES FORCE

The successful commercial exhibitors used entertainment to gather their audience, to lift the crowds above the humdrum routine, to shake their minds loose from worries and preoccupation. With entertainment as the background, they so interwove their product story with the entertainment setting that the public accepted both together as logical, interesting, and understandable.

What had Tony Sarg's marionettes to do with groceries? The Great Atlantic and Pacific Tea Company found a connection so admirable that the majority of the visitors rated this exhibit one of the most successful on the grounds.

What inherent relation was there between television and terraplaning? Hudson-Essex created one that jammed their theater for twenty shows a day so that the pulling power of a scientific novelty was effectively interwoven with a merchandising story of an automobile.

It is interesting to note that these highly effective entertainment and built-in ideas are adaptable to many types of products. Television or marionettes might have been used as crowd getters for any one of a score of products.

MAN'S INTEREST IN MAN

In the spacious Hall of Science, with its nine acres of medical, chemical, and related exhibits, the four displays that commanded overwhelming popular attention had to do directly with man himself. Their success proved again that the average citizen's thinking begins in terms of his own body and never gets very far from it. The more directly a story can be made to touch the public's self-absorption in itself, the more certain it is to win favor.

At the Ovaltine's Wonder Robot theater, there was always a crowd to hear and watch the lecture on vitamins and digestion, illustrated by the illuminated ten-foot interior of the mechanical lecturer. There was the same overwhelming interest in the embryology exhibit, seen by vast crowds of people, most of whom stood in line forty-five minutes or more and then spent another half hour filing slowly by the tiny specimens that showed the development of the human embryo from one week to birth. The transparent man, with the ten-minute lectures on human anatomy five times each hour, always drew capacity audiences. There was the same overwhelming interest in the intimate and, in many cases, displeasing revelations of appendicitis operations, stomach disorders, and thyroid glands at the Mayo booth.

It is evident that the human body and all it entails has come into its own and that prudery and blushes are publicly outmoded. An enlightened public demands a new deal in increased frankness, honesty, and intellectual content when it comes to matters relating to its own health and personal well-being. No merchandiser of foods, drugs, or cosmetics can afford to underestimate the importance of this trend toward increased frankness in what may be termed a physiological appeal.

BACKSTAGE COURTESIES

People are vitally interested in actually seeing how things are made, in wanting to understand what goes into a product and how that product can be of benefit to themselves. A sure way to call attention to a product is to stage the process by which it is created or assembled.

Over ten million people entered the General Motors building, attracted primarily by a desire to see automobiles assembled. Firestone officials checked an attendance of from eight to ten thousand people an hour passing along their tire-assembly line on busy days. Crowds took an intense interest in seeing Ipana tooth paste packaged and in watching girls sew on buttons at the Big Yank Workshirt demonstration. Almost invariably those manufacturers who showed how their product was made drew crowds of surprising size, about equally divided as to men and women.

While it is undoubtedly true that a certain portion

of the buying public has become more skeptical of advertising claims and is resentful of overstatement, yet at the same time the buying public welcomes the voice of authority and is seemingly well pleased to accept it. The more disinterested it is, the more powerful. Because of his fundamental curiosity about things that interest him, the average citizen lays his doubts aside with evident relief and wholeheartedly follows the sales story offered him by the voice of authority.

SELF-PARTICIPATION PAYS

It takes two to make an agreement, and it takes two to make a sale. Every salesman tries to get his prospect to take part in the discussion, to draw him into the picture. You can readily see why those manufacturers who let the public take part found that a small effort on the public's part registered much more effectively than many times its equivalent on their part. Safety Glass applied this principle with a vengeance, for everyone who wished could satisfy a long-suppressed desire to break a window!

The clever use of this same principle of self-participation was partly responsible for the phenomenal success of the most profitable concession along the Midway—the weight-guessing scales used as a ruse to sell canes.

It is the utilization of this self-participation principle which also accounts for the wide popularity of many radio programs and of all advertising campaigns using contests or other devices whereby the reader is invited to take part.

But this self-participation must always be part of an understandable story. That was the weakness of the costly Playground of Science, which shot completely over the understanding of any save the trained engineer.

SHOWMANSHIP SELLS THEM

The most ordinary subject, properly dramatized, can be made an object of novelty and interest to the consuming public. Few things today are more commonplace than the telephone. Yet its story, dramatically done, stole the show in the Communications Building. Sunbeam Mixmaster dramatized the commonplace story of peeling potatoes and outdrew many more costly nearby exhibits, meanwhile successfully selling as many as 100 machines daily. Union Carbon and Carbide, the Wings of a Century, and others personalized their story in highly dramatic form. The significant point is that this dramatization, in its most successful applications, was told in stories of ordinary, everyday human behavior.

The Chrysler exhibit was typical. At first their outdoor quarter-mile track was merely an adjunct to their main exhibit building—an afterthought for free demonstration rides. Then someone saw its dramatic possibilities. Every hour, a show was staged on the miniature race track. Stock cars raced around hairpin turns while tires smoked and brakes squealed. Within the race-track oval "hell-pit" of loose sand and deep ditches, other cars were subjected to more abuse in a few minutes than most cars receive in years. Not infrequently cars completely overturned, but always without crumpling the all-steel bodies, breaking safety glass, or injuring the drivers.

The crowds gasped at the daring maneuvers of Barney Oldfield's crack drivers and roared their approval. It became necessary to add a large grand-stand to accommodate the throng that packed every seat at each show. The Chrysler Company did not originally plan a show—they found themselves with a show on their hands, a show that sold deeper and more effectively than any number of exhibits. They made their building an adjunct to their track, and dramatized entertainment enabled them to hold their own against both Ford's and General Motors's much greater Fair investments.

Standard Oil learned to their sorrow that beautiful but obscure symbols were not enough. The average citizen simply will not make the mental effort to respond to expensive decorations and fanciful lines and curves.

Wisely, Standard Oil changed their tactics. In place of a symbolic film depicting the contributions of oil to industry, they substituted a thrilling wild-animal act with Allen King and his den of tigers and lions. Hourly it crowded the big stands to overflowing and sent the throngs away with an indelible impres-sion of the meaning intended in the merchandising slogan: "Live Power."

Ford's "Rhapsody in Steel," the motion picture shown in the Ford Building theater, was personalized through the friendly antics of a mischievous little imp. And The Human Ford was the acme of personaliza-tion plus the always helpful element of mystery. The

General Motors's mechanical talking Indian, Chief Pontiac, was another successful adaptation of the same principle.

One of the most popular units in the Radio Corporation's exhibit was a crude, animated diorama, making little pretense at expense, that in two brief scenes enacted a touching drama of the seas. Act one featured a doomed vessel of thirty years ago sinking at sea; act two showed a modern liner afire, but this time equipped with radio. Frantic S.O.S. signals are heard, nearby ships respond, and all aboard are saved. In melodramatic fashion a canned voice interprets the action. No one seemed to mind the crudities of the device, any more than comic-strip readers object to the artistic crudities of their favorites. As old and obvious as is the appeal—to sympathy, suspense, relief, fear—it rarely lacked an appreciative audience of men, women, and children.

DINOSAURS ON THE SALES FORCE

It is the human import, not the product itself, that registers with the average citizen. For ideas not necessarily inherent in a product itself can be built into it by skillful merchandising and an effective and entertaining sales story thereby created, in which the product and the extraneous idea become inextricably interwoven. Sinclair's deservedly popular animated dinosaur zoo is an example. When the story finds favor with the crowds, the product happily is carried along with it.

The public is rarely analytical. Drama to them is more important than logic.

An uncritical and admiring audience required no further evidence for the statements that Sinclair crudes actually are older than competitors, or that the oldest crudes do make superior oils. The zoo was a visual and physical proof of the slogans. Witness the lad who related that the "Sinclair" was the world's oldest animal.

General Electric's House of Magic demonstrated the wizardry of electricity by scientific vaudeville before packed audiences. Even the power companies in the Central Station Exhibit employed marionettes to personalize their story. Dutch Cleanser's first effort was built around a scientific display of crystalline structure. Later they pulled many times their former attendance with a marionette story of romance in a kitchen setting.

Similarly many of today's winning advertisements take slices out of life, little intimate dramas of everyday happenings in which each of us can see himself. Sometimes, to our discomfort, they tell us a story which we are inclined to accept because we have in many cases already lived through such happenings ourselves. And fortunately a pleasing, practical solution for our difficulties, a way for us to help ourselves is provided through the skillful interweaving of the product story.

SYMBOLISM A POOR SALESMAN

Symbolism proved to be of little value as a salesman. The classic example of this was the failure of the exhibit sponsored by a large food company to draw the crowds that the costliness of the exhibit and its

An Exhibit Primer for Merchandisers

1. *Attract Attention.* Competition for the visitor's limited time is keen at trade, exposition, county, or world's fairs. Liven the exhibit with motion, color, lights, motion pictures, moving signs, or operating devices. Make certain your exhibit will build an audience. Remember, successful exhibition is first, last, and always putting on a show to sell a product, a service, or an idea.

2. *Dramatize Your Story.* Even the most commonplace product can present its story dramatically and thereby draw and hold crowds. But don't simply glorify the product. Dramatize what it will do for the visitors to your exhibit.

3. *Demonstrations Popular.* People like backstage privileges. Showing how a product is made, taking people behind the scenes, will draw crowds.

4. *Self-participation Pays.* Let the public take part. Give your visitors something to do. A little effort on their part is worth more than many times its equivalent by the exhibitor.

5. *Use Entertainment.* Sugar-coat the pill. People like to be amused and expect to be at expositions. Use entertainment as your crowd puller.

6. *Built-in Ideas.* Related ideas, not necessarily a part of the product story, when skillfully interwoven with the sales story, are effective.

7. *Trained Attendants.* The point of contact with the ultimate consumer is vitally important. Be on hand

yourself or have your best people at your exhibit to greet your visitors, and explain your story properly. Don't forget that the people the public meets at the exhibit booth largely typify the sponsoring company. Don't give this all-important job to the office boy!

8. *Service Appreciated.* Administering to the public's comfort is appreciated. Convenient rest rooms attract crowds. People become extremely tired at expositions. They like to sit down and rest. If they can do both while viewing a commercial moving picture, the sponsor receives high audience concentration from gratified visitors.

9. *Building an Audience.* Publicity should be used to tell the story of your exhibit; to create interest in what you are doing; and to make people want to see your exhibit. Feature your exhibit as an incidental part of your newspaper, magazine, or radio advertising. Include notices in your direct mail. Use every possible method to build an audience of visitors. Remember that a much larger audience will not get to the exhibit, and they, too, should know about your activity.

10. *Study Your Visitors.* The primary purpose of your exhibit is to sell your product. You can also use it as a laboratory in which to study mass human nature. You can test the opinions of your visitors about your products, your advertising activities, your personal sales strategy.

favored location indicated it should. The so-called "Beautiful Mausoleum," with its highly artistic frieze depicting the speed with which the sponsor's products are rushed to the grocer, was not direct and practical as a selling vehicle. It needed an interpreter to tell the story to the public, and the public resents the necessity of making its own interpretations.

Costly trimmings, beautiful arabesques, clever and original symbolic designs, when observed at all, attracted more attention to the novelty of the display or the originality of the designer than to the product itself. United States Steel had a failure along these lines in its highly symbolic Tower of Steel. So did Pennsylvania Railroad and many others.

The value of an outstanding special feature—what Kenneth Goode calls "soloism"—was dramatically verified. Washington's artificial teeth won the spotlight for the dental exhibit. Swift focused attention by importing the entire Chicago Symphony Orchestra. The Chicago Art Institute rallied around Whistler's "The Artist's Mother," the largest paid admission ever to attend an art exhibit; but later, when they neglected to install a widely publicized favorite, they suffered a serious drop in attendance.

When the Italian Village added Sally Rand to its program, the reputation she had gained the previous summer served to pull it from sixth to second place, in point of attendance, among the foreign villages— passing the Streets of Paris. Yet there were other shows on the grounds which quite surpassed Sally in daring and originality.

An exposition offers certain unique advantages that

every copywriter or art director who has struggled to get a three-dimensional idea across within the limitations of the two-dimensional printed page will readily appreciate.

The printed page, the radio, the billboard are, at best, selling at a distance. There must always be a gap remaining between the actual product and the customer. Everyone who has talked into a radio microphone knows that feeling of lack of direct, personal contact with the audience. This is not intended in any sense as a disparagement of these media. They are essential avenues of selling. But the handicap is there; and the ability to overcome it so largely is one of the striking characteristics of modern sales promotion.

At an exposition that handicap is eliminated. Your prospects, millions of them, stand before you in the flesh. You can demonstrate the actual product to them, instead of talking about it or drawing pictures of it. You can reach out and figuratively "rub their noses in it."

And the simpler and more obvious your story can be made, the better. Subtlety is not for the masses. Sunbrite Cleanser, as the hero in an amusing marionette comedy, pulled as big an audience in the aggregate as the Chicago Symphony Orchestra. Union Carbide had an animated cartoon strip planned for juveniles, called "Freddie Flash Joins the Boy Scouts." It drew fully as many adults as youngsters.

"The majority of self-made famous men," says Pearson, "achieved their eminence by virtue of their excessive ordinariness, by the extremity and inten-

sity of their reactions to the commonest impulses."
This applies in selling to the masses: the simplest
story—plain and friendly—is the best liked.

OBJECT LESSONS IN HUMAN NATURE

The most important lesson to be learned from this
or any other study of mass human nature, for both
the merchandiser and customer, is a relatively simple
one. It is an attitude of mind, a manner of thinking.
Properly understood and applied, it will move mountains. Essentially, the lesson is always to work back
from the customer toward the product, rather than
from the product toward the customer. The modern
merchandiser is trying to get inside the head and
look out at the product through the customer's eyes,
with his perspective, his personal interest, and his
wants. He is finding this not only a fascinating adventure, but a most profitable one. Here lies the road to
quick profits—selling around known sales resistance
instead of against it.

Furthermore, if you like your fellow human beings
or are curious about them, or if your business or
personal success is dependent upon people, remember
that the greatest exhibit at any fair is not listed on
the programs or ballyhooed along the Midway—the
fair's chief wonder is always the people who throng
its grounds!

  ❖ ❖ **W**HAT do the American people like?

A study of forty million consumers' reactions to a variety of appeals affords an authentic object lesson in human nature and salesmanship which has a memorable dollar-and-cents value for merchandisers. These methods are most effective:

1. Entertainment, properly used, is a valuable sales tool.

2. Built-in ideas add greatly to a product's appeal.

3. Backstage privileges tickle the buyer's ego.

4. Self-participation by the public rouses interest.

5. Dramatization of your story will intensify the power of your selling appeal.

6. People are absorbed in themselves. Build your sales story with this in mind.

An Exhibit Problem

Your company manufactures laxatives. Your product is sold to the general public. Valuable good will has been established with the medical profession.

Your company has decided to take a relatively small exhibit space at a world's fair. The amount of money available for the exhibit itself and for its maintenance is relatively small.

The purpose of this exhibit is to acquaint more people with your product; provide a proper background for your sales story; impress people with the standing of your firm; and build further good will among doctors.

What type of exhibit would you recommend? How a manufacturer of laxatives successfully solved the problem is told on page 478.

VII

Understanding the Customer's Viewpoint

The customer is always right. So goes the saying that defines the attitude of modern merchandising and takes the place of the discarded theories that found expression in the curt: *Let the buyer beware!* Through all lines of sales activities now runs this reasoning: "The consumer is our sales manager. He defines our sales policies; he determines how many salesmen we shall employ; he decides when, where, and how we shall sell; he actually fixes the price of our merchandise."

In this is a smooth blending of practical philosophy and rugged truth. No one can deny that today the Consumer reigns supreme. Only the short-sighted will argue against his controlling influence and fail to take into consideration the qualities inherent in him. The astute merchandiser will investigate this King Consumer, find out how he thinks, feels, and acts; what are his interests and his desires; what he is seeking in the products that are offered him. In doing so, the merchandiser equips himself to sell around known entrenched sales resistances rather than wasting time and money bucking them.

WHO IS KING CUSTOMER?

The first step in any successful selling program is taken long before the salemen go out on the road,

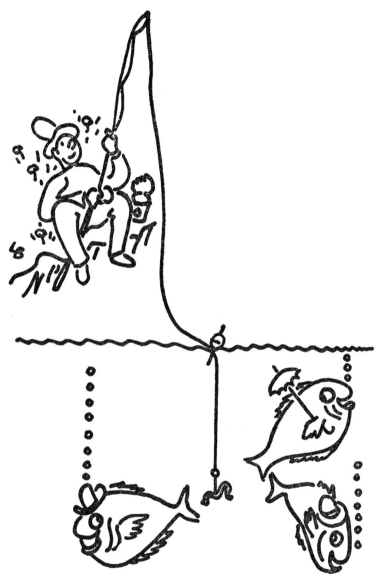

It's the taste of the fish that determines the kind of bait to be used.

long before any advertising copy or preliminary lay-outs are made, long before printers' bids for sales-promotional materials are received. The start of the truly effective sales effort is made only when the sponsor gains a thorough and sympathetic under-standing of the "average" people in his market and their needs and desires.

Who is this average American? Statistically, he is a completely imaginary person; as an entity, "the average man" does not exist except as a card in a business filing machine, one among millions used for plotting purposes.

The "average citizen" is the female head of the family (women now outnumber men), but her hus-band might reasonably object to this assumption, and his children might also claim recognition. Their in-clusion brings the age of the "average citizen" to about twenty-eight and leaves her still female, but by so narrow a margin that she would probably devote her leisure time to trapshooting or pipe collecting.

No, "the average man" doesn't exist. But the ordinary man, the representative, typical American, exists by the scores of millions. He is a nonconformist. He may be as jealous as he pleases about his individ-uality. Since no two persons are exactly alike, the essence of science is to discover identity in difference. And the law of averages, whether applied to atoms or human nature in the mass, is relentlessly dependable.

This representative American is a composite of the primitive and the civilized, of blind instincts and enlightened ideals. Somewhat facetiously he has been described as one who "believes that a couple of quinine pills and a stiff drink of whiskey will cure a cold; that the Masonic Order goes back to the days of King Solomon; that it is practically fatal to eat lobster and follow it with ice cream; that all Swedes have thick skulls and are stupid; that red-haired people always have quick tempers; that dew falls; that morals were purer twenty years ago; and that the winters were longer and the snows heavier and more frequent when he was a boy." And the average woman has aptly been referred to as the wife of this representative American.

HE WANTS WHAT HE WANTS

While the average person's actual needs are few, his wants are many. For the most part, he wants things he could live without, but his desire for them is more intense than for the few simple possessions that are essential to life.

The average person knows what he wants, but coupled with his knowledge there is little understanding of why he wants it. The impulses that force him in relentless fashion to seek this, that, or the other spring from his subconscious mind. All the modern girl may be aware of consciously is that she wants, more than anything else, a riding habit to wear every minute of the day. She does not know, as the psychoanalyst does, that she wants this riding habit because it resembles masculine apparel and she has seething in her subconscious the wish that she had been born a boy. Beneath everything that people want with a singleness of purpose is some profound, elemental reason, of which, in most cases, they are never really aware.

It has taken over a half century of spying for psychoanalysis to pierce the average person's mask and discover what is down deep inside that makes the wheels of his head go round. What such analysts as Sigmund Freud, Carl Jung, and Alfred Adler have uncovered about man's mental life now gives the merchandiser a practical perspective by which the specter of high sales costs can be viewed with more of a possibility of lowering them.

There is an interesting analogy between this pull and force of the subconscious mind of human nature in terms of millions of people and the performance of the iceberg in the open sea.

To the landlubber, who sees only the exposed above-the-surface portion of the iceberg, it is the force of the winds that blow upon it that determine the course taken.

To the wise ocean navigator this naïve assumption is poppycock, for he knows that what really determines the course of the iceberg is the flow and pull of the oceanic currents on the five-sixths of the iceberg's volume not visible on the surface.

Similarly, the astute merchandiser who understands mass psychology knows that it isn't logic or reason that moves the majority of people to action. Instead, it is the pull of the subconscious forces or emotions that prompts them to act and decide and buy as they do.

It is vanity, fear, hate, love, immorality, curiosity, ambition, science, evil-doing, veneration, morality, selfishness, amusement, heroism, superstition, culture—one or more of these elemental human urges—that need to be appealed to by a basic selling idea to produce outstanding sales returns.

BUYING SATISFACTION

What the manufacturer may think of his product has no real significance. Far more important is the point of view of the Average Person, for products are not bought for their own sake—they are a means to an end. *The real commodity purchased is the satisfaction of a desire.* The wise advertiser concentrates on telling people not so much what he puts into his product as what the consumer can get out of it in increased happiness, health, affection, protection, comfort, ease of mind, or other human wants.

Imagination is a prime essential to effective sales appeal. The automobile purchaser is not buying four wheels, an engine, and so many pounds of steel. He is concerned more with the romance and adventure of the open road, the sense of freedom, the "excuse my dust" attitude which this new car will give him.

> *Less lingo and more life is what is needed in most selling. The real flair for salesmanship consists largely of the ability to see inanimate things living which other men think are dead.*

People buy ideas when they buy products. Their preference between similar products is an idea preference. The idea makes the original contact with the buyer's mind and has much to do with his final decision to buy or not to buy.

That is why it is so important to send a product to market armed with a distinctive and basic advertising idea—something the mind of the buyer can grasp and comprehend readily.

Chrysler's famous "Look at All Three" advertising did just this for Plymouth cars. The force of this ingenious basic advertising strategy promptly lifted Plymouth into the public consciousness on an established footing with Ford and Chevrolet, its well-entrenched competitors, and sold the idea that there were not just two important low-priced cars, but three. Furthermore, this idea closed the door to competition from other makes by firmly implanting in the public mind that there were *only* three low-priced cars to consider. At the same time, it emphasized the importance of looking at Plymouth.

The more graphically an idea can be presented to lure the eye and capture the prospective buyer's imagination, the quicker it catches his real interest— the first spoil of this battle known as selling.

SEE THROUGH HIS EYES

There is a popular fallacy that an advertising man is a sort of genius, an odd fellow who goes into a trance when a sales problem is presented, snaps his fingers, shouts "Eureka," and produces the advertising that opens the floodgates of popular demand.

Quite to the contrary, a period of painful, hard thinking frequently coupled with research in the field comes first. "Painful" is used advisedly because the first thing an advertising man must do is forget himself, his cleverness, high tastes, and nobility of purpose. His ego must be trampled into the sod of common instincts and, as he succeeds, he becomes truly a "ghost thinker and ghost writer for the masses."

He identifies himself with the housewife as she goes through her daily tasks, planning meals, getting children off to school, mending clothes, running a household on a limited budget while all the time her imagination is playing with thoughts of mink coats, jewels, and a few sympathetic words from the movie hero of her fancy.

A good merchandiser, selling to the mass market, so orients his vision that he is able to see and think of life through the golden haze of youth, as a young father sees it. He recognizes the fact that in hundreds of homes tonight's discussion may center around the subject, "Which will it be, spark plugs or a new tea-kettle? We can't afford them both in one week." He views life through the eyes and with the emotions of the waitress who served you at lunch; the mechanic in Michigan who helped assemble your car; the tenant farmer in the South who grew the cotton for your wife's summer dress; and the woodcutter in Oregon who felled the trees for your home. He believes in the philosophy of reaching for his hat before reaching for his pencil—in other words, before preparing plans he goes out and gets facts.

SPEAK HIS LANGUAGE

Along with the necessity of gaining a genuine understanding of the nature of the person one is attempting to sell to comes the need of proper consideration of the limitations of one's audience as to vocabulary and pocketbook.

Vocabulary comes first because words, the stuff with which ideas are expressed, are the working tools of the advertiser. A mass market composed of erudite men and women who are quick on the intellectual trigger may be pleasant to think about, but to the merchandiser of a volume product such a picture is just a mirage, which for sheer deception surpasses even those desert phantasies that delude and confuse the weary traveler.

Few errors in marketing are so common as a too-lofty estimate of mass intelligence. Few mistakes are so costly as the tendency of advertisers to talk to the millions in much the same language they would employ when addressing their own friends.

The working vocabulary of the average man or woman is limited indeed. If proof be needed, try mingling with the shopping crowds or the throngs along the boardwalks at your local Coney Island. Listen to their conversations. Notice the kind of language they use. Then, impersonally, read some of your promotional material. Is it down to earth? Will it make *sense* and *reach* and *sell* those millions of average citizens who had their last peep at a textbook when summer rang down the curtain on their sixth or seventh grade? Don't forget that 107 words comprise the working vocabulary of the average housewife; 159 words meet the everyday requirements of the high-school graduate; and even the college alumnus in the top 1 per cent stratum of our

Intelligence Rating of the Public

A major waste in promotional activity is traceable to the misconception of the audience to be addressed. The trouble lies in forgetting or overlooking the intelligence rating of the public. The educational background of 86,000,000 adults, the total population twenty years old and older, according to figures released by the Bureau of the Census, is as follows:

Grammar school or less	48,000,000
Incomplete high school	14,000,000
High school	14,000,000
Incomplete college	5,000,000
College	4,100,000
Illiterate	1,000,000

Few people who buy your product have had the advantage of a college education. Did you know that out of every hundred boys who entered the fifth grade with you,

—only 77 went on to enter high school?
—only 14 or 15 became freshmen in college?
—and only 7 became college graduates?

Most people think the rest of the world lives on a plane equal to their own. But few of those who read your advertising even approximate your own level of intelligence, living standards, or purchasing power.

population gets along with a day-by-day vocabulary of approximately 330 words.

Consider the situation in which the judge queries the officer and the two unruly citizens with, "Who's the aggressor here?" And the cop replies, "Aggressor? Search me, sir, but this guy threw the first punch!"

Remember, too, the young bride who startled the highbrow rental agent with the statement, "I don't care about the vista, but I'm nuts about the view."

Smile if you will, but these are not extreme cases. Granted that most people do have a general idea of what is meant by a word, the fact remains that if the term is not frequently used in their everyday language it has no place in a sales argument. Merely getting the drift isn't enough to arouse *desire;* at least not the kind of desire to make the millions reach into none-too-brimming pockets to trade hard-earned dollars for merchandise.

Dr. Gallup, of the Institute of Public Opinion, in his nationwide reader-interest surveys for newspapers, finds, time and time again, that the best read parts of the daily paper are: first, the pictures; second, the comics and continuity strips. This was equally true of both men and women readers. It is equally interesting to note that the far-famed editorial page stood in tenth place in the list of popularity of various newspaper features among men and in nineteenth place for women readers.

And don't forget that vocabularies themselves change. The idiom of last year's class won't do for the graduates of this one; change there must be, even if only in name. If your sales story isn't linked to the oncoming generation, you may find, by the time you realize that the audience is beginning to tire of your act, that a competitor has already stolen the show!

The one sure way successfully to adver-
tise a volume product to the masses is to
tell them about it, clearly but forcefully,
in the language they readily comprehend.

Headline, illustration, text, radio script, any sales message—all should be simple and direct enough to ease their way into the average person's mind without a single obstruction.

Do not confuse *simplicity* with crudity. To write understandingly for the man in the street you need not skirt the borders of illiteracy. Nor do you need to violate good taste in order to be interesting. What you must do is exercise your *selective* powers to the utmost and chart your course by those things which you know register most conclusively with the great majority of people. There is cynical wisdom in the remark attributed to Mencken: "No one ever lost money by underestimating the intelligence of the American public."

A gentleman has been defined as "a man who would never intentionally permit another person to have a sense of inferiority." Not only is this a perfect definition of a gentleman, but also it has great significance in every relationship of life, especially the one existing between merchandisers and their prospects. For the man who does allow another person to have a sense of inferiority not only loses caste as a gentleman but also becomes an undesirable person with whom to do business.

Reflect a moment and see how you react toward any human being whose attitude makes you feel snubbed or small and how very differently you feel toward the person who makes you feel important. And when you have that picture clearly in your mind, go one step further and think which one of these two types would get your business if both were trying to sell you something. It is, therefore, of paramount importance that the marketer of a product sold to the masses, while fully appreciative of the educational limitations of his audience, never gives his customers any idea that he is talking down to them, because proper respect for the prospect almost invariably pays out in cold cash.

GAUGE THE CONSUMER'S POCKETBOOK

The sponsor of the promotional effort should also give serious thought to an accurate evaluation of the buying power of his market.

How easy it is to make the mistake of mentally endowing the average prospect with an affluence which in reality he does not possess! For every household that boasts a maid, a car, and a ready checkbook, there are ten thousand average homes where folks must frequently choose between new dishes for the table or a new tire for the car, or between a new roof for the house or a vacation trip for the family. Here is a competition that oversteps product lines. A competition in which refrigerators vie with automobiles, radios with washing machines, gasoline with theater tickets, cosmetics with stockings, lingerie, and gloves.

Does your sales planning recognize this? For remember, more than 50 per cent of the families and single persons in cities must keep their extravagance within the bounds of $2,700 a year or less—$52 a week to pay for food and clothing, for rent and fuel, for education, entertainment, and the dozen and one little comforts that must be indulged in to make life worth while.

Research in one market shows that over twenty million families, representing 72 per cent of the market, cannot afford to spend more than $50 monthly for housing; that houses costing not more than $6,500, including lots, are within the price range that two-thirds of the families can afford to buy. The national income last reported was 158 billion dollars, but despite this staggering total, only one American family in thirty-four had an annual income of $7,500 or more per year and only one in ten had $4,000.

Unless your sales activity is adjusted to realities such as these, unless it is marked by uncommon skill and better than average showmanship and salesmanship, unless it really has the customer's point of view, and *puts the prospect above the product*, it is likely to fail in its real job of building increased profitable sales.

"The quickest way to profits," says Alfred P. Sloan, of General Motors, "is to serve the customer in ways the customer wants to be served. In the final analysis the critical and all-important factor in advertising is its vital connection with the habits, interests, emotional patterns, and experience of the people who constitute the market."

KNOW YOUR MARKET FIRSTHAND

A sales-promotion program that clicks with the heartbeat of humanity seldom emanates from the walnut-and-chromium sanctuary of a Manhattan skyscraper. The most effective sales activity comes into being on the ground while its originators are rubbing shoulders with the consumer for whom the program is planned—visiting, talking, listening—and always learning more and more about the idiosyncrasies, the wants, the needs, and the desires of the people who comprise the market for the product to be sold.

Sales plans originated in the field and based on a genuine understanding of the consumer's point of view are not "impersonal" sales helps despite the fact they take form in printed advertising material or an announcer's voice over the air, without direct personal contact with the prospect. Sales plans of this type might more aptly be termed "un-personal" selling. Investigation shows that the most successful promotional plans are always of the "un-personal" type, characterized by more "you" in their sales message and less of the manufacturers' "me."

The writer believes so strongly in the wisdom of knowing your market firsthand before you attempt to sell it that over a period of years he has purposely spent a good portion of his time out in the field. Perhaps this point of view is due to an experience of some years ago, when, as an inexperienced trout fisherman decked out with expensive trout flies, he made his first trip to Maine. Casting these high-priced trout flies hopefully into a trout pool, the novice Izaak Walton was dismayed to find they brought no response. Then the remarks of the Maine guide, "You know, son, it ain't the taste of the fisherman that decides the kind of bait. It's the taste of the fish," brought home a moral equally applicable to fishing and merchandising.

Marketing, like fishing, is essentially the art of persuading potential customers to action. People are no more likely than trout to rise instantaneously to any kind of bait and swim gratefully ashore holding it in their mouths.

Yet strangely enough, many merchandisers appear to expect just this. They remind one of the rookie on the target range who, when reprimanded by the instructor with the question as to where all his bullets went replied, "I don't know, sir, they left here all right."

THE NATION'S "PURCHASING AGENT"

Women are credited, according to the Hearst Magazine Report, with influencing the purchase of 75 per cent of men's underwear, 97 per cent of the food-stuffs, 48 per cent of all drugs, 49 per cent of hardware, and 98 per cent of home furnishings. They influence the selection and purchase of 50 per cent of all automobiles sold, and they actually buy one out of every ten. If further proof be needed that women are the shoppers of the world, consider the fact that they buy 75 per cent of all neckties, 60 per cent of men's sportswear, and 68 per cent of men's shoes.

Today women own 50 per cent of all privately owned stock in large corporations; they file 42 per cent of all income-tax returns; they are beneficiaries of more than 80 per cent of all privately owned life-insurance policies; and two-thirds of all privately owned war bonds are in women's names. One out of every three women is expected to be gainfully employed in 1950.

How should marketers approach this great buying group of women, who annually make 90 per cent or more of all the purchases? Is there a specialized feminine style in writing advertising? Do women respond more readily to highly emotional appeals than men? Do they welcome more details? Are they less imaginative? Are women greater value seekers than men? Do women more frequently buy on the basis of a sudden impulse than do men? What types of sales appeal should retail clerks use when making contacts with women prospects or customers?

These are not rhetorical questions. The correct answers, in relation to an individual product or a specialized market, are worth real money to the merchandiser, large or small. The more the marketer studies his goods with the feminine viewpoint in mind, the more successful will be his sales efforts. Never forget that in this so-called "man-made" world, men may scrape up the money, but the women actually spend it!

Exactly the same goods are bought by men and women, but chiefly for widely different reasons or because of totally different consumer responses.

Women will buy a certain type of roofing, for example, primarily because of its colorful beauty in lending architectural charm to the castle of their dreams; men are influenced more in their buying choice because the roofing material possesses inherent characteristics of durability and economy.

Feminine automobile purchasers are usually more impressed by the appearance of the car than are men. Style and luxury details are of greater importance in influencing their buying decisions. In the "feel" of the upholstery, many women, because of their experience with clothes and furniture and their more highly developed senses, get an impression of the intrinsic value of the entire automobile.

A large automobile concern has found that the points about their car which make a special appeal to women are:

1. Pride of ownership
    Appointments
    Appearance inside the car
    Color
    Style of fittings
    Quality of upholstery
2. Protection and safety
    All-around safety
3. Comfort and convenience
    Ease of operation
    Riding quality
    Comfortable seats
4. Gain and economy
    Low first cost
    Low operating cost

It is significant that these same sales appeals apply generally to men customers, but in a different order of importance.

FEMININE BUYING CHARACTERISTICS

Wherever women buyers may live throughout the country, it is conceded that they buy goods for about the same reason. The mother of five in a Georgia crossroads village buys ironclad shoes for Junior in order to stretch her funds over five sets of restless feet; and so does the ranchwoman in California who heads a vigorous, growing family. The New York society girl and the clerk in the office of a Montana mining company overspend on dresses for the Saturday-night celebration on exactly the same principles: either to catch the eye of an indifferent suitor or to turn green with envy the stare of a feminine rival. We all know the stews and bread puddings that grace the table the week Mrs. Housekeeper indulges in a permanent wave. In the final analysis, "Women are people."

In handling women, salesmen can benefit from the knowledge that the primary feminine interest is in their personal life. Women have been taught from childhood to place chief emphasis on children, home, and family. If they are working, most of them do not use their jobs as careers. Men will put up with inconvenience and deprive themselves of many personal pleasures in order to promote their careers. Outside of a few really ambitious women, women will chuck the career under similar conditions.

If the salesclerks, salesmen, and manufacturers

understood this, if they had a better understanding of the impulses behind the buying habits of women, lower sales costs would be theirs, and fewer disappointments. And if some women understood themselves better, they could help lower sales costs and make their weekly budgets buy more.

Women are first, last, and always shoppers. They are slower in their mental reactions than men; as a result, they are less quick in making up their minds when and what to buy. Women are greater value seekers than men; they are more thrifty. The woman shopper is a hard buyer. When buying clothes or shoes, the thought of economy is uppermost in her mind. But economy, to the average woman shopper, means more than a low price; it means good quality as well, at a higher price than she would like to pay. Perhaps these buying characteristics help account for the fact that women return, on the average, 15 per cent of the purchases made at department stores.

The woman shopper is a great bargain purchaser. She finds it hard to resist something, almost anything, that is marked down in price. She will frequently make these bargain purchases whether or not she likes or needs the product. Actually, she may never use it; witness the unused "bargain" dresses in milady's wardrobe.

Because women are on the lookout for economy and bargain sales, merchandisers find them receptive to such phrases as "marked down," "greatly reduced in price," "more for your money." Special offers, prizes, something free, and coupons also find a wide acceptance among the sex.

Women, as shoppers, are undoubtedly more sensitive than men. Salesclerks, retail salesmen, house-to-house canvassers must treat them with great deference lest they offend, thereby losing sales. Department stores find that more than 20 per cent of their loss of customers can be ascribed to the supposed indifference, high-hat attitude, or sales pressure of their salespeople.

WHAT INTERESTS WOMEN?

Each week 1,500,000 women, most of them wives and daughters of the 1,800,000 men readers of *Time*, prove they are interested in all the news of the world a busy person needs to know.

Based on Crossley studies of men-women readership, the ratios below are of women readers to men for each of *Time's* departments, according to a continuing study of *Time* readers:

DEPARTMENT	WOMEN READERS FOR EVERY 100 MEN
Art	99
Books	115
Business	68
Canada	76
Cinema	121
Education	96
Foreign News	81
International	82
Latin America	75
Letters	97
Medicine	102
Milestones	107
Miscellany	101

DEPARTMENT	WOMEN READERS FOR EVERY 100 MEN
Music	107
National Affairs	86
People	102
Press	81
Radio	85
Religion	104
Science	74
Sport	52
Theatre	118

WOMEN'S INTERESTS GROWING

Once woman's sphere was the home—completely. That was the position accorded her by man-made conventions. But she has long since upset these conventions. While the woman today takes just as much interest as her forebears in the administration of her home, her horizon no longer stops there. Her interests have widened. She is concerned with what is going on. Current topics are mental food for the wife as well as the husband. If you doubt this, review the editorial content of the current issues of the leading women's magazines. There you will find stimulating information and provocative articles, not only on the problems of the home but on the world outside as well. It is on such a vigorous, thoroughly modern journalistic platform that the knowing editors of the women's magazines base their appeal.

Merchandisers should realize that the interests of women are growing rapidly. Studies show that women magazine readers' interest in fiction has declined, as has the interest in style and beauty. Interest in food remains the same but women's interest in current events, social and economic problems, advertising, home management, and home decoration have all increased since 1939. In this broadened viewpoint, the discerning marketer will find chances for new sales appeals that will find ready response among the most important buying groups in the country.

GET OUT AMONG CUSTOMERS

How can the merchandiser get and keep in constant touch with his market, realizing always that markets are people?

> *First*, by getting out among the people who comprise his market and, by personal observation, make his own deductions and interpretations of his complete merchandising activity. The higher placed the individual is in his own marketing setup, the more important is the need for his doing so. A competent sales or advertising manager, with his accumulated knowledge of all the variables inherent in his sales problem and distribution setup, can frequently reach sounder conclusions about a marketing problem affecting consumer relations after a hundred interviews with typical customers than he would discover by an extensive marketing survey, made by others, covering thousands of interviews.

One of the chief causes of the unnecessary waste in distribution is the fact that the men directing sales and advertising activities are, by the very nature of their positions, their abilities, and their educational and social backgrounds, far removed from the point of view of the average people who comprise their markets. The higher placed these executives are, the more far-reaching their sales and advertising program, the greater is this gap likely to be between their point of view and their customers.

It would be an interesting matter of record and probably a serious indictment of American business if a poll were made of the major executives of leading concerns to determine how much time they spend during a normal business year away from their main offices and out among their customers and prospects.

Second, the merchandiser can keep his hand on the pulse of the customer's point of view by making periodic market studies of a limited or national scope, specific or general in nature, dependent upon his needs. Details of how to do so and the types of information attainable are outlined in Chapter V, "Knowing Your Market."

Third, the merchandiser can keep accurate check on the effectiveness of his advertising and sales-promotion activities, both prior to their widespread use and during the time individual campaigns are being conducted, by copy testing and other checking methods.

Today's merchandiser can and should know the answers to such questions as these:

How popular is my radio program? How does it compare with competitive programs?

What percentage of the readers of any national magazine read my advertisements? How does my whole advertising program compare in its attention-getting values, in its urge to sales desire, and in actual results produced with the advertising activities of competitive products?

What general trends of public opinion are prevalent today that have a bearing on my merchandising activities?

What is the reaction of my own sales force to my promotional activities? What does the trade think? Are both the sales force and the trade using the sales aids effectively?

Any competent merchandiser can expand this list to cover many subjects of paramount importance to his specific needs. The vitally essential matter is to accept the premise that the customer's point of view is well worth knowing and to keep everlastingly at the attempt to understand that point of view.

The surest way to profits lies through placing the prospect above the product!

❖ ❖ THE Customer is King! The more you know about him, the better you understand his point of view, the easier your selling job will be.

Put your prospect before your product. What you think about the product is of little importance; what the customer thinks is largely the key to your sales problem.

Consumers do not buy products. They buy satisfaction of desires. Learn what the customer expects from your product so that you may talk his language and sell him most effectively.

Don't overestimate either the intelligence or the pocketbooks of the people who make your market. Get out among your customers and study your market firsthand. You can't formulate sound sales plans in the cloistered sanctuary of a city skyscraper.

Make a special effort to understand women. They are the nation's purchasing agents.

A Consumer Problem

A LEADING paint company spent a sizable sum annually in national advertising which appeared in the leading consumer magazines. The advertising appeal was directed at home owners.

The advertising copy told in detail why this paint was a good paint. Sound logical reasons were cited explaining the reasons why the finest ingredients obtainable were used in the manufacture of the paint. Emphasis was placed on the skill and experience of the manufacturer and his unrivaled manufacturing facilities. The illustrations used in the advertising usually featured the can of paint itself.

Before any advertising copy was used it was reviewed and approved by a committee composed of the three vice-presidents in charge of sales, manufacture, and research.

Results from the advertising have been disappointing. A new advertising manager has been employed. He is now preparing a report for the board of directors outlining the advertising policy for the coming year.

What kind of a report would you write? Turn to page 477 and compare your report with that written by the advertising manager.

VIII

Keeping Ahead of the Parade

"How does your company stand in the automobile industry?" asked the new-found Pullman companion of the sales manager, thereby unconsciously naming the industry in which the sales manager did his largest volume.

A pleasant person by nature, the sales manager did not show his impatience with what must have been considered a very silly question.

"How do we stand?" he repeated. "Why, first, of course. We're the largest and the oldest company in the field, with a reputation for quality. Our sales to that industry last year were more than double those of the previous year and four times as great as three years ago. Furthermore, our shipments to that industry last year were actually larger than our shipments in our peak year."

That should have squelched the inquirer, but it didn't. "Sales figures speak for themselves, but they do not tell the whole story," he calmly replied. "True, your company may be outselling its competitors in this field. True, its dollar volume may have kept pace with the production during the last four years. But there are many things other than sales volume which should be taken into consideration in appraising the position of a company in a given industry.

"For example, are your products now used in the many applications for which they were practically standard a few years ago? If not, what is being done to regain that business? What applications in the swiftly changing automotive industry are you apt to lose this year? Or next year? What steps are being taken to prevent their loss? Are you developing new uses for your product? What is being done to offset the gains of competitive materials? What are you doing to anticipate the further development of competitive materials?"

The sales manager sensed the thinking process behind the apt questions of a chance companion. He was not too complacent about his sales figures. He knew he had been fortunate in that new uses for his products, developed by the automotive industry, had offset some of the inroads of competitive materials. He, too, was disturbed about developments and trends in his biggest market. He was not at all sure that sales figures for the year would again parallel the industry's curve. He realized the need for definite, authoritative answers to a number of important questions about the rapidly changing conditions in the automobile industry.

What, for example, was the attitude of the development and design engineers of the industry? Did they expect to continue their development work in making improvements in his own and other suppliers' products, or did they feel that now such development was not properly the work of the automotive industry? What were these engineers primarily interested in—products that gave better car performance and cut

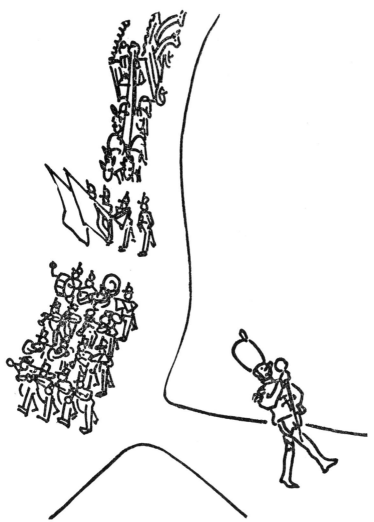

Keep up with and know where the parade is going.

car-operation costs, or products priced lower to the maker but less efficient in the completed car furnished to the ultimate consumer? How would the new assembly-line machinery being installed in the plants of four large customers affect the packaging of the new products his company was developing?

These and other related questions flashed through the sales manager's mind as the train sped back to Detroit.

> *Effective marketing requires a far-sighted anticipation of market trends and changing conditions, and, equally important, a mental attitude that encourages a willingness to meet the changed situation.*

EVER-CHANGING CONDITIONS

Change is inevitable. The statement is simple, but the task of accepting it is not. For changing conditions are much like a river flowing along quietly and minding its own business. The river on the surface looks innocent enough—yet its force, in its gentle way, is invincible. Changing conditions are just as powerful. They rarely get agitated or out of bounds. You can dam them up temporarily, even ignore them, but in the end Father Time, Mother Invention, and Dame Fashion will have things the way they want them.

Because of these beneath-the-surface characteristics, because change is not spectacular but, rather, slowly inevitable, it behooves the modern merchandiser not only to keep pace with the business trend, but also to have a shrewd anticipation of the direction it will take in accordance with the wishes of the buying public.

Silently, with no fanfare of trumpets, every day and hour and minute, these forces are at work altering the foundation of established order. Every day hundreds of new inventions are filed at Washington. Every day energetic competitors are devising new ways to win the public to their products. Every day great masses of the people are deciding to fly in airplanes instead of riding in trains, or to use composition materials for the side walls of their houses instead of lumber, or to shift from one well-established brand to another or to a newcomer in its field. And your customers and prospects are changing. For example, a recent analysis of McGraw-Hill Publishing Company circulation records reveals that during a twelve-month period

> Out of every 1,000 industrial buyers (the men who recommend, influence, and order goods) only 371 make no change in job, title, company, or address; while 241 buyers remain with the same company but change their title or address; and 388 new buyers replace those who die, retire, or shift to other companies.

CONSUMERS ARE CHANGING

Simple, obvious, yet of inestimable importance to any business are the facts of life and death.

Population trends are changed markedly by the recent upsurge in births. Once, in the late 1930's, experts calculated that the country's population might begin to decline after a peak of 159,000,000 in 1980. Later, when war stimulated the birth rate, the experts advanced the peak to 165,000,000 in 1990. Now both the population peak and the time are being put still further ahead.

This means the United States can count on a growing population for a longer period. Out of this growth will come a greater demand for houses and school facilities, for infants' wear and toys, and for all the goods that a larger population will require.

A higher birth rate in the years ahead also is suggested by the postwar marriage rate, thus modifying a 100-year trend toward smaller families. Sample surveys indicate that there is a larger proportion of married persons in the population than ever before, and that portends more births. The birth rate per 1,000 population, at a low of 16.6 in 1932, currently is running above 28 births per 1,000.

The question for the merchandiser to ask himself is, "What shall I do about it?" In a few short years, the total changes in a market due to the inevitable laws of life and death make for great changes with which the merchandiser must keep abreast.

ARE MORALS CHANGING?

From many self-appointed critics, we have been hearing that the decadence of America is rapidly arriving. Both clergy and press point a finger at the morals of the younger generation and the faults of us oldsters—and utter dire warnings.

This situation is a matter of importance to any

merchandiser in America, for all business is based on integrity between the consumer and the producer. Is there any real cause for alarm? Everyone with a stake in the future of the United States should be interested in the answer.

To find this answer, the *Ladies' Home Journal* sent investigators the country over to women representative of every classification, young and old, married, single, divorced, widowed, of every religious faith—from the millions of women who manage homes, raise children, and spend the preponderance of the national income of the United States.

These investigators asked: "Do you think the moral standards of youth today are lower than they were twenty-five years ago?"

"Plenty happened then, too," was the reply of a garage worker's wife in New York. A Detroit widow took a realistic view. She said "The youth of today are the outward expression of our suppressed desire in former years." The minister's wife in Arkansas, who said, "There's a frankness and we hear more about them; of course, some things are shocking, but I'm for the youth," echoed the tolerance expressed generally. For 58 per cent of the women of America are satisfied that morals of today's youth are no worse than those of former generations.

The next question put by the investigators was: "Do you think petting is indulged in by most young people today?"

The vote was overwhelmingly affirmative, 88 per cent of the women agreeing that they do. There were some who did not restrict it to youth, like the professor's wife in New Jersey, who said, "Many adults are worse than young people."

To the next question, "Do you believe it is right for young people to pet or kiss any person but the one they expect to marry?" 59 per cent of the women answered an emphatic "No!" The percentage ranged from 56 per cent among city women to 76 per cent among the women over forty-five, but one surprising reaction was that of a fifty-seven-year-old mother with three children, who opined: "I don't want any one to marry the first one they kiss. Try a few first."

It is recognized that getting married today has problems that did not face the prospective bride and groom of earlier days, so the investigators then asked: "Do you think the difficulty of getting married nowadays ever justifies young people in having sexual relations before marriage?" Nationally, 86 per cent of the women disapproved of such relations. Only 14 per cent said "Yes." On the other hand, 22 per cent of the women under thirty would not condemn sex relations before marriage. Almost unanimous, too, was the reaction to the question: "If you had a daughter that got in trouble before marriage, would you stand by her?" Mother love proved more powerful than moral scruples, for 97 per cent of the women declared firmly they would stand by their daughters in their hour of great need.

To the question, "Where should the responsibility for character and morals rest chiefly—on the schools, the home, or the church?" 88 per cent answered in favor of the home, 7 per cent for the church, and 5 per cent for the school. The majority of the women feel that parents' conduct is the most important factor in moral guidance, for to the question, "Are good morals in the home best taught through parental example, punishment, or praise for good conduct?" 72 per cent said parental example would do most to elevate the standards of young people. Praise for good conduct came next with 21 per cent; only 7 per cent believed that morals could be beaten or scolded into the young.

The survey disclosed, too, that American women's faith in their fellow Americans has not been shaken. To the question, "Do the majority of rich people get their money by means that are not entirely honest?" 66 per cent said "No." Only 34 per cent felt there was any relation between wealth and crookedness.

A majority of the women of America believe that the moral standards of youth are just as high as they were twenty-five years before this study was made. But the *Journal* survey proved more than that—it proved that the women of America are just as good a business risk as ever. If this report were taken as a character reference on which a business contract was to be based, the women's credit rating would be AAA. For the stability, sanity, and fairness of their answers to the questions revealed a moral integrity that should be inspiring and reassuring to every business-man. For times *have* changed. Automobiles, movies, woman suffrage, closer world communications—all have played a part. But, in the midst of economic chaos, of shifting standards of behavior and living, women are absolutely sound on the fundamentals of living and of integrity in their dealings.

This survey of public opinion completely discredits a rather widely held viewpoint. It is cited here in detail as a concrete case illustrating the necessity of not only keeping abreast of changing conditions but knowing the actual facts before accepting or reaching conclusions that may prove erroneous.

HAVE WOMEN CHANGED?

How much women change—and how little—is revealed in studies made over half a century, based on actuarial tables, research papers and monographs, and files of ladies' magazines of the 1890's.

Dr. James F. Bender, Director, The National Institute for Human Relations, specializing in vocational and marital problems, writing in *The New York Times Magazine,* provides the answers to thirty searching questions.

Do women really change? It is the general impression that during the last few generations women have become leggier and slimmer—but have they? Most people would say more and more women are entering professions such as medicine—but are they? Women are as much interested in fashion as ever—but do they have the same attitude toward it?

Some of these questions, and a few more, can be answered on a fairly accurate basis. Starting about fifty years ago, men began to take more of a scientific (though no less personal) interest in women. More or less definitive studies were made and, in the years since, there have been many new ones. As a result, certain aspects of change—or lack of it—can be determined. Here are thirty questions and their answers, tending to show just how much and how little women have changed.

PHYSICALLY

Are today's women taller than those of fifty years ago?

Yes. The average height of college women in 1892 was 5 feet 3 inches. Today it is about an inch and a half greater. Generally speaking, "as education has become broader, women's figures have become narrower." (*Sources: Dr. Dudley A. Sargent's exhibit at Chicago World's Fair of 1893–94; Dr. E. A. Hooton's "Twilight of Man."*)

Are women getting thinner?

Yes. In all age groups they are losing weight. The average decline in feminine weight in a recent decade was almost five pounds. (*Source: Metropolitan Life Insurance Company.*)

Are women's physical contours different from what they were fifty years ago?

Yes. In the 1890's the hourglass figure was the vogue; the ideal waist measure, often attained by tight lacing, was nineteen inches. Today the average woman has broader shoulders, a better developed chest, more prominent abdominal and back muscles, a less slender and fragile waist, slenderer legs. There is also a decrease in the breadth of her hips, but hip and arm girths have increased. (*Sources: Elsie Clews Parsons' "The Old-Fashioned Women"; E. A. Hooton's "Up From the Apes."*)

Have women's feet become larger?

Yes. Twenty years ago the so-called "sample shoe," worn by footwear models, was officially size 4B. This year the size was officially raised to 7½B. (*Source: National Shoe Manufacturers Association.*)

Are American women warmer-blooded today than their predecessors of fifty years ago?

No. Female body temperature fifty years ago averaged 87.7 Fahrenheit. Today it averages 80.6 Fahrenheit. The difference is explained by the decline in the weight of clothing worn.

(*Source: Dr. Donald A. Laird's and Charles G. Mullen's "Sleep."*)

Are American women becoming blonder?

No. The number of American women darker in hair color and eye color has increased in recent years. (*Source: E. A. Hooton's "Twilight of Man."*)

Are American women turning gray earlier than they did thirty years ago?

Yes. Premature *canities*, technical term for grayness or whiteness of the hair, is on the increase among women generally in civilized countries. (*Source: H. Stanley Redgrove's and Gilbert A. Foan's "Blonde or Brunette?"*)

Do modern women eat more than their predecessors?

No. Thirty years ago a woman of twenty was able to eat 2,800 to 3,000 calories a day and still maintain a fashionable figure. Today, with many labor-saving devices around the house and with cars instead of foot locomotion, women use up less energy and average only about 2,200 calories a day. Some, intent on slimming, go as low as 1,500. (*Source: Dr. Margaret A. Ohlson, Michigan State College.*)

Do women of today live longer than those of fifty years ago?

Yes. Their life expectancy (at birth) is now about 69 years—about eighteen years more than fifty years ago. The comparable figure for men is now 63—an increase of fifteen years. (*Source: Metropolitan Life Insurance Company.*)

PSYCHOLOGICALLY

Do women weep and cry as much as they used to?

No. Much of women's crying has always been due to a sense of frustration. Today, as women more closely approach sex equality, their sense of frustration is less acute and weeping and crying are declining. (*Source: Dr. M. F. Ashley Montagu in Psychiatry.*)

Are women becoming less sensitive personally?

Yes. The consensus is that increased freedom and better educational advantages have made today's women less sensitive than their predecessors. Nevertheless, they are still more sensitive than men; in a study of 500 members of each sex, one-third of the women were deemed to "take things too personally," whereas only one-fifth of the men reacted that way. (*Source: Dr. Harry Hepner, Professor of Psychology, Syracuse University.*)

Are women as conservative—as averse to accepting new ideas— as they used to be?

No. They are accepting many ideas that fifty years ago would have been almost unthinkable. Within the past decade, in polls, a majority of women stated that they approved of legalized prostitution to combat venereal disease, and a majority indicated approval of divorce, only 11.2 per cent saying no divorce should be allowed. Women of higher income levels have changed their attitudes most in regard to sex and marriage. (*Sources: Fortune and Prof. Theodore Newcomb in American Sociological Review.*)

Are American women becoming less feminine?

Yes. A recent study by a psychoanalyst concludes that modern women's greater intellectuality is to a large extent paid for by the loss of valuable feminine qualities. (*Source: Dr. Helene Deutsch's "Psychology of Women."*)

Do women select their clothes on the same psychological basis as women did fifty years ago?

No. Formerly style was the single criterion, regardless of how a given style suited a given woman. Today the tendency is to pay more attention to selecting clothes that "capitalize on assets" and cover up defects. (*Source: Dr. Elizabeth B. Hurlock, consulting psychologist on fashion.*)

Are contemporary women more satisfied with their lot than women used to be?

No. Despite women's rapid social and economic progress, one-fourth of the women of the United States are disturbed "about their lot—as women." Their chief complaint as homemakers is isolation and inability to have outside interests. (*Source: Dr. Margaret Mead in Fortune.*)

Are women less prudish than they used to be?

Yes. A study of women's attitudes during the past century designates the Nineties as "The Decade of Prudery," and notes a successive decline in prudishness in ensuing decades. (*Source: Dr. D. Willett Cunnington's "Feminine Attitudes in the Nineteenth Century."*)

With the waning of prudishness, are contemporary women considered less strict in their morals?

Yes. A recent survey addressed this question to women: "Do you think that during the last ten years women in general have become more strict in their morals, less strict, or stayed about the same?" In the answers, only 11.1 per cent said "more strict"; 51.4 per cent said "less strict"; 32.3 said "about the same"; 5.2 per cent said they didn't know. (*Source: Fortune.*)

Are there more "heavy drinkers" among women than formerly?

Yes. The number of women who drink excessively has risen in a decade from 6.3 per cent to 17.3 per cent. (*Source: Dr. Robert V. Seliger, psychiatrist.*)

INTELLECTUALLY

Are contemporary women considered more intelligent than their predecessors?

Yes. A half century ago many universities refused to allow women to pursue graduate studies, women being judged incapable. More recently, experiments at Johns Hopkins show that women can do more mental work than men in a given time and do it more accurately. (*Source: Dr. William Moulton Marston, reporting experiments at Johns Hopkins University.*)

Do today's women think differently from their predecessors?

Yes. The "women's angle" is tending to disappear. About fifty years ago at the University of Wisconsin, in a free-association word test taken by both men and women and requiring 100 entries from each, ten categories cropped up much more frequently in women's lists than in men's. The categories were: wearing apparel, interior decoration, food, buildings and building materials, jewels, etc., stationery, education, the arts, amusement and families. The test was repeated recently and only one category—wearing apparel—cropped up with markedly greater frequency in women's lists than in men's. (*Sources: Dr. Joseph Jastrow; National Institute for Human Relations.*)

IN BUSINESS

Do modern wives prefer working careers to tending a home and children?

No. A survey showed that only 11 per cent of working wives actually preferred such careers; the rest said they had to work, most of them because the husband was not making enough, others because of sickness, separation, etc. (*Source: Dr. Gwendolyn Hughes Berry's "Mothers in Industry."*)

Are women doing a better job than they used to of being bosses in the business world?

No. In 1928 a study concluded that women bosses were too personal in and oversensitive to criticism; too jealous of one another; didn't work well with other women; didn't have a sense of fair play. From a study made in 1942, similar conclusions were drawn. (*Sources: Dorothy Dunbar Bromley in Harper's [1928]; Dr. Beatrice M. Hinkel in Harper's [1932].*)

Is there a greater trend of women into medicine than formerly?

No. In 1890 there were 4,555 women physicians in the United States; today there are fewer than 8,000. The female population has more than doubled in the intervening time. (*Source: Thomas Woody's "History of Women's Education in the United States" and American Medical Women's Association.*)

IN MARRIAGE

Are women exercising their traditional Leap Year privileges more than they used to?

No. While it is admittedly difficult to account for all factors operating in marriage censuses, there has appeared to be a tendency in the marriage rate to fall off in recent Leap Years. (*Source: Dr. Paul Popenoe, director American Institute of Family Relations.*)

Do more women, proportionally, marry today than formerly?

Yes. In 1885 the figure was 8.9 women marrying out of every 1,000 in the population; in 1945 the figure was 12.3. (*Source: U.S. Census Reports.*)

Do American women marry earlier than they used to?

Yes. Since colonial times there has been a steady decline in the age at which women marry. Today half of all native white women are married by the time they are 22. (*Source: U.S. Census Reports.*)

Have women's ideas of what they want out of marriage changed?

No. Today, as for several generations, the two most common objectives of marriage given by women are "children" and "economic security." They believe the "best solution to the love problem is marriage." (*Sources: Dr. Olga Knopf's "The Art of Being a Woman"; Prof. Willard Waller, Prof. E. R. Groves.*)

Has the American woman's conception of her role and her husband's changed in recent years?

Yes. She is less willing to accept a passive role, preferring to think of her husband as a partner rather than a patriarch. She is willing to take on wider responsibility in the affairs of the family. She reveals a strong tendency to emphasize the "mating gradient," seeking to marry above her own level. (*Source: Dr. Paul Popenoe.*)

IN THE HOME

With all their enlightenment, are women doing a better job of being mothers—i.e., are they turning out a "better grade" of children?

No. Authorities who have reached this conclusion point out that since the turn of the century mothers have more and more been shifting their responsibilities of child-rearing to the schools and churches; that today's children are overstimulated and therefore less well adjusted. (*Sources: David Snedden, professor emeritus of sociology, Columbia; Dr. A. E. Watson and others.*)

Are contemporary women better cooks than their grandmothers?

Yes. They do a better job of food conservation, know the value of vitamins and how to improve cookery through "gadgets," how to prepare well-balanced meals. In former times food was likely to be cooked too long and in too large quantities. (*Source: Blanche Stover, editor of "Practical Home Economics."*)

BUSINESS PROBLEMS CHANGE

Not all the problems facing the modern merchandiser in keeping in step with the parade are restricted to his product, his customer, or the activities of his competitors.

What is happening in Washington and in the halls of the various state capitols and what is going on in the other industries is usually more vital in determining policies, in affecting plans for the future, and in fixing the attitude of executives toward their own business than the purely internal methods of procedure used in the operation of the individual business.

This does not mean that successful methods and techniques are not of enormous importance. The distinction, however, is that they can be controlled by the alert merchandiser, while these other important factors have to do with pressures from the outside which he cannot ordinarily control.

Thus there is an increased demand from businessmen for information and the interpretation of information which will keep them oriented to the sweeping changes occurring in the political, social, and economic world.

The modern merchandiser must assume and absorb this additional burden, if he is to keep up with his fast-moving competitors. He can best do so, can best keep himself well posted, by a careful reading of the better business papers and by close attention to the valuable services his trade or other business organizations can or should render.

WARS BREED CHANGES

All great wars breed great economic changes. The Second World War was no exception—in fact, changes in population, income, purchasing power, savings, wage levels, industrial employment, and trade activity are apparent to those observant merchandisers who know the facts about their markets.

With all the statistics at hand the figures must be fitted together, since the statistics by themselves may or may not reveal new, continuing, or resumed market trends.

Here are four market facts, selected from the many available, that typify some of the factors merchandisers must analyze today if they are to keep ahead of the parade:

1. Since 1940, ten million people have been added to the U.S. market. That's more people than live in nations the size of Hungary, Austria, or Czechoslovakia.

2. The U.S. program for peacetime national security is costing U.S. taxpayers thirty billion dollars annually—about 15 per cent of the nation's annual national production. Before World War II we spent one-half billion dollars annually for security.

3. U.S. farmers have thirty billion dollars in cash to buy equipment and buildings to lower farm production costs. For the first time in U.S. history farmers have money at hand and face no need to liquidate livestock, etc., to get funds for such purposes.

4. With the great wartime Army-Navy demobilized and more men than ever back as breadwinners, there are still five million more women working in business and industry than in prewar 1940. Since that year male employment has climbed 20

per cent. But women at work have increased 50 per cent to well over sixteen million. High prices and ambitious living are the chief reasons why.

NO COASTING

This whole question of change may be summarized in the statement: "There is no such thing in life as standing still. You are on the way up or on the way down. You can't coast."

Neither can a business concern. Henry Ford's Model T might have tried to coast along on its successful record; there was plenty of this apparently successful precedent in the industry for doing so. Instead, a new and better car was produced and its makers have profited ever since.

Sapolio, Rubifoam, Pearline, to mention only a few once well-established household necessities, tried coasting on the soft cushions of a national reputation until public demand slowly but surely subsided toward the vanishing point.

Human nature being what it is, some phase of a business is always starting to coast. Some department head or sales manager or branch executive is everlastingly getting satisfied with the way things are going. He may not know it but he is on the way down.

What activities of your business are coasting now? Conceivably there are uncultivated markets or new uses for your product that a skillful and thorough market study would reveal. Such studies—when properly made—seldom fail to contain a surprise.

The essence of the problem of keeping pace with changing conditions lies in a personal experience.

The author called, with other executives of an advertising agency, on a client, to inquire if he was satisfied with the work being done.

"Absolutely not," was the answer.

This was a shock, because the executives believed they had done a good job and could verify this opinion by demonstrable sales returns. The natural query was raised as to what the gentleman was dissatisfied with.

"I'm not dissatisfied with anything," was the answer. "Neither am I satisfied. I'm just eternally conscious that as soon as I become satisfied, I'm on the way out; I'll get the feeling I've arrived.

"We've made a good sales record this past year. Profits, too. But no one knows better than I how many chances we have overlooked and how many problems we must overcome before we can get where we should. So I'm always trying to be constructively dissatisfied. I'm always trying to figure out where we will be five years from now and how we can make things better when we do get there."

Nothing will ever stop a merchandiser with that brand of foresight. He knows the secret; his business will never coast or be caught napping by the often invisible and yet inevitable changes carried on day by day by Dame Fashion, Mother Invention, and Father Time. For no business can stand still. No manufacturer can do things as he did them yesterday.

Without constant improvement a business may continue on its own momentum for a few years, but the end is sure, inevitable. No business stands still.

✤ ✤ CHANGES in your market are inevitable. If you are to be as successful in your selling next year as you are now, or more so, you cannot afford to overlook the powerful forces constantly at work. Some of the more important changes concern:

1. Your customers. The recent sharp increases in births may not continue indefinitely.

2. Your market. The people in it will be more numerous in the next few decades. There will be increased demand for all the goods a larger population will require.

3. The language used and understood by your customers. Keep abreast of the changes in popular expressions and vocabularies.

4. The moral attitude. Morals may undergo little real change, but the point of view may become more liberal. Keep closely in touch with the reaction of women to such questions.

5. Business problems. Important changes occur almost daily in both world and national affairs. Legislative activities, national, state and local, must be more closely followed than previously to assure sales success.

✤ ✤ ✤ ✤

A Problem of Changed Conditions

THE ABC Company manufactures a line of wallboard products. Dealers secure more favorable prices, owing to lower freight rates, if they can purchase this bulky product in carload lots.

The RP Company originally sold rock wool insulation products, distributing its products through the same dealers that handle the wallboard products of the ABC Company. Recently the RP Company added a line of wallboard products similar to those sold by the ABC Company. Dealers, therefore, are now able to buy mixed carloads of both products, thereby securing the benefits of smaller initial purchases of both products without paying higher freight rates for less-than-carload shipments.

What should the ABC Company do to meet this changed market condition? Compare your conclusions with those of the sales manager of the ABC Company shown on page 479.

IX

Planning and Working Your Plan

THE visitor to the Canadian Rockies who travels on a well-known transcontinental train will pass through the famous Spiral Tunnels, one of the world's most notable engineering feats.

Formerly, the stretch between the Great Divide and Field, just west of Banff and Lake Louise, was a difficult route, the grade being 4.5 per cent. Train hauling costs were excessive; heavy snow frequently made this trip impossible and dangerous. Now these problems have been solved and the grade reduced to 2.2 per cent by the Spiral Tunnels. From the east, the track enters the first tunnel under Cathedral Mountain, 3,206 feet in length, and, after turning almost a circle and passing under itself, emerges into daylight 48 feet lower.

The track then turns back again and, crossing the Kicking Horse River, enters the second tunnel, 2,890 feet long, under Mount Ogden. Again turning part of another circle and passing under itself, the train comes out into daylight 45 feet lower and continues westward to Field. The whole performance takes place in a maze of tracks, the railway doubling back upon itself twice and forming a rough figure 8 in shape while doing so.

If the train is run in two sections, passengers are

Sound planning is the foundation of success in all competitive activity.

able to see the other section at a higher or lower level (according to the one on which they happen to be) making its way down the big grade.

Before the first shovelful of dirt was dug in these tunnels under the towering mountains, the mind of man had planned their function. Before a single spike was driven into place in this intricate network of tracks, careful planning charted the position of each rail and beam. Before the overhead load of the towering mountains could be maintained, engineering brains weighed each stress and strain of the materials used in the tunnels to assure the safety and utility of the finished project.

THE FOUNDATION OF GREATNESS

Sound planning is the foundation of greatness in all kinds of competitive activity—in the engineering profession, on the football field, in military operations, and in marketing procedure.

No architect or engineer can long survive a mistake obviously due to faulty planning or to lack of planning. He can't bury his mistakes; they are there for all to see—in physical evidence, in stone and concrete and steel, or in completed projects that fail to perform as expected.

Marketers, however, do make mistakes, costly mistakes, and yet because these are not so easily seen they continue to make them. Primarily these mistakes are caused by incorrect planning or by failure to make any plans, or by lack of courage or vision or the conviction needed to carry a sound plan through to completion.

The value of this is so apparent that it need only be stated to be accepted, and yet in practical application far too often it is disregarded.

Sixty years ago the average businessman had a comparatively easy life. The high pressure of modern business was unknown. Today businessmen are often required to be almost literally in two places at once, for modern business can afford no lapse between conception and execution. Time is money. The active businessman's greatest problem is to find time for thinking. How to clear his desk of mail and other messages and to supervise local problems personally in big cities by making quick hops to these points and yet have time to think and plan for the present and the future is the marketer's most perplexing and difficult task.

In marketing operations you have to get in gear to go up. Your product, your selling, your distribution, your sales promotion, your merchandising, and your market in terms of consumers must all be as synchronized as are parts of a smoothly purring motor, if you are to get where you should at the rate of speed your machine is capable of producing. There is no alternative—sound planning is the answer.

PLAN YOUR WORK; WORK YOUR PLAN

Planning in marketing work is usually concerned with the determination of policy, practice, and objectives that provide the answers to these fundamental questions, thereby serving as a basis for a plan of both immediate and long-range action. Acknowledgment is given Harry C. Marschalk, president of Marschalk & Pratt, Inc., New York advertising agents, for permission to include certain questions originally prepared by his organization in the following list:

Your Product: Is it the best value for the money that you know how to produce? Does it sell at a fixed price, or is it a "football"? Is its value obvious? If not, is its value explained on the package? Is it offered for sale in easy-to-buy price units? Does it compare favorably with competitive products? Does it "sell itself"? Repeat on its own merits? Has it any avoidable drawbacks, such as unpleasant color, odor, flavor? Is the package honestly and plainly labeled? Does it meet the various trademark regulations? Are its disadvantages, if any, warned against, to guard consumers from misuse or disappointment? Is it easy to pick up in the hand? Easy to open? If the contents are not used all at one time, can the package be easily closed again? Is it easy to find in a home pantry or on a medicine shelf? On a retail-store shelf? Will it fit in the ordinary pantry or medicine chest? Is it attractive to the eye? (Other questions and suggested procedure regarding the product merchandised are discussed in Chapter II of this book.)

Your Distribution: Is your product available to purchasers or do they have to hunt for it?

Is it readily bought in multiple units? Is it fairly priced to the trade, so that it is carried willingly, not grudgingly? Is its sale forced by means of special deals or other concessions? How much sales efforts do various markets deserve? How can the sales power available be best used? Where should salesmen be routed? When? Is the creative sales effort of distributors, dealers, dealers' salesmen effective? If not, how can you improve it? (Other questions and detailed comments on the distribution of the product are outlined in Chapter III.)

Your Market: Who buys your product? Why? What competitive products do potential customers buy? Why? Are you gaining or losing competitors? Why? What market areas or income groups buy most readily? Why? What basic trends are apparent in the market? How do they affect your product? What relative weight does the consumer give to quality, style, service, cost of operation of similar merchandise? Is similar merchandise being sold on the time-payment plan? At what season of the year is buying most active? Could the selling season be lengthened? Could the product be sold in the export market? Is your product keeping pace with the changing buying habits of the public? (See Chapters V and VIII for further facts about the market for your product.)

Your Customer: Are your name and reputation already established among customers with regard to similar products, quality, dependability, and other virtues? Is your firm name or trade-mark susceptible to further explanation among prospects and customers? Has your product ever been under attack by the Department of Agriculture, the Fair Trade Commission, the Consumers' Union? Have writers criticized your product in books, such as "Your Money's Worth"? Is your product used in schools, business courses, manual-training classes, domestic-science classes? Is your product publicized or featured by women's magazines, newspaper women's pages, radio speakers, Boy or Girl Scouts? (Refer to Chapters VI and VII for more information on the subject of your customer.)

Your Sales Strategy: Are your sales plan and sales strategy designed automatically to take full advantage of favorable circumstances, emergencies, or conditions created by unusual seasonal, style, or climatic factors? Is your promotional activity motivated by a genuine sales idea? Is your personal sales effort geared into your promotional activity and vice versa? How are you measuring up to your immediate objectives? Your long-range objectives? Are you using the best selling aids for maximum results? Is your sales strategy easily under-

stood by your own salesmen, your wholesalers, dealers, dealers' salesmen? Does the
public get the "reason why" your product
is best for them? (Review Chapters X, XII,
and XVII for more facts about selling
activities.)

Your Public Relations: Are you personally
available to the reporters of all newspapers?
Do you hold regular or periodical meetings
with them? Do you cooperate fully with the
press? Or do you, rather, "fight shy" of
them and attempt to suppress news that
might be unfavorable? Do you send out
occasional news releases, or "handouts," or
publicity photographs? Do you welcome,
under proper safeguards, trade or news
photographers? Have you any contact with
newsreel photographers? Have you any contact with the editors of, or writers for, such
magazines as *Fortune, Business Week, The
Nation's Business*, etc.? Instead of cultivating news writers and cooperating with
them, has your company ever attempted to
put over any publicity stunts? Do you cooperate and cultivate the following: schools
of business administration, including those
of Harvard, Dartmouth, University of
Pennsylvania; other colleges and universities, especially cooperating with the in-
structors in economics; the high schools
located near your factory town or towns;
the grade schools; the civic organizations;

the police and fire chiefs; the churches; your stockholders? Does your company support the national, state, and city chamber of commerce? Do members of your company participate in representative business gatherings? Do you advertise in general business papers? Is your company active in promoting the fullest possible legal cooperation with competitors? Do you support and participate in the organized activities of your industry?

THE NECESSARY COURAGE AND VISION

Answers to such questions as these (and the list just given, despite its length, is by no means inclusive, inasmuch as each industry and each individual marketer has specific basic questions of his own) determine the objectives, the goal of the marketer's program.

When he knows what the objectives are, the modern marketer can work toward them. Webster defines the planner as one who "arranges beforehand," a definition which is satisfactory as far as it goes, but which does not go far enough. Not only must the marketer arrange in advance to provide maximum results. He must also have the strength and the faith to stick to his plan and make it work. This does not mean mule-headed obstinacy in clinging to a product or a plan that is outmoded or out of step with the buying public's desires; it does mean the business fortitude to remain with a plan that is sound, despite temporary setbacks or temporary conditions beyond the marketer's control that only for a short time affect the possibilities of the final success of the plan.

Many well-conceived marketing plans are discarded or sidetracked because cold water is thrown on them by the top executives of a company who do not fully appreciate their potentialities. Other plans are dropped because executives charged with their active operation, cursed with desire for immediate volume and willing to sacrifice planned policy for expediency, get cold feet when they are on the very threshold of success.

In other situations those who have made the plans do not have the realistic sense fully to acquaint their board of directors with the hardships involved in their final success; in their desire to get the plan approved, they will oversell and promise impossible returns either as to actual results or as to the time in which they can be produced.

Probably in no other field of business activity are the qualities of acumen, vision, and the courage of conviction so needed as in the formulation and operation of a marketing plan. And in the preparation of a marketing plan, no other phase requires such careful planning as the advertising and promotion program.

PLANNING YOUR ADVERTISING BUDGET

Too much emphasis cannot be placed on the importance of planning and budgeting advertising expenditures in advance. Any intelligent decision as to the amount of money to be spent requires a basic conception of the objectives and sales possibilities, which in turn are based on sound planning. The hit-or-miss operation of a sales-promotion program invariably results in more misses than hits and is primarily accountable for many wasteful uses of promotional effort.

> *The more successful marketers, large or small, plan and budget promotional costs and, having set aside a definite sum, spend it to get the desired results.*

The determination of the sales-promotional budget should be based on a definite procedure and should have a definite relationship either to actual or estimated sales or to the estimated costs of accomplishing a specific task. Some concerns determine their promotional budgets by the unscientific and shortsighted procedure of spending the amount of money necessary to meet the activities of competition.

One of the following four methods or a combination of parts of two or more is almost universally used to establish the promotional appropriation, irrespective of the size of the business involved:

1. A fixed percentage of actual sales for the past year or an average of sales for several previous years is budgeted.
2. A fixed percentage of estimated sales for the coming year is set aside.
3. A definite estimated amount is set up to accomplish a given end.

4. A definite amount is established to meet the
   efforts of competitors.

The majority of marketers determine their promotional appropriation on the basis of sales income,
either past or anticipated. Each plan has its advantages. The first plays safe by fixing the appropriation
on the basis of a known figure. Its chief disadvantage
is that it may overlook current sales opportunities
and prevent profitable expansion because of limitations set as to the moneys available for promotional
expenditures during a given period.

Some marketers find it more logical to base the
budget on anticipated sales or profit for the ensuing
year. If you are experienced and accurate in establishing sales quotas and estimating sales, the second
method will make a strong appeal. If you use the
first method, be certain to adjust your figures to
allow for any unusual condition that may have
produced abnormally high or low sales figures in the
previous year.

In theory, the third method, the setting up of a
definite amount to accomplish a definite task or
given end, is sound. It is, however, based on a more
accurate knowledge of all the variables inherent in
the task to be accomplished than most marketers
possess. Not only is it frequently difficult to establish
the task or objective definitely, but it is also difficult
to determine just how much money will be required
to accomplish the given end. The average marketer
who uses this method is undoubtedly basing his
estimate more on guesswork than on tried advertising
experience in the market involved.

Many experienced sales and advertising executives of the author's acquaintance prefer to use a combination of the second and third methods. They actually use the third method with the safeguard that the total must not exceed the figure established by the second method. As one man expressed it, "It's like going into an à la carte restaurant with a dollar in your pocket. You go down the left side of the menu and decide what you'd *like* to have. Then you go down the right side, check the costs, and adjust your choices to coincide with what you can spend."

The fourth method, that of appropriating enough money to meet the efforts of competitors, is a short-sighted one. Few successful marketers operate solely on this basis, but all give it some consideration. Every marketer is influenced to some extent in the determination of his own advertising budget and in his planning by the activities and expenditures made by his more formidable competitors.

Irrespective of the methods used, tradition and experience have established certain rather widely accepted levels of expenditure for typical percentages of consumer advertising expenditures in relation to net sales volume. These useful figures, summarized from an analysis of national advertising budgets, issued by the Federal Trade Commission, should be considered only as representative of the general practice. Individual companies in any industry may spend considerably more or less than the percentages quoted, dependent upon the needs, their conception of the importance of advertising, their profit setup, and a number of varying factors.

CONSUMER ADVERTISING EXPENDI-
TURES IN RELATION TO NET
SALES VOLUME

An analysis of the amount spent by 548 corporations, whose advertising expenditures aggregated $71,498,607, in seventeen industries, showed the following percentages:

Medium	Percentage
Radio	18.3
National magazines	17.4
Newspapers	15.2
Miscellaneous	13.3
Material furnished dealers	13.0
Outdoor posters	7.3
Joint advertising	6.4
Letters and folders, mailed by manufacturer	5.7
Trade journals	2.6
Indoor posters	0.8

The seventeen industries were manufacturers or processors of meats, canned foods, cereals, flour, biscuits, and crackers, coffee, women's dresses, women's hosiery, men's and boys' suits, men's shirts, carpets and rugs, lumber, cement, paints and varnishes, farm machinery, gasoline and lubrication oil, and rubber goods.

SPENDING THE APPROPRIATION

With the total sales-promotion appropriation established, the marketer must next determine in advance how he plans to invest these moneys in sales-building activities. Each business organization has certain ideas and more or less definite policies to be followed in the attempt to achieve those objectives. Sales promotion is simply one of the means employed by management to attain the desired end—more sales.

It is not possible, of course, to give an accurate breakdown of an advertising appropriation to be followed as a guide in setting up other appropriations. Each advertising appropriation will vary because the needs and objectives of the individual marketer will differ; furthermore, these needs and objectives will fluctuate from year to year as conditions change.

A workable, sensible promotional budget of a typical building-materials dealer, operating in a local market, is itemized below to illustrate the way an appropriation may be planned for coordinated effort. In this particular instance, the dealer based his promotional budget on a percentage of estimated sales for the ensuing year of $150,000; this figure representing an anticipated 5 per cent increase over sales for the last year's operations. It was concluded, based on previous operations and anticipated profits, that 3 per cent of this total, or $4,500, could be spent advantageously on sales promotion, divided as follows:

Expenditure	Per cent	Amount
Newspapers............................	15	$675
Directories............................	8	360
Direct mail............................	20	900
Radio (local).........................	12	540
Billboards and signs....................	9	405
Showroom maintenance.................	6	270
Novelties.............................	5	225
Price lists, catalogs, and other printing...	15	675
Reserve for contingencies..............	10	450
Total..........................	100	$4,500

The percentage figures established for each activity in this budget reflect the dealer's judgment as to their relative effectiveness in his market. Naturally this varies with local conditions. In some instances it is conceivable that no local radio station would produce the desired results. In that case, the 12 per cent, or $540, planned for this purpose in the budget under discussion might be used by another dealer to increase the scope of his newspaper campaign, enlarge his direct-mail activities, or for other purposes.

In the typical budget given, you will note the last item is "reserve for contingencies," an extremely important item in any advertising appropriation. It enables the marketer to capitalize immediately on unforeseen opportunities. It permits him to take advantage of unusual sales opportunities created by emergencies, fortuitous news events, unusual climatic conditions, or unanticipated sales trends dictated by style or seasonal factors.

Suppose, for instance, that a disastrous fire occurred in the residential district of this dealer's town. Without disturbing his carefully planned advertising schedule, he could immediately use advertising in his newspaper stressing the desirability of fireproof roofs. This 10 per cent (it should not be less) emergency fund is needed in the advertising appropriations of both large and small concerns.

WHEN TO SPEND YOUR APPROPRIATION

The dealer under discussion has established how much he will spend and how he will spend it. It is equally important to determine (in advance, again) when he will spend it. Too many advertisers who overlook this essential point discover to their sorrow that they have spent or committed their whole appropriation in the first six or eight months and have little or nothing left for the remaining months of the business year.

In determining when to spend your advertising dollars, it is necessary that your schedule be closely allied with your selling plans and to the natural seasonal variations of your business. In this dealer's business, home-insulation products, for example, should receive part emphasis in May and June (the summer-comfort story) and again in October and November (the winter-comfort and fuel-savings stories). Roofings, also, have spring and fall characteristics. Interior materials can be featured in off seasons. And so on, through the whole line of materials on which the dealer wants to place advertising stress.

> *There is a proper time for all promotional and selling effort, and only when this effort is planned ahead and expertly timed are maximum sales returns possible.*

BALANCED BUSINESS SUCCEEDS

Some businessmen are excellent salesmen but poor manufacturers. They can sell at a profit in spite of the fact that their production procedure is inefficient. Some businessmen are very good manufacturers but very poor salesmen. They are able to stay in business because they manufacture products that people want and will buy, in spite of the fact that the quality of salesmanship is poor.

But such businesses are lopsided, are not so secure as balanced, well-organized businesses, and are easily upset by changes in conditions. An inefficient manufacturer can get by as long as he can sell at high prices, but when hard times make it impossible to get high prices, the inefficient manufacturer will lose money and may fail.

A skillful manufacturer can get by with inferior salesmanship as long as many people prefer his product, but if he hasn't enough sales sense to understand changes in habits and styles, he may go broke manufacturing efficiently products that people have ceased to want. There was no profit in the efficient manufacture of the old-fashioned type of corset when it went out of style, and some corset manufacturers lost a lot of money because they failed to sense the change in the buying habits of their customers.

Businessmen who operate unbalanced or lopsided businesses may be well educated, may be experienced and intelligent about the particular divisions of business in which they were trained, but they are not necessarily capable businessmen.

A capable businessman realizes the importance of a good organization of people who can help him to achieve a reasonably balanced and properly organized business that will sell intelligently, manufacture efficiently, and finance soundly. A capable businessman appreciates and employs the abilities of people who can do things that he cannot do himself.

A businessman cannot command the full benefit of

the abilities of other people unless he can earn and hold their respect for his own ability and integrity. If he lacks either ability or integrity, his capable associates will not stay with him, he will not enjoy the benefit of intelligent assistance, he will not enjoy the security of a balanced business. So he will not be a smart businessman and he probably won't last very long in business.

The men who build businesses that are permanent and profitable are capable men. Many of them started as errand boys and apprentices and never got past the eighth grade in school. Most of them don't know how to score a polo game or play a deep-sea fish. But they are earnest, honest men who can win the confidence, trust, and loyalty of other good men and thus surround themselves with assistants of fine integrity and high ability who combine their efforts to create balanced and successful businesses.

Of course, it would be foolish to assume that all the men in business are capable men with fine characters, because some are not smart and some are not entirely honest. Nor are all of them successful. It is fairly easy to go into business in the United States, and many men who are unfair and unqualified to run businesses will, nevertheless, go into business for themselves. A few such men appear to succeed, somehow or other, and people take notice. But most people fail to take notice of the high percentage of failures in business.

In a typical year, 382,000 businesses failed (according to statistics supplied by the United States government). During the same period 408,000 new businesses were started. These figures mean that, for every 100 new businesses that started in that year, there were 93 businesses (old or new) that failed.

Some of the businessmen who failed that year were honest, capable men who had runs of bad luck. Some were honest men who were capable in some respects, but who operated poorly organized, lopsided businesses because they didn't know any better. And undoubtedly some of the 382,000 failures occurred because the management was lacking in character and failed to fulfill its obligations to be fair and honorable to the employees, the stockholders, the customers, and the competitors.

This large proportion of failures in business is reasonably constant in normal years and is higher in years of depression. The failures are largely the result of incapable or shortsighted or unethical management and represent the process by which business purges itself of the inexperienced, the unfit, and the characterless.

The businesses that survive this constant and automatic house-cleaning process and continue to operate and to provide employment, year after year, are those that possess a high average of integrity and ability. The men who manage those permanent businesses are capable businessmen; in most instances they fully appreciate the necessity for sound, careful planning in all their operations—selling, manufacturing, and financing. The large majority give a high percentage of their time and effort to the careful planning and correlation of the varied activities of their business. They develop plans and have the vision and courage to carry their plans through to completion.

A MANY-SIDED SCIENCE

One day a member of the famous Sales Executive Club of New York spent some time outlining the subjects that were of immediate or general interest to him as a sales executive. His outline is well worth study as a check list for sales executives whose interests may be developing in a lopsided manner.

INTERESTS OF ONE SALES EXECUTIVE

I. Market analysis
II. Product
   1. Product research
   2. Product standardization
   3. Packaging
III. Marketing
   1. Marketing policies
   2. Price policies
IV. Sales organization
   1. Organizing the selling force
      a. Home office
      b. Field
   2. Supervision of branches
   3. Mapping of sales territories
V. Sales planning
   1. Competitive analyses
   2. Sales engineering
   3. Consumer research
   4. Marketing legislation
   5. Sales budgets
   6. Sales forecasts
VI. Sales operation
   1. Getting distribution
   2. The sales force (wholesale, retail)

a. Selection	*d.* Stimulation
b. Training	*e.* Supervision
c. Equipment	*f.* Compensation

3. Sales planning
4. Sales quotas
5. Sales conventions
6. Sales control
   a. Sales analysis
   b. Sales expense
   c. Customer control
7. Sales campaigns
8. Selling techniques
9. Sales promotion—the energizing force in sales
10. Advertising
    a. Publicity   *d.* Outdoor
    b. Films   *e.* Radio
    c. Newspaper   *f.* Ad testing
11. Demonstrations
12. Slogans
13. Credits and collections
14. House organs
15. Direct-mail campaigns
16. Mail-order selling
17. Missionary work
18. Dealer helps
19. Sales manuals
20. Sales contests
21. Point-of-sale merchandising

VII. Management
1. Management policies
2. Management controls
3. Administrative thinking

VIII. Topical interests
1. Trends in business
2. Trade-organization activities
3. Public relations
4. Taxation
5. Political and economic subjects of the day, domestic, foreign
6. Manufacturer, dealer, and jobber relations

7. Chain stores, supermarkets, and independents
8. Price maintenance; loss control
9. What department stores want
10. Personal efficiency
11. Talks by business-book authors
12. Inspirational material with practical slants
13. Dramatizing sales education
14. Financial problems of the day
15. Today's manufacturing problems
16. Reselling and the service problem
17. The businessman in politics
18. Studies of specific sales-department operations
19. Some selling inefficiencies
20. Employee relations

This list, while not all-inclusive, deserves attention also in that it gives tangible evidence of the many-sided activities that go to make up modern marketing. The need for planning your work and working your plan seems obvious.

❖ ❖ Most business mistakes are due to faulty planning, lack of planning, or lack of courage or vision to carry sound planning through to completion.

If you are to be a successful merchandiser, you need a set of practical, plans.

Planning should be related to these aspects of your business:

1. Your product

2. Your distribution

3. Your market

4. Your customers

5. Your sales strategy

6. Your sales-promotion program

7. Your employee and public relations

❖ ❖ ❖ ❖

A Planning Problem

Assume that you are the advertising manager of a company which has never used national advertising. Your careful research has convinced you the company is overlooking profitable opportunities for increased sales by failing to use national advertising. The sales department agrees with your conclusions.

You have recommended that a national advertising program should be undertaken. You have set up estimates of costs, amount of consumer coverage required, and possible anticipated returns. The major executives of your company have somewhat reluctantly agreed "to give national advertising a try for the first six months of next year."

What is your reply?

The reply of one advertising manager is briefed on page 479.

X

Promoting Sales Aggressively

THE regular Wednesday executive meeting in the president's office had the following item on the agenda:

> Formulate plans and procedure for announcement of new product to dealers. Factors to be considered are promptness, complete coverage, and economy.

In opening the discussion, the president reviewed briefly the steps taken to date concerning the new product in which the company placed high hopes.

"I have here," he said, "the report of our director of research, together with the final report of the outside research engineers we employed so as to be doubly sure the product was right before beginning to sell it. They agree that it is as near perfect as human skill can make it; furthermore, they both conclude that the defects discovered during the first six-month testing period have now been eliminated.

"I think we can safely say that the product is satisfactory and will do all we claim for it, which is vital to the permanent success we hope to achieve. A concern like ours, with an established prestige for quality products and valuable good will built up over a period of years with both the trade and consumer could not afford to offer a product which it was not sure of—that's one of the quickest forms of business suicide I know.

"I also have here the final report of our own advertising department, the report of our advertising agency, and the report of the outside marketing bureau employed for this special job, copies of which you have had for several days. All concur in their basic conclusions that their research among consumers proves that there is a real and as yet untapped market for this product. They confirm our judgment that we are in the forefront in anticipating the needs and desires of customers for this product, at the price we propose to charge.

"The special investigation conducted among a carefully chosen list of our dealers, located in all sections of the country, adds their endorsement to the product, its salability and profit potentialities.

"The important question of color preferences which will have a real bearing on sales, since women will play so prominent a part in the actual buying of the product, has been carefully determined by a special research made among 5,000 women. This study shows that, of the ten colors tested, four will satisfy 90 per cent of the present needs. By starting with and concentrating on a line of these four colors, we will cut manufacturing and inventory costs and simplify stocks and speed up turnover for dealers. Should other colors be required, they can and will be added to the line as the need for them develops.

"The durability and low-cost features of the product have been checked with these women prospects

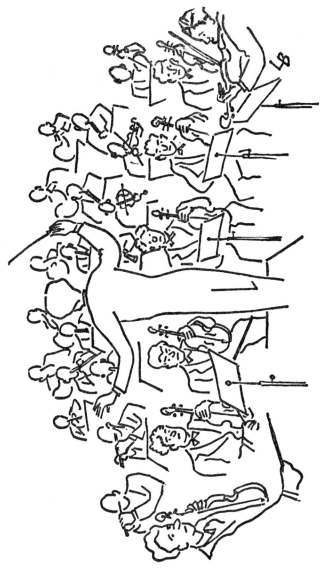

The marketer, too, knows how and when to call on his sales aids.

and also with the husbands of about two-thirds of this group, because experience shows that men help make the buying decisions; furthermore, these technical and economy features of the product are of particular interest to them. In their case, too, these prospective male purchasers believe the product serves a real need and is priced reasonably.

"The Board of Directors has given me every backing, so that we have spared no legitimate expense to make certain that the product is right and that it will serve a real need in a market susceptible to an aggressive interpretation of the inherent values built in the product. We have tried to avoid all guesswork and to eliminate all personal whims and preferences. Incidentally, two of the colors turned down most emphatically by our prospective customers were the shades my wife and I preferred.

"Our immediate concern, as the agenda states, is 'to formulate plans and procedure for the announcement of the product to our distributors'! Let's discuss this aspect of the problem."

"Here's the immediate problem from my angle," said the sales manager. "We want to get the jump on competition and bring this story promptly to 5,000 customers, and about double that many good prospects. We have 120 salesmen. Normally, they would not call on some of our customers for ninety to 120 days, unless we had them double back on their routes. Were we to do so, travel expenses would be excessive for the next sixty days: also, if we used our salesmen for this work, we'd be bound to have a loss in actual sales and profits on our present line for the next thirty days or longer."

"Look at it this way," commented the treasurer. "Our average sales call costs us better than $10, dependent on the salaries paid and the travel expense involved. Records show that our most active men never make more than 1,000 bona fide sales calls a year; a great many of them make an even smaller number of calls. These costs of ours, by the way, are not out of line with average costs for most industries. Can we afford an expenditure of about $10 a call to explain this new product? I don't believe the profit possibilities will stand such a load, either now or later when we have actual distribution and volume sales."

"They most certainly will not," declared the president. "We cannot and should not make our salesmen responsible for this entire 'drumming' function. Naturally they must help but we can't afford to disturb their normal routine."

"This seems to be the answer to the problem," said the advertising manager. "It is more efficient and economical to accomplish the 'drumming' function by the printed word and to use our salesmen's limited time for real sales calls on qualified prospects. We have to use these $10 calls to close orders and build sales on an economical basis; not to do missionary work which can be accomplished much more rapidly and far more cheaply by mail.

"Here's the program I wish to propose: First, we will send this letter to our salesmen today, describing the new product, its merits and main sales advantages. In the same mail, via parcel post special delivery, we will send each salesman a dozen samples of the product, so that by actual handling and inspection he can determine for himself the merits of our claims for the product, and also demonstrate the product to the customers he is now calling on. We will explain to the saleman what we propose to do to get our story across to the trade. This procedure will be about as follows:

"1. Within five days we will mail every customer and prospect an announcement broadside like this dummy I have here. Page 1 will contain a letter signed by our sales manager that emphasizes the merits of the product and its profit possibilities for dealers. Pages 2 and 3 will be devoted to a complete story about the product. Pictures and pictographs will be used so that the story may be quickly grasped and easily understood. Page 4 will be filled with facts about the market for the product and will tell dealers what we will have available in sales aids to help them sell the product. Enclosed in the letter will be a self-addressed return card which dealers can check, asking for a sample, for further information, or the call of a salesman. This card will also be used as an order form; in fact, it will stress the desirability of ordering now; it will make a strong bid for immediate stocking of the product by dealers so they may capitalize on the demand created.

"2. Seven days after the first mailing, we shall send this small booklet to all dealers and prospects. This will do a rather complete job on the product itself and will contain many valuable merchandising suggestions, which dealers can adapt to fit their specialized needs. We may, if returns warrant, enclose a flier, a two-page printed sheet, telling about the response so far received from the trade, as to comments and orders. This mailing will also have a combination order blank and return card, which dealers can use as a convenient order form, or to request further information, the forwarding of a sample, or the call of a salesman.

"3. In next month's business publications we will feature this new product in page space to reach large-scale repeat purchasers of our product. To build consumer demand, we will start announcing the product in our radio program starting next Sunday. Within three to six weeks' time we will be devoting a sizable part of our space in national magazines to the story about the product. We shall use the copy theme and art visualization which our copy pre-testing has shown to have the greatest appeal to consumers. Specialized campaigns will be used in the business and general magazines. Publicity stories as outlined in this folder will go out tomorrow to all trade publications and a little later to newspapers and general magazines.

"4. Each salesman will understand our plans fully, not later than the day after tomorrow. As the promotional pieces, publicity releases, radio announcements, and advertising proofs are ready, they will be sent to salesmen with an explanatory letter telling how each can be merchandised to the trade.

"5. As replies and inquiries come in from our mailings to dealers, these data will be forwarded the same day to each salesman. As salesmen go about their normal business, they will naturally tell the story of the new product along with their regular sales work. Within 10 days, we will have a complete sales manual for all our salesmen; perhaps later it may prove advisable to develop a sales-training course for our dealers' salesmen so that they may get maximum returns from their sales effort.

"6. You will note that we have timed every step in this promotional program to take full advantage of every existing market opportunity. Our paid advertising and publicity have been carefully scheduled so that they gear in closely with our personal selling activity to assure maximum sales results."

"Just a minute, Tom," interrupted the president. "That sounds like a pretty complete program and it all makes sense to me, but how much will it cost?"

"The major items of expense will be as follows," the advertising manager replied:

"1. Preparation of the announcement broadside, 11- by 17-in. size, two-color-printing line engravings or 12- by 18-in. size, one color, with combination half-tones, and the return card, and mailing to 15,000 names, including postage, at the rate of 15 cents a name—$2,250.

"2. Second mailing to same group consisting of sixteen-page booklet and two-page flier and return card, including postage, at the rate of 40 cents a name—approximately $6,000.

"3. Publicity releases, radio announcements, and the necessary changes in the story in our trade and general advertising will cost very little. New art work will be necessary and this should not add more than $2,500 to our already budgeted expenditures for radio, publicity, and magazine advertising.

"An appropriation of from $10,000 to $11,000 will enable us to get off to a fine start. Later, if sales returns and estimated potentialities warrant, we may find it good business to spend a sizable sum, say $10,-000, on the sales-training course. The manual, which we will prepare at once for our own salesmen, will not cost more than a few hundred dollars, as all the creative work will be handled by our own advertising staff working closely with the general sales, research, and manufacturing departments."

"As I understand it," said the president, "you are proposing an immediate investment of about $11,000 for which you plan to make two calls by mail on 15,000 persons, actual customers and prospects, within the next two weeks. That's 30,000 calls at a cost of about 37 cents a call.

"To use our 120 salesmen for this job, assuming each man would make four calls a day, and allowing only one call per dealer, would take five to six weeks or longer and cost us, in the final analysis, at least $150,000, provided each call cost only $10. Obviously, your proposal is the one we will follow. One thing concerns me, though. Can you deliver on the time schedule you have outlined?"

"We can," responded the advertising manager. "Of course, it will mean a week or so of fourteen- or fifteen-hour days for our staff, and it may mean that we will have to sacrifice some of the artistic perfection we normally strive for as a creative ideal. But the realistic aspects and the needs of the situation come first, and, in the time allotted, we can do a good, practical, hard-selling job within the costs estimated."

MODERN SALES TECHNIQUE

In this business conference, it will be noted that the manufacturer followed these steps in a carefully correlated plan:

He made certain the product was right, prior to its release to the trade. His own research department and outside engineers conducted a testing period and eliminated defects discovered in the product.

He predetermined the consumer's approval of the product. His own advertising department, a marketing bureau, and his advertising agency conducted market researches to determine color preferences, product appeal, and consumer reactions (men and women) as to value and price.

He conducted special investigations among dealers to make certain the product, from their viewpoint, met a real market need, had profit possibilities, and was priced correctly.

He made plans to use all available sales tools to speed profitable sales. Direct mail, publicity, radio, general-magazine and business-paper advertising, and sampling were coordinated.

He arranged for his sales representatives to be kept fully informed on all developments and to receive, prior to their release, copies of all direct mail, publicity, radio announcements, and advertising proofs, so that they might merchandise these sales aids to their dealers. His salesmen were to be provided with complete product information in sales-manual form, possibly to be followed later on by a more intensive form of sales training.

He developed a plan whereby dealers would promptly receive product information, data about markets and profit possibilities, samples of the product, and information about the promotional materials to be made available for speeding sales.

All these plans were made by the manufacturer with the full realization that the primary purpose of this activity was to promote the production of sales at a profit.

Thus "sales helps help sales." In just four words, a progressive policy is stated. When this policy is put into operation efficiently, it not only moves every salesman further along the road to more sales and larger earnings, but it also enables the manufacturer to plan and correlate the entire sales program for maximum effectiveness, by making use of some or all of the modern sales tools available.

XI

Sales Promotion

SELDOM, if ever, does the modern merchandiser maintain a sales force of such size that his men can call on all their customers and logical prospects as often as is desirable. Few businesses would find it economical or efficient to do so; most of them use sales promotion to enlarge, widen, and intensify the selling force; to back up their salesmen and dealers; and to carry the missionary or pre-selling sales story to a wide audience of present and potential customers.

Sales promotion is a characteristic feature of modern merchandising. It is distinguished by the use of intelligence and originality in selecting and devising the best selling tools and the aggressive, energetic, and consistent use of these sales helps.

Since sales promotion is dependent largely upon human behavior for its results, it is not and never will be exact science. There are no hard and fast rules for its success; no mysterious formulas to guarantee results; no slide rules which can be used to predict or measure results with scientific accuracy.

There are, however, certain time-tested principles and methods which have proved to be efficient in promoting the sale of products and services. These basic principles, successfully applied by the more important corporations, with adaptations to fit local market needs, can be used favorably whether you are merchandising automobiles or groceries in New York City or Keokuk, Iowa.

In almost every type of business, during every working day, some form of sales promotion is being used or misused. Very few sales are made without it. For such promotion, in its broadest sense, does not mean a magazine advertisement, a printed folder, or a direct-mail letter.

Sales promotion consists of everything done to bring the business favorably to the attention of prospective buyers, to make the business better and more widely known, to increase sales and profits, and to build good will.

The two methods by which you can bring your products or services to the attention of prospective buyers are personal contact and sales promotion. Personal contact, though limited, is admittedly the more effective, but sales promotion, although impersonal in its nature, can reach infinitely more prospects, more quickly and more economically.

Sales-promotion activity is not a substitute for personal selling, but it can and will complement, amplify, and assist selling efforts.

TWO BROAD DIVISIONS

The sales department of the average business is composed of two broad divisions—sales management and sales promotion.

Sales management is primarily concerned with a knowledge of markets, the close following of sales and stock, the direction of branch managers and salesmen, the development and pricing of products, the providing for deliveries, and other related trade and sales services.

Sales promotion includes all the rest of the various activities used in modern selling. Stated most simply, it means helping the salesman and the dealer to sell— making their jobs easier. The sales-promotion aids precede the final charge made by salesmen on prospects, thereby making the selling job easier and more likely of accomplishment.

Beyond, around, and mingled with sales management are a variety of essentials which must be handled capably to hold sales management and sales promotion in effective relation to each other and in complete coordinated working order within themselves.

Sales promotion, both direct and indirect, has a definite place in the sales plans of any business. Intelligently superintended, properly planned, and consistently used, it can be an invaluable selling tool. The job of the manager of a business is to use this tool in such a way that maximum results are received from a minimum investment.

SALES-PROMOTION DUTIES

Rather than attempt further to define sales promotion, we shall list some of its duties and tasks without particular regard to the name of the individual department which may actually perform them. The list is more than imposing.

> Direct and coordinate the activities of the advertising agency in its program of national advertising in magazines, newspapers, and radio.
>
> Exchange experiences within the far-flung parts of a large organization and make prompt use of current data suitable for promotional purposes.
>
> Gain publicity for new products introduced and maintain a continuous, sound public-relations policy and program.
>
> Prepare and supervise salesmen's and dealers' training, the programming of meetings, and instruction in product facts.
>
> Originate the production of direct-mail material, display advertising, circulars, and publicity for use by local outlets.
>
> Conduct sales research to determine trends, seek causes, and interpret conditions.
>
> Plan and supervise market research to uncover possibilities and anticipate needs.
>
> Maintain mailing lists and handle consumer inquiries.
>
> Catalog products in the most convenient and most effective way.
>
> Exhibit products in branch houses, at trade meetings, and in dealers' stores.
>
> Develop sales-facilitating services such as time-payment plans.
>
> Develop the use of pictorial (film) presentations of all kinds.
>
> Guide trade relations through education, trade associations, meetings, product information, dealer helps of all kinds, and selling aids.
>
> Act as a clearinghouse to forward leads from advertising, professional services, and other sources to the right persons or departments.

Publish and distribute a house magazine, either for employees or for the trade, or both.

Coordinate the programs and itineraries of traveling representatives from the home office to branches so that there will be no overlapping or backtracking of effort.

Keep in touch with competitors and associations or related concerns.

Gather testimonial data and photographic evidence of use of products.

Develop periodic reports to stockholders such as mailings with dividend checks and annual reports that combine news features with financial data.

Prepare specialized advertising, direct mail, signs, displays, and other sales aids for dealers' use in local marketing areas.

USE ALL SALES AIDS

This list, although incomplete, is impressive. It segregates a great many necessary activities that are aids to sales, either directly or indirectly. If responsibility for these activities is not definitely placed, some are likely to be lost in the shuffle or inefficiently performed. Aside from activities that are strictly sales management or advertising, there are so many of these supplementary and coordinating services to be performed that no firm, large or small, can afford to have them slighted, performed inadequately, shunted off, or overlooked, even partially. To get the most out of selling, it is important that these secondary activities be carefully provided for. They are not extraneous; they are inherently important, and someone or some unit in the selling organization should be given the job of seeing that they are all keeping in step.

Printing Problem

A nationally known manufacturer wanted an advertising folder to announce a new product.

The job was dropped in the lap of an advertising agency which, being well versed in graphic techniques, designed and planned the folder. Furthermore, in an attempt to save some money, the agency calculated the size of the folder so that six of them would cut evenly out of a standard (or stock) size sheet of paper.

The piece was approved (by the manufacturer), the art work was finished, the engravings were bought, printing estimates were received, the printer was selected, and the job was sent out for production.

Now that the engravings were all made, the printer sat down to print it. He found that, instead of printing six at a time as the agency had planned, four at a time was more economical; because, while printing six at a time would have meant fewer "press impressions," the cost of two extra sets of plates was more than the press saving. But four at a time required a press sheet which left one third of the basic sheet unused, and printers always charge the customer for such leftovers.

However, this printer wanted to save the customer money, so he took advantage of the large quantity to order a press sheet to fit.

Paper (in large quantities) can be bought in special sizes at no extra cost. The printer, therefore, ordered the paper to fit exactly four folders.

By this time the manufacturer began to want the job so the first two (of the four) colors got done in a hurry.

Then the trouble began. The newly delivered paper was not and, in a short space of time, could not be seasoned to the temperature and humidity of the press room. With half

Printing Problem

the job done, the paper shrank. Therefore, the third and fourth color plates would not strike the sheet exactly where the first two had. This condition ("out-of-register") slowed up the job still more.

Finally these things resulted—

1. The folders were late in delivery.
2. The color was not in register.
3. The manufacturer was understandably "upset."
4. The agency was "on the spot."
5. Instead of a profit, the printer came out with a net loss of $400, to say nothing of press waste.

This is one item that too many people neglect. For instance, even though the unlucky printer was correct in running four folders at once, his total printing surface was much smaller than the press capacity. The manufacturer paid $8.50 an hour for the use of a particular press and only two-thirds of its capacity was used. Therefore, it is apparent that knowing and designing advertising pieces to fit standard size sheets of paper is only the beginning. Especially is this so when we discover that the same area of paper with different dimensions (that is, the folder of slightly different shape) would have eliminated all the waste.

In order to plan printing easily and efficiently, a sales-promotion department needs a set of standards which are founded on:

1. Knowledge of *raw materials* (paper, ink, type, etc.)
2. Knowledge of *converting equipment* (printing presses, bindery equipment, cutting devices)
3. Knowledge of *production methods* (as, for instance, whether to print one, two, four, or six folders at once)

To the head of a sales division, an alert, aggressive sales-promotion department is indispensable to his efforts to stimulate smooth operation of the business-getting machinery, in his aim to have the various parts of the division aid each other's activities satisfactorily, in his desire to get the most done with the least friction, and in the necessity to keep all units in tiptop form and fully equipped to tackle the problems immediately ahead.

A FLEXIBLE PROGRAM

Sales promotion must be adaptable and able to carry new burdens as fast as they arise; able to shed old routines and methods when a real need for them no longer exists. Sales promotion must be elastic, able to expand overnight and able to contract even quicker in meeting the requirements of the day.

Sales promotion should never grow large and bulky, because the moment it does it becomes sluggish and there is no room for sluggishness here. The well-directed sales-promotion program exemplifies mental trimness, demonstrates alert execution, and exhibits a versatility which accomplishes a wide variety of changing duties in the quickest and most effective manner.

Only in this spirit can a sales-promotion department guide itself

—to prevent an overbalancing of effort in the wrong direction, as, for instance, an inequitable demand upon the attention of the sales force as between one product and another or one department and another;

—to get the most out of all sales and advertising effort through a program whose parts dovetail with and supplement each other;

—to obtain the power and momentum in any drive or special campaign, which can come only from a coordinated effort of many different units; and

—to act efficiently as a clearinghouse for relaying information, doing liaison work, timing efforts, and getting the best concerted participation from all sides.

Sales promotion may be a catchall for sales helps and selling services, but it must never allow itself to be bogged down helplessly. It may be loaded with odds and ends of supplementary jobs that others cannot find time to do, but under no condition should it become barnacled with useless duties.

Once sales promotion becomes entrenched as a mere department, it is on the road to ineffectiveness. It should knit the various activities and units of a sales division together, enabling them to function as a coordinated whole.

DON'T STOP PROMOTING SALES

Regardless of the many ingenious methods that are tried, nothing has ever been invented to take the place of time. It is well, too, that this should be so. Rich tobaccos and fine wines are cured by an aging process for which there is no substitute. Expensive bond papers are still loft-dried. True, substitutes have been devised, but at their best they are not the real thing.

It is the same with sales-promotion activity. Nothing can ever do the job as thoroughly as time. If it were not so, the element of continuity would not be such an important necessity. There is no short road to royal success. It is the persistence of keeping on with a sales-promotion program that makes the sales curve maintain its steady upward climb.

Stop a moment and recall that:

> The price of grain tumbles, but housewives keep on buying Kellogg's Corn Flakes.
>
> New soaps bob up on grocers' shelves but the white bars of Ivory leave them more rapidly and in greater volume each year.
>
> The owners of the smallest men's-wear stores know that the shirts labeled "Arrow" outsell all others.

Remember this. None of these firms have a patent protection or an exclusive ingredient. Neither have they any advantage over anyone else for their source of supply. They know only one thing. Nothing but gross neglect and time can destroy them. They also realize fully that a continuous sales-promotion program and time made them.

The failures are caused by too many businessmen who try to find substitutes for advertising and time. There are none. Others try too many kinds of promotional activity for too short a time. It has been truly said that the memory of man is only two seconds long. In order that you may impress your product indelibly on the minds of those you want to sell, you must repeat your message over and over and over again. All this takes time, for which there is no substitute. The point of this whole matter is that a genuine, lasting sales success can be built only if you keep on keeping on.

A study of the sales-promotion materials used in industry after industry proves conclusively that where price, product, and distribution are nearly equal, sales leadership follows the flag of the best promotional efforts. It makes little difference whether you are selling soup, tobacco, furniture, dry goods, or the luxury items, whether you distribute your products nationally or sell direct from your own Main Street store, your problem is sales. You either sell or sink! And if you are to continue to sell profitably, you must everlastingly promote your products by using the sales helps best suited to your particular needs and market requirements.

BUSINESS MODERNIZATION PAYS

America's Main Street is not only its longest street but its busiest street, too! Statistics show that over half of the consuming public, approximately 70,000,-000 people, do most of their shopping on Main Street. Usually they do so in the stores that are modernized; for merchants are learning that attractive stores, inside and out, attract business and actually increase profitable sales volume.

The old dingy store front and the dark musty interior with poorly arranged merchandise are as outmoded as the cracker barrel and the oil lamp. Study the service stations, restaurants, and the stores in your town that are doing the biggest business. These stores are dressed up, made to look as modern as tomorrow. They reflect up-to-date progressiveness and the ultimate in service and reliability. They inspire confidence in and help speed the goods they have to sell.

FOUR STEPS TO SUCCESS

The ultimate success of a sales-promotion program is usually dependent upon four fundamentals:

1. *Timeliness.* Does the promotional plan take advantage of an existing market opportunity?
2. *Utility.* Does the promotional plan embrace practical and proved aids to speed sales? Can the plan be understood easily and put into operation with minimum effort by wholesalers and dealers?
3. *Adaptability.* Is the promotional plan flexible enough so that it can be adapted to fit the varying conditions and needs of local markets?
4. *Salability of the Plan to the Trade.* Will the manufacturer's salesmen accept the plan and sell it to their trade?

The first three fundamentals—timeliness, utility, and adaptability—are built into the campaign by those who create it. The degree of success achieved by the promotional plan is, in the final analysis, dependent largely upon the understanding and personal ability of the manufacturers' sales representatives, in whose hands the plan is placed for interpretation to the trade.

This fourth fundamental, *the salability of the plan to the trade*, is all too frequently overlooked amidst the smoke and fire of the creative activity necessary to bring the promotional plan into being. And yet, unless each individual salesman clearly understands the plan; sees how it will help produce more sales in his territory; and has faith in the practical utility of the plan in terms of the local dealers and people who comprise his market, it is doomed to failure despite the excellence of the basic sales idea and the cleverness of its presentation.

Too many merchandisers overlook the vital importance of this fourth and final step. They fail to realize that neglect of this phase of the promotional program is just as incongruous as would be the sending of soldiers into battle equipped with machine guns they do not know how to operate.

TYPICAL PROMOTION PROGRAM

The operation of the usual sales-promotion department may include the planning, execution, and administration of any or all of the following major activities:

> Advertising to both the consumer and the trade. Cooperative dealer advertising in newspapers. Trade-paper advertising in dealer and professional magazines. Consumer advertising in national magazines and newspapers. Radio advertising on national hookups. Spot radio announcements and local radio programs.

Direct-mail materials and campaigns directed to consumers to be distributed through dealers in local markets. Direct-mail campaigns sent direct to the trade or to consumers by the manufacturer. Also periodic mailings to stockholders.

Trade promotion to improve the selling and operating efficiency of the dealer's or distributor's business.

Sales training for the manufacturer's sales force and the dealers' and jobbers' salesmen.

Research and investigation among consumers, distributors, and special groups to seek causes, interpret conditions, and determine trends with regard to products, sales, distribution, and advertising policies.

Publicity releases for newspapers, trade papers, and general magazines dealing with sales plans, product improvements, new uses, and company policies.

All or some of the foregoing activities are usually being carried on continuously and are coordinated in relation to the major activities of the sales department, thereby assuring maximum sales returns.

In the operation of the sales-promotion program a variety of modern sales aids are used. The characteristics, functions, and uses of the more important are outlined in detail on the following pages.

❖ ❖ FEW businesses find it economically possible to provide enough salesmen to call on their customers and prospects as often as is desirable.

Modern marketers, therefore, use a wide variety of impersonal sales tools:

1. To enlarge, widen, and intensify their selling force.

2. To back up their salesmen and dealers.

3. To carry the missionary or pre-selling story to a large audience of present or prospective customers.

This sales-promotion activity must be flexible, timely, adaptable, practical, and salable to both the trade and the manufacturer's sales force. To be productive of results, sales-promotion activity should be continuous.

❖ ❖ ❖ ❖

A Promotion Problem

A^N association of lumber manufacturers is interested in encouraging
home-building activity. Careful research
shows that the majority of prospective
home builders do not have incomes large
enough to enable them to buy the type of
homes which builders are accustomed to
build. Few plans for good desirable low-
cost homes are available to dealers,
builders, or prospective home owners.

What type of promotional program
would you recommend? What sales tools
would you use if you had a moderate sum
available for this program?

Compare your recommendations with
the promotional plan used by the association. Refer to page 480.

XII

Advertising Tools and Procedures

THE more important promotional tools, effectively used by modern marketers in sales-building programs, include:

Newspapers	Direct mail
Magazines	Catalogs
Business papers	Billboards and car cards
Public relations	Motion pictures and slide films
Radio	Window and store display

No attempt is made to evaluate these selling tools or to list them in the order of their importance or effectiveness. To do so would be misleading and stupid, for their utility usually varies greatly with each sales situation. Neither should the reader infer that the number of pages devoted to reviewing the purposes, uses, advantages, and limitations of any individual sales aid is a measure of its importance in relationship to any other sales aid or to any given sales problem.

Furthermore, this list of sales aids is not and should not be considered as all inclusive. There are additional sales helps less commonly used but deserving of mention that are effective as applied to individual sales situations. Space limitations preclude their review here.

ADVERTISING

Advertising, which has carved for itself a clear-cut niche, is now universally recognized as a powerful business force. It is defined as "salesmanship in print" (before radio or television), as "a business force, which through the printed word sells, or helps sell, builds reputations, and forms good will," or "as the paid form of the impersonal presentation of a proposition to the people in such a way that they may be induced to act upon it favorably."

The primary purposes of advertising are to assist consumers as an aid in buying, thereby performing a legitimate news function; to influence more people to use a product, or a service, or ideas that are offered for sale; and to influence people to use the product or service more extensively, that is, to buy in greater quantity. Advertising helps also in preparing the way for sales, in removing obstacles to the sale, and in encouraging continued patronage of the sponsor's product or service.

Through the printed word in newspapers and magazines, in business papers and agricultural, college, and religious publications, on car cards and outdoor billboards, by the spoken word over the radio, and by sight plus sound through television, advertising aids the efforts of salesmen as well as of management, and supplements in many other ways the job of selling, for the present and for the future.

Many costly mistakes are made by merchandisers that undoubtedly arise because of the lack of a clear conception as to what advertising really is and what it is expected to accomplish.

Advertising, in itself, represents nothing. Advertising is only a means to the end—and the end is increased sales activity. If advertising does not achieve its objective, it does not exist as advertising.

Consider the situation where a manufacturer buys a page of advertising space in a magazine. He prints on that page, "Best Wishes of a Friend," and nothing more. That is not advertising, for the manufacturer has failed to utilize the medium of the magazine, with its hundreds of thousands of readers, to increase his commercial activity.

Now, assume that the manufacturer uses this same page to tell a creative sales story, based on sound selling strategy. Let us assume he is a food manufacturer and the advertisement carries the offer of a novelty for children if the coupon is filled out and accompanied by a box top of the product. In this case the manufacturer may receive several hundred thousand, possibly more, signed coupons accompanied by box tops of his product. That's advertising—measured not by the test of how beautiful or artistic the advertisement is—but by the commercial yardstick of demonstrable cash returns.

WHAT ADVERTISING DOES

Advertising has, to the individual businessman, three basic functions of interest, with commercial, social, and psychological implications.

1. The practical or commercial function of stimulating the sale of goods, services, or ideas.

What Is Advertising?

Much of the criticism of advertising and much of the regulation which has followed are based on what seems to be an important misconception of its character and function. A clearer picture of what advertising actually is and of the part which it is presumed to play in business promotion, would change the character of regulation by directing it toward those definite misstatements of fact which involve essential misrepresentation of advertised goods and services.

Advertising is not primarily a catalog or description of the qualities and characteristics of products. Yet many consumers who criticize advertising base their objections entirely on their conception that it is intended only to provide detailed information about products. And governmental authorities who are enforcing laws having to do with advertising insist on putting copy under the official microscope, entirely with reference to its factual content.

Most advertising, to be interesting, must be informative, but the big fact which is disregarded by its critics is that disseminating product information is not its primary function. As a matter of fact, the best product advertising and the most successful campaigns frequently have very little to do with factual information, because the public is already entirely familiar with the facts. The purpose of advertising under these conditions is to remind, to persuade, and to present familiar facts in a new guise.

Since persuasion, which is mainly an appeal to the emotions rather than to reason, is the primary purpose of advertising, the character of the persuasive argument should be regarded in the same light as the conversation of a salesman who is endeavoring to crystallize the decision of a reluctant buyer, and who uses arguments which are not factual in a scientific way, but which are intended to create confidence of satisfaction in use. The buyer who has been assured by the salesman of ultimate satisfaction with his purchase, like the housewife who is convinced by advertising that the product she buys will make her look better or feel better, signs the order because the salesman has succeeded in establishing a favorable attitude toward the product in the mind of the purchaser.

With control of advertising copy becoming more and more severe, and with expanding governmental facilities for checking advertising and prosecuting assumed failures to meet the requirements of the statutes, advertisers themselves should emphasize the character of their copy as salesmanship in print, and not as a catalog of descriptive information. Statements of fact must be supported by proof, but purely persuasive material need not be of a scientific character. If every adjective must be subjected to the test tube of laboratory analysis, advertising will soon be deprived of the color and interest that make it effective.—*Advertising Age.*

A Conception of Advertising

T. H. Young, Director of Advertising, United States Rubber Company, and Chairman of the Board, Association of National Advertisers, Inc., defined advertising in these words:

"To me advertising is a business just like any other business. It creates. It manufactures. It sells. It uses research. It has people who keep books; those who work at benches; some who draw pictures; others who write.

"Advertising tumbled out of its cradle in this land of ours and has grown with it. It is distinctly an American product. It is a method of communication which is as American as mass production, the conveyor line, the automobile, the telephone and, yes, freedom itself.

"It is a form of communication that has been developed in no other nation in the world to the extent to which it has been developed here. Yes, we find it in Canada. Yes, in a small way, it can be found in the British Isles and in other parts of the British Empire, but in the remainder of the world, by and large, because of the rules which hem it in and stifle it, it has failed to flourish, as freedom has failed to flourish in those same spots.

"It has taken the dreams of courageous manufacturers and inventors to a people who bought those dreams and thereby produced the greatest material civilization ever known to man. It has been called the handmaiden of mass production and is a definite part of the American distribution and sales structure. It is the lowest cost means of fast communication that has yet been devised.

"In many ways it might be called the youngest part of business. Vital in its youth, reckless in its statements at times; yet generally picturing a better and brighter future. It wakens each morning to tell you and me and all America what is new in our world that day; what is now in the shops,

A Conception of Advertising

in the stores and what is coming from the laboratories and great plants of the nation. It has been laughed at by its critics and abused by its friends, but it has lived and grown steadily.

"It makes you and me work harder for the things it offers. It quickens the pulse of the ambitious and has even kicked the pants of the lazy at times to obtain the things it tells about. It enters sales meetings and brings salesmen up on their feet. It enters homes and makes people want the things it tells about.

"It is you. It is I and millions of others. It is our hopes and desires spread into pictures and words. It is what we want for ourselves and ours.

"Before the war it was used to tell the story of products. During the war it became a real power for the molding of public opinion. It sold war bonds. It recruited nurses. It obtained men for industry in vital spots where men were needed. Its messages caused housewives to save fat. It went to work on salvage drives and brought in rubber and old steel and metal to the scrap piles.

"It is truly as American as we are ourselves. Laugh at it, make fun of it, but without it America would be different. Take it from our newspapers, our magazines and from the radio—take it from our daily lives and you would find a drab world.

"America will not be America if advertising ever ceases to exist, for then our businessmen will not be telling the people what they want them to know about their industrial dreams and products. The books, newspapers and the radio will be in the hands of those who will decide what we are to read and hear, for freedom will have disappeared. That gives you my picture of advertising."

2. The social function of using appeals that are defensible morally and socially so that the effect of this impersonal selling generally will be continuously wholesome and beneficial.

3. The psychological function of reacting upon mental processes so that attention may be secured that compels favorable associations of ideas with the brand, store, or manufacturer's name.

AVENUES TO MARKETS

Since advertising is impersonal selling, the advertising media used are potentially significant. A medium, in the advertising sense, may be defined as any means whereby the advertiser's message is carried to the public. As advertising has evolved, the list of media has likewise developed so that the following listing, lengthy as it is, is incomplete and merely suggestive:

ADVERTISING MEDIA
(Not listed in order of importance)

Magazines	Signs	Store displays
Newspapers	Matches	Theater curtains
Radio	Moving pictures	Truck panels
Catalogs	Souvenirs	Window displays
Programs	Novelties	Yearbooks
House organs	Letterheads	Loud speakers
Packages	Posters	Exhibits
Car cards	Direct mail	Slide films
Taxi signs	Calendars	Bags
Television	Business papers	Package inserts

249

The more important media used as avenues to markets, measured in terms of dollars spent, are newspapers, magazines, radio, direct advertising (that is, direct-mail and mail-order advertising), and business papers.

It is impossible to determine the exact amount spent annually for all advertising purposes, since the amount spent on direct advertising and the total advertising done by many small concerns in little-known publications are difficult to estimate. The total annual expenditure for advertising is currently considered to approximate 3.8 billion dollars in an average "normal" business year, an amount constituting nearly 2 per cent of our national income. This sum of money is said to be distributed among the various media in about the following proportions:

MEDIUM	PERCENTAGE
Newspapers	31.5
Direct mail	12.5
Magazines (weeklies, women's, general, farm)	12.7
Radio	13.7
Business papers	5.0
Outdoor	3.1
Farm papers	0.5
Miscellaneous*	21.0

* Cost of advertising departments, sales helps, transportation advertising, and other expenditures not assessable to the main media.

ADVERTISING EXPENDITURES IN LEADING MAGAZINES

Based on data from the Publishers' Information Bureau, advertisers spent the sums indicated on page 251 in the magazines listed in the five-year period,

Rank	1942 Magazine	1942 Revenue	1943 Magazine	1943 Revenue	1944 Magazine	1944 Revenue	1945 Magazine	1945 Revenue	1946 Magazine	1946 Revenue
1	Life	$27,369,394	Life	$33,903,059	Life	$37,725,005	Life	$41,136,693	Life	$56,422,472
2	S. E. P.	23,653,121	S. E. P.	29,276,379	S. E. P.	31,571,784	S. E. P.	34,379,779	S. E. P.	47,755,345
3	Collier's	13,914,248	Collier's	17,584,752	Collier's	18,790,286	Collier's	19,570,765	Collier's	22,476,827
4	Time	9,718,180	Time	12,267,564	Time	13,742,612	Time	13,910,407	L. H. J.	19,630,595
5	L. H. J.	8,975,816	L. H. J.	11,067,439	L. H. J.	12,233,234	Amer. Weekly	13,285,217	Time	18,537,057
6	Amer. Weekly	7,479,562	Amer. Weekly	10,273,112	Amer. Weekly	11,553,308	L. H. J.	12,845,069	Amer. Weekly	13,312,632
7	Good House.	6,450,000	Good House.	8,110,896	Good House.	8,695,981	Good House.	10,145,323	Good House.	12,440,407
8	This Week	6,224,093	This Week	7,973,407	McCall's	8,204,088	McCall's	8,962,508	McCall's	10,263,034
9	McCall's	6,107,932	McCall's	6,975,242	This Week	8,145,254	Newsweek	8,217,409	This Week	9,739,873
10	W. H. C.	5,828,530	W. H. C.	6,935,264	W. H. C.	7,611,706	W. H. C.	7,780,671	Vogue	9,125,761
11	Newsweek	3,906,270	Newsweek	6,358,500	Newsweek	7,115,462	This Week	7,321,131	W. H. C.	9,053,011
12	B. H. & G.	3,401,921	Look	5,623,179	Look	5,665,104	Look	6,355,394	Newsweek	8,867,910
13	Business Week	2,865,553	Cosmopolitan	4,263,410	Vogue	5,164,456	Vogue	6,031,101	B. H. & G.	8,737,868
14	Cosmopolitan	2,818,140	B. H. & G.	4,149,244	Cosmopolitan	4,876,397	Cosmopolitan	5,457,262	Harper's Baz.	6,865,247
15	Country Gen.	2,809,908	Business Week	4,100,990	True Story	4,785,051	True Story	5,320,372	Look	6,428,872
16	Amer. Home	2,645,591*	American	4,034,721	B. H. & G.	4,672,072	Liberty	5,214,830	Cosmopolitan	6,219,577
17	Fortune	2,537,353	Country Gen.	3,718,860	American	4,657,358	B. H. & G.	5,203,980	Esquire	6,193,086
18	Liberty	2,531,270	Vogue	3,715,239	Fortune	4,609,287	American	5,065,417	American	5,802,498
19	True Story	2,522,531	Fortune	3,537,580	Bus. Week	4,589,828	Fortune	5,055,979	New Yorker	5,721,901
20	Look	2,472,393	Farm Journal	3,441,486	Amer. Home	4,298,374	Bus. Week	4,726,159	Mademoiselle	5,514,507
21	Vogue	2,345,596	U. S. News	3,395,825	Country Gen.	4,252,235	Amer. Home	4,700,955	Amer. Home	5,494,366
22	Farm Journal	2,304,274	Esquire	3,189,622	Farm Journal	4,033,639	Farm Journal	4,601,203	Country Gen.	4,975,347
23	New Yorker	2,157,435	True Story	3,141,734	Esquire	3,914,113	Country Gen.	4,491,230	Farm Journal	4,937,578
24	American	2,132,100	Amer. Home	3,099,752*	Liberty	3,689,536	Harper's Baz.	4,304,427	Bus. Week	4,932,864

* National edition.

1942 to 1946, inclusive. During three of these years, 1943, 1944, and 1945, it should be noted that all magazines operated on a wartime rationing of paper.

INCREASES IN MAGAZINE CIRCULATION

According to The Association of National Advertisers, the average circulation per issue of *ABC* member magazines totalled 161 million during the last half of 1946, as stated in a report issued by the Magazine Advertising Bureau. This average—the highest on record—represents an increase of 8.9 per cent over a corresponding period in 1945 and well over double the circulation of the predepression year of 1929.

Since 1929, the average circulation, in millions, of *ABC* member magazines has shown the following changes:

Year	Single Copy*	Subscription*	Total*
1929	28.0	49.2	77.2
1934	25.9	48.6	74.5
1939	39.4	57.4	96.8
1944	81.8	55.3	137.1
1945	92.1	55.8	147.8
1946	94.5	66.5	161.0

* Second six months of each year.

EXTENT OF NEWSPAPER MERCHANDISING HELP

The extent to which newspapers provide merchandising assistance to advertisers has been measured in a survey recently completed by Deutch & Shea, Inc., advertising agency, as announced in an A.N.A. News

Associations, Organizations, and Trade Groups Serving the Advertising, Graphic Arts, Marketing, Media, and Sales Professions*

ADVERTISING COUNCIL
11 West 42d Street, New York
ADVERTISING FEDERATION OF AMERICA
330 West 42d Street, New York
ADVERTISING RESEARCH FOUNDATION
11 West 42d Street, New York
ADVERTISING SPECIALTY NATIONAL ASSOCIATION
1426 G Street, Washington, D. C.
ADVERTISING TYPOGRAPHERS ASSOCIATION OF AMERICA
461 Eighth Avenue, New York
AGRICULTURAL PUBLISHERS ASSOCIATION
333 North Michigan Avenue, Chicago, Illinois
AMERICAN ASSOCIATION OF ADVERTISING AGENCIES
420 Lexington Avenue, New York
AMERICAN COMMUNITY ADVERTISING ASSOCIATION
1846 Summit Avenue, Madison, Wisconsin
AMERICAN INSTITUTE OF GRAPHIC ARTS
115 East 40th Street, New York
AMERICAN MANAGEMENT ASSOCIATION
330 West 42d Street, New York
AMERICAN MARKETING ASSOCIATION
School of Business, Indiana University Bloomington, Indiana
AMERICAN NEWSPAPER PUBLISHERS ASSOCIATION
370 Lexington Avenue, New York
AMERICAN PHOTO-ENGRAVERS ASSOCIATION
166 West Van Buren Street, Chicago, Illinois
AMERICAN RAILWAY MAGAZINE EDITORS' ASSOCIATION
c/o Norfolk & Western Railroad, Roanoke, Virginia
AMERICAN SOCIETY OF SALES EXECUTIVES
90 West Street, New York
AMERICAN TRADE ASSOCIATION EXECUTIVES
1427 K Street, Washington D. C.

ART DIRECTORS CLUB OF NEW YORK
115 East 40th Street, New York
ASSOCIATED BUSINESS PAPERS, INC.
205 East 42d Street, New York
ASSOCIATION OF ADVERTISING FILM COMPANIES
c/o United Film Ad Service, Inc.
2449 Charlotte Street, Kansas City, Missouri
ASSOCIATION OF EXPORT ADVERTISING AGENCIES
c/o Gotham Advertising Agency
2 West 46th Street, New York
ASSOCIATION OF INTERNATIONAL PUBLISHERS REPRESENTATIVES
19 West 44th Street, New York
ASSOCIATION OF NATIONAL ADVERTISERS
285 Madison Avenue, New York
ASSOCIATION OF NEWSPAPER CLASSIFIED ADVERTISING MANAGERS
122 East 42d Street, New York
ASSOCIATION OF PUBLICATION PRODUCTION MANAGERS
c/o Street & Smith Publications, Inc.
79 Seventh Avenue, New York
AUDIT BUREAU OF CIRCULATIONS
165 West Wacker Drive, Chicago, Illinois
BUREAU OF ADVERTISING
American Newspaper Publishers Association
370 Lexington Avenue, New York
COMMITTEE ON CONSUMER RELATIONS IN ADVERTISING
420 Lexington Avenue, New York
CONTROLLED CIRCULATION AUDIT
420 Lexington Avenue, New York
COOPERATIVE ANALYSIS OF BROADCASTING
330 West 42d Street, New York
COPY RESEARCH COUNCIL
c/o McCann-Erickson, Incorporated
50 Rockefeller Plaza, New York
DIRECT MAIL ADVERTISING ASSOCIATION
17 East 42d Street, New York
EASTERN LITHOGRAPHERS ASSOCIATION
1776 Broadway, New York

* This listing, though not complete, contains most of the more important services available

253

EXPORT ADVERTISING ASSO-
CIATION
20 Vesey Street, New York
FINANCIAL ADVERTISERS ASSO-
CIATION
231 South LaSalle Street, Chicago, Illinois
FM BROADCASTERS, INC.
21 Brookline Avenue, Boston, Massa-
chusetts
HOUSE MAGAZINE INSTITUTE
c/o Sperry Gyroscope Company
Manhattan Bridge Plaza, Brooklyn, New
York
INDEPENDENT RADIO NETWORK
AFFILIATES
c/o Station WFIL, Philadelphia Pennsyl-
vania
INTERNATIONAL AFFILIATIONS OF
SALES AND ADVERTISING CLUBS
225 Norwood Avenue, Buffalo, New York
LABEL MANUFACTURERS NATIONAL
ASSOCIATION
1700 Eye Street, Washington, D. C.
LIFE INSURANCE ADVERTISERS
ASSOCIATION
215 Pershing Road, Kansas City, Missouri
LIFE INSURANCE SALES RESEARCH
BUREAU
64 Pearl Street, Hartford, Connecticut
LITHOGRAPHERS NATIONAL ASSO-
CIATION
420 Lexington Avenue, New York
LITHOGRAPHIC TECHNICAL
FOUNDATION
220 East 42d Street, New York
MAGAZINE ADVERTISING BUREAU
271 Madison Avenue, New York
MAIL ADVERTISING SERVICE ASSO-
CIATION, INTERNATIONAL
1005 Park Avenue Building, Detroit,
Michigan
MARKETING EXECUTIVES SOCIETY
330 West 42d Street, New York
MARKET RESEARCH COUNCIL
c/o New York University
Washington Square, New York
MEDIA MEN'S ASSOCIATION OF
NEW YORK
c/o Wm. Esty & Company
100 East 42d Street, New York

METAL ADVERTISING SIGN & DIS-
PLAY MANUFACTURERS ASSO-
CIATION
836 North Humphrey Avenue, Oak Park,
Illinois
MIDWEST NEWSPAPER ADVER-
TISING MANAGERS ASSOCIATION
c/o Pittsburg Publishing Co.
Pittsburg, Kansas
NATIONAL ADVERTISING NEWS-
PAPER ASSOCIATION
c/o Shopping News
5309 Hamilton Avenue, Cleveland, Ohio
NATIONAL ASSOCIATION OF BETTER
BUSINESS BUREAUS
1921 Oliver Building, Pittsburgh, Pennsyl-
vania
NATIONAL ASSOCIATION OF BROAD-
CASTERS
1626 K Street, Washington, D. C.
NATIONAL ASSOCIATION OF CREDIT
MEN
1 Park Avenue, New York
NATIONAL ASSOCIATION OF PHOTO-
LITHOGRAPHERS
1776 Broadway, New York
NATIONAL ASSOCIATION OF PUB-
LICITY DIRECTORS, INC.
420 Lexington Avenue, New York
NATIONAL ASSOCIATION OF TRANS-
PORTATION ADVERTISING, INC.
30 Rockefeller Plaza, New York
NATIONAL BETTER BUSINESS
BUREAU
405 Lexington Avenue, New York
NATIONAL CONSUMER-RETAILER
COUNCIL
8 West 40th Street, New York
NATIONAL COUNCIL ON BUSINESS
MAIL
Second National Bank Bldg., Washing-
ton, D. C.
NATIONAL COUNCIL OF INDUSTRIAL
EDITORS ASSOCIATIONS
c/o Monsanto Chemical Company
1700 South Second Street, St. Louis,
Missouri
NATIONAL FEDERATION OF SALES
EXECUTIVES
Hotel Roosevelt, New York

* This listing, though not complete, contains most of the more important services available.

Associations, Organizations, and Trade Groups Serving the Advertising, Graphic Arts, Marketing, Media, and Sales Professions* (Continued)

NATIONAL FOREIGN TRADE COUNCIL
26 Beaver Street, New York

NATIONAL INDEPENDENT BROAD-CASTERS
500 Edmonds Building, Washington, D. C.

NATIONAL INDUSTRIAL ADVER-TISERS ASSOCIATION
542 North Dearborn Street, Chicago, Illinois

NATIONAL INDUSTRIAL CON-FERENCE BOARD
247 Park Avenue, New York

NATIONAL NEWSPAPER PRO-MOTION ASSOCIATION
c/o Hartford Courant, Hartford, Connecticut

NATIONAL OUTDOOR ADVERTISING BUREAU
60 East 42d Street, New York

NATIONAL ASSOCIATION OF MAGA-ZINE PUBLISHERS
232 Madison Avenue, New York

NEWSPAPER ADVERTISING EXECU-TIVES ASSOCIATION
536 West Wisconsin Avenue, Milwaukee, Wisconsin

OPINION RESEARCH CORPORATION
10 Rockefeller Plaza, New York

OUTDOOR ADVERTISING ASSO-CIATION OF AMERICA
165 West Wacker Driver, Chicago, Illinois

PACIFIC ADVERTISING ASSO-CIATION
215 Bank of Commerce Bldg., Oakland, California

PACIFIC NORTHWEST NEWSPAPER ASSOCIATION
604 Journal Building, Portland, Oregon

PACKAGING INSTITUTE
342 Madison Avenue, New York

PERIODICAL PUBLISHERS ASSO-CIATION OF AMERICA
271 Madison Avenue, New York

PHOTO-ENGRAVERS BOARD OF TRADE OF NEW YORK, INC.
60 East 42d Street, New York

PHOTOGRAPHERS ASSOCIATION OF AMERICA
520 Caxton Building, Cleveland, Ohio

POINT OF PURCHASE ADVERTISING INSTITUTE
16 East 43d Street, New York

PREMIUM ADVERTISING ASSO-CIATION OF AMERICA
608 Fifth Avenue, New York

PRINTING INDUSTRY OF AMERICA, INC.
719 15th Street, Washington, D. C.

THE PSYCHOLOGICAL CORPORATION
522 Fifth Avenue, New York

PUBLIC UTILITIES ADVERTISING ASSOCIATION
c/o Amarillo Gas Company, Amarillo, Texas

PUBLISHERS ASSOCIATION OF NEW YORK CITY
280 Broadway, New York

RADIO EXECUTIVES CLUB OF NEW YORK
347 Madison Avenue, New York

SALES EXECUTIVES CLUB OF NEW YORK
Hotel Roosevelt, New York

SOUTHEASTERN PHOTO-EN-GRAVERS ASSOCIATION
c/o Dixie Engraving Company, Savannah, Georgia

SOUTHERN NEWSPAPER PUB-LISHERS ASSOCIATION
312 Times Building, Chattanooga, Tennessee

SOUTHWESTERN ASSOCIATION OF ADVERTISING AGENCIES
Chamber of Commerce Building, Dallas, Texas

SOUTHWESTERN ASSOCIATION OF INDUSTRIAL EDITORS
Oklahoma A. & M. College
Stillwater, Oklahoma

STARCH, DANIEL & STAFF
420 Lexington Avenue, New York

TRADE ASSOCIATION OF ADVER-TISING DISTRIBUTORS
1918 Washington Avenue, St. Louis, Missouri

* This listing, though not complete, contains most of the more important services available.

Bulletin. Over 370 papers in cities of 50,000 or over responded to the questionnaire. Results show that:

> Merchandising assistance is provided by 88 per cent of the papers.
>
> Only a very small percentage charge for their services.
>
> Twenty-six per cent of the papers specified minimum contract requirements.
>
> The most frequently offered services are (1) letters to distributors and dealers; (2) information on dealer names and route information; (3) market data; (4) calls by newspaper representatives on dealers, and (5) mat services for retailers.

The greatest difference between papers in large urban centers and those in smaller communities concerns providing dealer names, route lists, and mat services. Metropolitan papers find these services beyond their scope. On the other hand they are more likely to prepare trade surveys and create sales-promotion material.

MECHANIZED SELLING AT WORK

The McGraw-Hill publications point out, in the interest of more effective advertising, that "Mechanized selling at work recognized that American business has grown and prospered as it has learned to mechanize. It submits that our industrial executives have demonstrated more initiative and ingenuity in adapting mechanization to the steps in production than they have to the steps of distribution. It suggests that the basic principle of mechanization—which reduces the cost of making the product—can be more effectively applied toward lowering the cost of taking it to market. It recommends that management men give more thought to, and make a careful analysis of, the specific functions which can be delegated to well directed and properly executed advertising. Objective: Larger possibilities for a stable and continuing profit."

Continuing this reasoning the observation is made that the ultimate answer to the problem of making a profit usually lies in better methods of manufacturing and better methods of distribution. American industry has traditionally met, and is constantly solving, the manufacturing phase of this problem through an increasing investment in "Mechanized Equipment," which permits higher worker productivity at lower unit cost.

Mechanization in its simplest and most basic application is a multiplier of man's productive power. The farmer cultivates more acreage with a tractor. The trucker couldn't haul much without a good truck. The machinist steps up his productive capacity with a modern power lathe. Which, of course, is why management consistently provides its production workers with more and better tools.

When the problem (or opportunity) is production, it's up to methods engineers to determine the answer. In order to reduce the unit cost of production, methods engineers constantly study and analyze each step in every operation with the express purpose of placing a larger portion of the total manufacturing load on machines instead of hand labor. They break down every job, analyze each component part and process, and utilize as high a ratio of automatic equipment per employee as is feasible in order to obtain a higher degree of speed, precision, and lower unit cost.

When the problem (or opportunity) lies in distribution, the same techniques which lower the cost of manufacturing the product can be generally applied to reducing the cost of taking it to market; that is, mechanized selling—the technique used by progressive business management to (1) increase the productivity of salesmen, (2) lower the cost of distribution, and (3) enlarge possibilities for profit.

Reducing the unit cost of selling the product requires in the final analysis thorough and intelligent utilization of the most economical means for reaching and preconditioning the prospect by telling him what it is, why he needs it, and what it will do for him. Mechanized selling involves taking full advantage of the high-speed, low-cost selling tools of advertising to perform the preliminary and intermediate steps in the manufacture of an order, thus permitting salesmen to concentrate on the steps necessary to close the sale.

Advertising is a mechanical tool. Its effective application requires the engineers' approach to the problem of manufacturing a sale. First, a careful appraisal of the basic steps that lead to the production of a finished order. Before he decides, the buyers want the answers to questions like these: What is it? Who makes it? What will it do for me? Where can I buy it? Can I buy it now? What does it cost? What is it made of? How do I order it (size, type, model, etc.)? How do I install it? How do I operate it? How do I maintain it? How much does it cost to operate? How long will it last? Are replacement parts available? What special servicing does it require? Why should I buy from you? Then, determine how much of the job can be mechanized in order to increase the productivity of the salesman's working time.

Let's examine the salesman's working time and calling power. Deducting Saturdays, Sundays, holidays, and a two-week vacation period, there are 244 working days per year. Multiplying 244 times 8 (hours per day) gives 1,952 hours of working time available per salesman per year. Surveys show that the average industrial salesman spends 50 per cent of his time with customers and prospects, 38 per cent of his time traveling and awaiting interviews, and 12 per cent of his time on reports, office work, etc.—or 976 hours in actual selling.

The industrial salesman handles an average of 488 accounts. If he called on them twice a year he could spend 1 hour with each company—there is an average of three persons in each company who should be contacted. This allows 20 minutes per person (1 hour per company) twice a year.

Your salesman is the skilled workman—the specialist. He is the most important and at the same time the most expensive factor in your selling program. His value to you and to himself lies in his ability to provide the personal touch between your firm and the prospective customer, meet and overcome specific selling obstacles, apply the product to the customer's specific needs and problems, and close the order.

Obviously, if he is to make most effective use of his productive ability, he cannot afford to devote his valuable time to the dozen and one chores which can be more economically performed by mechanization. But when mechanized selling is performing its important functions, consistently, he can concentrate much more of his limited working time on the jobs that he alone can do—and do best. The end result is lowered unit costs per sale.

The job for mechanized selling is clearly defined. Mechanized selling is the best, quickest, and cheapest way to accomplish the first three steps in manufacturing an order: *Contact*—all men who directly or indirectly control the purchase of your product; *Arouse Interest*—in your product; *Create Preference*—for your product.

When your advertising is performing its function (steps 1, 2, and 3), your salesman can concentrate on steps 4 and 5, permitting him to make the maximum and most effective use of his productive time! Step 4—*Make A Specific Proposal*—applying your product to the prospect's problem. Step 5—*Close the Order.*

101 JOBS ADVERTISING CAN DO

Here is a check chart and reminder for the business-paper advertiser.

1. Establish and protect your company's standing by:
   Creating and retaining customers good will
   Tieing in with exhibits and trade shows
   Maintaining sound public-relations policy
   Dramatizing or emphasizing the trade-mark
   Promoting special services

Securing use of company's trade name by fabricators

Keeping your markets posted on new developments and future plans

Stimulating word-of-mouth advertising

Protecting patent rights

Keeping present customers sold on standing of the house

Establishing organization as authoritative headquarters (for engineering, etc.)

Discouraging substitution through product identification

Overcoming possible prejudices against your organization

Gaining good will of machine operators

Establishing the speed and scope of company's service facilities

Countering false or exaggerated rumors

2. Develop and maintain your markets by:

Citing performance tests

Showing how to make better products

Cultivating future buyers

Educating newcomers among your prospects

Promoting new uses for products

Overcoming seasonal slumps

Reaching all of the men who influence the buying

Promoting better product design

Teaching "value" to those who are not trained buyers

Offering samples for test purposes

Providing customers and prospects with helpful information

Educating your market on your product and its uses

Selling the services behind a product

Eliciting inquiries for a catalog or other literature

Demonstrating the labor-saving qualities of the product

Giving information about product advantages
Selling the idea of adopting a process
Featuring a maintenance service
Creating new and favorable buying habits
Maintaining a basic consumer educational job
Maintaining interest in the product after purchase
Establishing with the ultimate consumer a recognition of accessories or parts that are sold to manufacturers to be built into machines
Encouraging foresighted buying
Showing how to make or save money
Replacing foreign goods no longer imported
Educating consumers to more limited selections of merchandise
Conducting market tests
Protecting customers from buying old models
Assuring intelligent use and understanding of product
Securing acceptance of substitute product ingredients
Securing acceptance of simplified products

3. Develop and maintain your distribution outlets by:
Moving goods that have been sold to distributors
Building up dealer and agent standing with customers
Explaining house policies that may affect good will
Keeping present dealers sold on the standing of the house
Establishing jobber as source of supply
Attracting new distributors
Holding distributor loyalty
Helping dealers gain parts and repair business
Merchandising, advertising, and other sales helps to distributors and dealers
Showing buyers where stock is available
Helping establish new sales outlets
Attracting desirable dealers and agents

Building greater and more immediate product acceptance by jobbers, dealers, and consumers

Backing sales arguments with repetition

4. Increase the effectiveness of personal selling by:

Presenting a sales story without competition controversy

Helping pave the way for price changes

Helping maintain prices to wholesale and retail outlets

Paving the way for effective interviews

Placing repetition element behind sales arguments

Reaching buyers with a special message

Reaching buyers geographically out of range

Calling more regularly

Preparing the way for salesmen by selling the need, type, and make

Confirming the salesman's story with a printed statement

"Setting-up" the salesman by showing his special qualifications for service to the prospects

Setting a sales story pattern for salesmen exactly the way you wish it to reach your prospect

Attracting highest type of salesmen

Reaching "all" of the buying influences

Keeping contact with the buyer between sales calls

Reducing interview time, increasing enthusiasm of the sales force

Getting inquiries and leads for salesmen

Reaching buyers who are hard to contact

5. Safeguard the future of your company by:

Testing potential salability of new items or services

Opening new markets

Procuring new customers

Building up secondary items

Offsetting ill will of "neglected" customers

Maintaining the momentum built up by continuous advertising

Building confidence in the company's financial structure

Combating illegitimate practices in an industry through cooperative advertising

Protecting against the price competition of unadvertised brands

Explaining delays in deliveries or temporary shortages

Informing customers why special services have been eliminated

Telling the user how to make products last longer

Forestalling the competition of new companies

Maintaining constant contact with customers temporarily out of the market

Reselling lost customers

Showing your confidence in the future of American industry

Maintaining the degree of recognition which your advertising has built

Preventing industry from believing that the company is slipping

Offering substitute products for established needs

Obtaining an increasing percentage of existing business

When you take the methods-engineer approach to the manufacture of a sale, you are raising your advertising sights far above such sweeping generalizations as "increasing prestige" or "improving product acceptance." You are giving advertising specific functions to perform. You are making your advertising an integral part of the sales operation—a more important voice at the management table—an investment in economy for the cost-conscious executive.

For advertising—when efficiently applied—is not an item of expense. It is a method of performing certain operations in the manufacture of a sale quicker, and at lower cost. To progressive management it isn't something to be turned on and off with the shifting tides of business. There is no economy in liquidating a cost-saving piece of automatic machinery—either in production or in selling.

"You are making a profitable investment in mechanized selling when your advertising is performing its specific objectives more efficiently than they can be accomplished by any other method" is a concluding statement in this McGraw-Hill summary.

GENIUS OR ORCHESTRA LEADER?

Many mistaken notions prevail about the characteristics and qualifications found in the competent advertising man. By some, he is regarded as a genius who pulls rabbits out of hats in the form of sales ideas that are panaceas for harassed producers. Others regard him as a dreamy, "arty" sort of fellow who spends money with little regard for its value and even less for the sales returns its expenditure brings or should bring.

The really good advertising man is by no means a genius. In many instances he is not even artistic. He usually is a good showman, and he is versatile. Frequently he has a flair for common-sense, down-to-earth writing. The best advertising men are sound businessmen who take nothing for granted and continuously check the minute and varied details of copy, art, and typography. Many of the more successful advertising men known to the author have an uncanny ability to work long hours under high pressure without blowing up. Most of them, sometimes to the despair of their families, become completely oblivious of time, sleep, or food when concerned with the sales strategy of a promotional plan.

The superior type adds these two distinguishing qualities to his make-up: an instinctive competitive attitude toward business and a deep professional pride in his advertising output.

The role played by the typical advertising manager in the complicated marketing setup of which he is a part is similar to that performed by the orchestra leader conducting a symphonic orchestra through the varied moods of the music of a Wagnerian opera. The leader may not, and usually does not, know how to play each individual instrument in the orchestra, but he knows *how* and *when* the flutes, violins, drums, and other instruments should be played to create a harmonious effect.

Similarly, the advertising manager may not know all there is to know about media, copy writing, layout, art, typography, radio scripts, and the varied advertising tools at his command, but he does and must know how to weld these together and when to use them to attain the sales objective at hand.

THE ADVERTISING AGENCY

An advertising agency is a service organization specializing in the planning, preparation, and placing of advertising for manufacturers and other business firms. As such, the agency makes available to its clients the services of specialized advertising talent, it offers judgment gained from experience with a diversity of advertising accounts, and it provides an outside objective viewpoint that is useful in reaching sound advertising decisions.

Virtually all national advertising is handled through advertising agencies, while smaller business firms and local retailers are making increasing use of agency service to assist or replace their advertising departments.

ADVERTISING-AGENCY SERVICE

"Agency service," as defined by the American Association of Advertising Agencies, "consists of interpreting to the public, or to that part of it which it is desired to reach, the advantages of a product or service."

This interpretation is based upon:

1. A study of the client's *product* or *service* in order to determine the advantages and disadvantages inherent in the product itself, and in its relation to competition.
2. An analysis of the present and potential *market* for which the product or service is adapted:
   a. As to location
   b. As to extent of possible sale
   c. As to season
   d. As to trade and economic conditions
   e. As to nature and amount of competition
3. A knowledge of the factors of *distribution and sales* and their methods of operation.

267

4. A knowledge of all the available *media* and means that can profitably be used to carry the interpretation of the product or service to consumer, wholesaler, dealer, contractor, or other factor. This knowledge covers:
   a. Character
   b. Influence
   c. Circulation—quantity, quality, and location
   d. Physical requirements
   e. Costs

Acting on this study, analysis, and knowledge, the agency then carries out the following procedure:

5. Formulation of a definite *plan* and presentation of this plan to the client.
6. Execution of this plan:
   a. Writing, designing, illustrating of advertisements or other appropriate forms of the message.
   b. Contracting for the space or other means of advertising.
   c. The proper incorporation of the message in mechanical form and forwarding it with proper instruction for the fulfillment of the contract.
   d. Checking and verifying of insertions, display, or other means used.
   e. The auditing, billing, and paying for the service, space, and preparation.

268

7. Cooperation with the client's sales work to insure the greatest effect from advertising.

Beyond these basic advertising functions, many agencies are willing to assist the client with his other distribution activities—personal selling, display, and sales promotion. They may do special work in such fields as sales research and training, package designing, preparation of sales literature, designing of merchandising displays, public relations and publicity, etc.

THE ADVERTISING-AGENCY STRUCTURE

Agencies' *principal* source of income is the "agency commission" allowed by all major advertising media, usually 15 per cent of the medium's published rate. On the average, about three-fourths of agency income is derived from such commissions.

Advertising agencies receive—on the average—only about one-fourth of their compensation directly from clients.

This compensation from clients is of two kinds:

1. Service charges added to the cost of materials and services purchased by agencies in connection with their clients' advertising.
2. Service fees for special services performed.

These service charges and fees are arrived at by individual agreement between each agency and client.

Media set up the system of allowing agency commissions—the advertising-agency structure—in the early days of advertising, when publishers found that their white space was not particularly salable. Further, they found that they could not successfully prepare advertising for competing manufacturers. By allowing commissions, the publishers established advertising agencies to convert their white space into advertising influence and provided the advertiser with a specialized creator of advertising who could serve him more efficiently.

However, media allow commissions only to "recognized" agencies. This recognition of advertising agencies is a function performed by individual media owners and their associations. To secure recognition, an agency must satisfy the medium on at least the following points:

1. It must be a bona fide agency—that is, free from control by an advertiser, in order that it may not be prejudiced or restricted in its service to all clients; free from control by a medium owner, in order that it may give unbiased advice to advertisers in the selection of media.

2. It must keep all commissions (that is, not rebate any of the commissions to clients) received from media owners, in order to maintain media rate cards and to devote the commissions to such service and development of advertising as the individual media owners desire.

3. It must possess adequate personnel of experience and ability to serve general advertisers.

4. It must have the financial capacity to meet the obligations it incurs to media owners.

Beyond these four basic qualifications, some media-owner bodies impose others, such as the requirement that the agency must be currently placing advertising in certain types of media, or that the agency must have a certain minimum of liquid capital.

There are approximately 1,800 advertising agencies in the United States, as listed in the Standard Advertising Register. Of these, about 650 agencies are recognized by the American Newspaper Publishers Association and about the same number (but not all the same agencies) by the Periodical Publishers Association. The Associated Business Papers and the Agricultural Publishers Association each recognize approximately 850. Nearly 300 agencies are recognized by all four of these media associations.

AGENCY-MEDIUM CONTRACTS

The advertising agency contracts with media in its own name, as an independent contractor; it is not, legally, the agency of its client. The word "agent" or "agency" is, in a legal sense, a misnomer.

Certain basic principles in the agency-medium relationship have been established by custom:

1. The agency is solely liable for payment to media. If the advertiser fails to pay the agency, it is the agency's loss. If the advertiser pays the agency but the agency fails to pay the medium, it is the medium's loss.

2. The agency agrees, with the medium, that it will not rebate to its client any part of the commission allowed by the medium.

3. The medium agrees that its rates shall be published, that the rate at which it contracts with the agency shall be the lowest rate charged for the same service, and that the medium shall follow a uniform policy toward agencies, without discrimination.

4. The content of advertising prepared by the agency is subject to approval by the medium, but the latter may not change the content of the advertising without the agency's consent.

The principles are written into three standard contracts between agencies and media—the Standard Order Blank for Publications, the Standard Contract for Spot Broadcasting, and the Standard Order Blank for Transportation Advertising—developed by the American Association of Advertising Agencies in cooperation with the media concerned and now used voluntarily by the great majority of agencies.

THE AGENCY-CLIENT RELATIONSHIP

Because advertising agencies render a professional service that must be adapted to the client's needs, there is much flexibility and variation in the working agreements between agency and client. Several basic principles have been established by custom, however. When the agency undertakes to handle the advertising for a particular product, it is usually understood that the agency will refrain from handling at the same time the advertising of a competing product of another advertiser. (Larger agencies that have unit branch offices do sometimes handle advertising for similar products but in separate noncompeting territories.)

Likewise, the client generally agrees that he will not engage a second agency to handle part of the advertising of the product without the first agency's consent.

The agency customarily secures the client's approval on all expenditures connected with his advertising.

The client pays the agency at each medium's published rate, and the agency retains the commission allowed to it by the medium.

The client is obligated to pay promptly the agency's bills for publication space and time, so that the agency may pay media by their due dates. It is not a function of agencies to finance the advertising of their clients, and media object strongly to it. To do so would require large amounts of capital that would shut out of the agency business men with high talent but modest funds—men whose creative work might do much to increase the volume of advertising.

The agency regularly passes on to its client any cash discounts allowed by media, on condition that the client pays the agency's bill by the discount date. The client is entitled to the exact amount of cash discount allowed to the agency by the medium. (As allowed by the great majority of media, the cash discount is customarily 2 per cent of the net amount paid to the medium—*i.e.*, published rate less agency commission.)

The agency ordinarily is not responsible for the failure of media or suppliers of materials to execute their commitments.

AGENCY ETHICAL STANDARDS

In addition to the standards of practice defined in agency-media contracts and agency-client agreements, agencies have established for themselves a general code of good conduct embodied in the Standards of Practice of the American Association of Advertising Agencies.

The Standards condemn untruthful, indecent, or misleading copy practices. They also condemn rebating to the client, extra compensation from any third party unless disclosed to the client, the use of speculative material in competitive agency solicitations, and offering credit extension as an inducement in solicitation.

On the subject of rebating, the Standards say:

It shall be considered as rebating to supply materials for advertising on any basis that can be considered as direct, indirect, or secret rebating. It shall also be considered as rebating to place men in the service of the advertiser at the agency's expense, or to assume all or part of the salary of any employee of the advertiser, or to pay any fee or compensation to any one connected directly or indirectly with the advertiser, for obtaining or holding an account.

It shall also be considered as rebating to agree to allow cash discounts not earned.

Condemning the use of speculative material, the Standards say:

In view of its obligation to provide adequate service to clients, as well as the sound business principle of making a reasonable profit on its effort, the advertising agency should refrain from practices that dissipate its income in any unsound or uneconomic solicitation for new business.

In this connection, "making a reasonable profit" has become increasingly difficult for advertising agencies. Of the total received as agency income, about two-thirds is paid out in salaries and other compensation to those who work in the business. The remaining third must cover rent, traveling, taxes, other costs—and profit.

Agency costs have been materially raised by the addition of staff specialists to handle newer forms of media, by demands upon agencies to serve other needs of business beyond advertising, and by increased expenditures for market, media, and copy research.

While a net profit of 3 per cent of billings was once considered good by advertising agencies, recent studies show that it is now averaging around 1 per cent for all except the smaller, and usually more profitable, organizations.

Agencies are meeting this challenge through better management, by more careful billing to clients for production costs, and by undertaking special services only when properly compensated.

USING THE AGENCY EFFECTIVELY

Effective use of advertising-agency service depends to a large extent upon the degree of confidence and cooperation that exists between the advertiser and agency.

It is desirable that advertiser and agency agree upon a long-range advertising plan so that the advertising effort may have sustained direction and purpose. In many such plans, certain objectives are fixed for each year's work. By the "task-appropriation method," the advertising appropriation is then determined to attain these objectives.

It is desirable that the agency's contact should be as high as possible within the advertiser's organization. He should be an executive with enough information at his disposal to coordinate the advertising effort with the company's other distribution activities—with personal selling, sales promotion, and display. He should have enough responsibility to make routine advertising decisions without continuous reference to higher authority.

The agency should be given all information that may be necessary to develop sound advertising plans and campaigns and to measure the effectiveness of results. There should be an explicit business agreement between advertiser and agency, so that the company does not make demands in time and service that the agency can ill afford to carry out. Company officials should maintain a receptive attitude toward agency suggestions, being careful to avoid personal prejudices, so that the agency's creative ability has full play. This assumes that the company has engaged an advertising agency which it respects and trusts. If the agency does not merit this attitude, then a new agency should be sought.

The Old, Old Story

"Romeo and Juliet" and "Abie's Irish Rose" have the same plot—and this identical plot had already been used successfully for a short story, a novel, and a play fifty years before Shakespeare wrote his immortal classic in the sixteenth century.

Ann Nichols took one of the oldest of sure-fire stories, gave the characters new names and modern dialect, made more than a million dollars, and set a Broadway record for box-office receipts and 2,327 continuous stage performances, topped only by two other productions to date.

The only way to get a dollar's worth of sales effect from every dollar's worth of sales-promotion effort is to follow the storytelling technique to which people in the mass always respond.

Even a price ticket can be dramatized—if somebody who knows how remembers to do it. But it rarely happens.

Sales promotion, in many instances, is like the nursery-rhyme little girl with the curl—when it is good, it is very, very good, but when it is bad, it gets nowhere.

Some advertisers do the obvious and succeed handsomely—like William Shakespeare and Ann Nichols.

Other advertisers—who themselves listen to Charlie McCarthy—buy millions of dollars' worth of newspaper, magazine, and trade-paper space and fill it with words that nobody wants to read. And nobody does read!

What Does Your Advertising Money Buy

Mr. Howard D. Williams, president, Erwin, Wasey & Company, advertising agents, wrote the text of the advertisement below, which aptly details the services bought by the advertiser and the costs. This advertisement, one of a series by leaders in the field of advertising, was published by *The Wall Street Journal* to create a wider understanding of advertising and the contribution it is making to America.

"When sales are either extra easy or extra hard, the cold fiscal eye on the P&L statement often stops at 'Advertising'—and questions its values because they cannot be measured or weighed.

"Then is the time to remember that sales are not God-given. Advertising spearheads sales advances, and protects sales gains. Sales tides change, but steady advertising keeps the main channel open, at high water or low.

"The cumulative effects of consistent advertising reach so far they cannot be seen all at once, nor counted exactly in tangible units. Often the greatest values of advertising come by its by-products.

"Some of the more important values of advertising are briefly listed here.

"1. *Sales Value.* Advertising makes sales at lowest cost—not only to users, but throughout the whole distribution chain. Salespeople sell advertised items harder, more confidently.

"2. *Distribution Value.* The middleman buys more readily, and stays sold, when advertising makes his sales easier. He "features" advertised products because it pays him—in turnover, profits, and friends.

"3. *Name Value.* Often worth more, and longer lasting, than plants or inventories. Only advertising can maintain this priceless business insurance.

"4. *Profit Value.* In any conditions, products known through advertising are likely to command better market, better prices, better profits; and lower production costs.

"5. *Assets Value.* Not only good will but all the assets of a business known through advertising are more marketable, and so more valuable. Materials are often easier to get, in times of short supply.

"6. *Financing Value.* A business widely known through advertising has a readier market for securities. Usually also an enhanced credit position.

"7. *Labor Value.* Not even union regimentation can prevent workers from preferring employment in a business well known through advertising.

What Does Your Advertising Money Buy

"8. *Executive Value.* The best talents are attracted to progressive advertisers. Pride in the prestige of a well-known name stimulates better work and stronger loyalty—and reduces turnover of personnel.

"9. *Foreign Value.* Publications and people both move widely today. Often an American advertiser finds demand ready made for his products in a new foreign market.

"10. *Social Value.* A means of helping the cause of free competitive enterprise, and the advantages of American standards—which advertising has done so much to build, by creating mass sales.

"WHAT DOES GOOD ADVERTISING SERVICE COST?"

"Under the existing commission system, the services of a good advertising agency usually cost the advertiser nothing.

"But if advertising agencies were paid by fee—as are lawyers, accountants, and architects—the cost would still be extremely low with regard to results.

"The best advertising agencies today provide in effect an essential department of their clients' business.

"Since this department is shared cooperatively, by a number of clients, the agency can employ the best talent in many highly specialized activities, at no extra cost for this advantage to the individual advertiser.

"In the modern advertising agency, preparation of advertising is a vitally important end result. But it represents only a small part of the work and value a good agency gives the client.

"Equally important is the broad help and experienced counsel which the advertising agency can provide in every problem related to selling—merchandising, marketing, packaging, pricing, styling, designing, sales promotion, and often sales management itself.

"Many businesses have become highly successful through confining their major efforts to production and finance—leaving all sales activities to a competent advertising agency. What would you say they should answer to "What does good advertising service cost?"

Years ago advertising agents sometimes sold "genius." Like early aviators, they fostered an aura of mystery and glamor. But advertising has long since become a strictly practical, and highly efficient, adjunct to industry.

"Inspiration is still of the utmost importance, but today it is aimed with the aid of modern research, added to years of trial-and-error experience. Advertising can be the most profitable investment of American business, when effectively and consistently used."

Readers interested in more detailed information about the structure of the advertising-agency business are referred to the publications of the Special Committee on Education and Training for Advertisers of the American Association of Advertising Agencies.

SELECTING AN ADVERTISING AGENCY

When A. & M. Karagheusian, Inc., importers of oriental rugs and manufacturers of domestic floor coverings, wanted to select a new advertising agency, they asked a number of pertinent questions subsequently summarized by their advertising manager, Charles B. Konselman, in an article in *Printer's Ink*, titled, "We Chose Our Agency by Asking 36 Questions."

Several months ago, when it was decided to appoint a new agency to handle the Gulistan Rug account, the $64 question was, "What is the best, most practical way to go about choosing an advertising agency?"

We are satisfied that the method and procedure we worked out to answer this question resulted in an excellent choice and makes possible a mutually profitable and advantageous agency-client relationship for many years.

The basis of our method was a list of 36 questions which each agency soliciting the account was asked to answer in detail. This list was the development of our thinking as to our requirements in terms of agency advertising services.

The use of this list of questions had several important advantages. In the first place it saved us from the ordeal of the traditional high-pressure and elaborate advertising agency presentation, which all too often offers little or no real basis for judging the agency's suitability from the prospective client's viewpoint. Second, the list being essentially a set of specifications, outlining our needs as we saw them, required each agency to detail its services within a common framework. Comparison thus became relatively simple instead of practically impossible, as it is when each agency "shoots the works" on its own.

A third advantage from each agency's standpoint was the opportunity it had of determining beforehand whether its operation and services were such that our account was a desirable one to have in the house. This last consideration, however, was academic in our case since each agency invited to solicit the account was carefully pre-chosen.

While essentially our advertising and merchandising problems are similar to those of many other manufacturers, there are several elements peculiar to our own operation and business. In considering agencies, we believed emphasis should be placed on experience, size, service and operation that would most exactly fit our needs. And, since in the final analysis, agencies are people, and the success of an agency-client relationship depends upon the personalities of individuals, we were particularly interested in exactly who would work on our account. Our questions reflected both these important considerations.

On the assumption that no agency could intelligently handle the account without a study of the business, we made it clear that we were definitely not interested in presentations of ideas for new advertising campaigns as a basis for agency solicitation. Rather we stressed that we were interested in knowing the qualifications of the agency to study and learn our operation first—and later to make specific recommendations and develop campaigns.

In inviting each agency to solicit the account, several other factors guided us. First, the disadvantages of being the large account in a small agency, or the reverse, seemed obvious. Second, while high style, beautiful presentation, and appreciation of modern modes and fashion trends are essential in our consumer campaigns, basic, down-to-earth merchandising counsel in connection with our distributor and dealer promotion is also most necessary. Third, we strongly believe our agency must have the facilities and desire to work with us on our entire advertising operation including space, radio, promotion, and display. Anything less than full understanding of the need for all advertising activities to be closely coordinated would be unsatisfactory.

With these qualifications in mind, several agencies were asked to solicit the account and did so. Originally, our list of prospective agencies numbered eight. However, after several friends of friends had asked that their particular favorites be included, and after the grapevine had done its work, fifteen contestants were in the field. Before the final choice was made, representatives of each organization were interviewed at least once, and in most cases twice or three times; answers to the questions were analyzed; and supplementary information on several agencies secured.

As mentioned above, individual interviews were arranged with each agency, at which our general operation and requirements were outlined. Each was given a copy of our questionnaire, or "set of specs," as it was soon called, and asked to submit as brief or detailed answers as the agency felt necessary.

It was interesting to observe that the various agencies welcomed this "track to run on" in their solicitations. All expressed the opinion that the questionnaire not only gave them an opportunity to present their services in line with our needs and desires, but resulted in the elimination of considerable unnecessary or superfluous data.

The list of questions are themselves self-explanatory as regards the information we wanted, with the exception of No. 36. This was frankly a trick question included for the purpose of determining just what each agency would do with it. Actually the answer to it was contained in the answers to several previous questions. However, it was surprising how several agencies let themselves go on this one instead of using it as a basis for a summary of previous answers.

When all questionnaire presentations had been received, it was far easier for us to examine, analyze, and consider the various agencies involved. Final selection, however, was most difficult since several organizations, from our point of view, seemed equally well qualified. However, a first choice was made, with four others listed as alternatives if a final interview did not result in a favorable decision.

The advantages of the questionnaire as a basis for agency selection over the guessing game or personal contact methods seem manifest to us for many reasons. Not the least of these is that it affords an opportunity to consider objectively agency qualifications in line with the prospective client's own problems, with extraneous influences kept at a minimum.

Experience:

1. What accounts do you have that are closely allied in market, outlets or sales appeal to our business and products?

2. What experience have members of your agency had that is pertinent to the marketing, merchandising and advertising of rugs and carpets?

3. What products do you advertise which are retailed through department stores, furniture and specialty stores?

4. What products do you advertise which are sold primarily to women?

5. What accounts do you handle requiring a practical knowledge of home decoration and furnishings?

6. What accounts do you handle requiring an inherent flair for "style" in copy, layout and merchandising?

7. Name several publishing executives who are familiar with the work of your agency.

8. Name the executive of those accounts you are handling whose products or business is pertinent to ours, to whom we may write concerning their experience with your agency.

Size:

9. What was the total dollar volume of your agency last year?

10. How many people are in your organization?

11. What is average billing of all accounts? What was low billing for 1945? High?

12. How do you rank in size among all agencies?

13. Are you a member of the 4 A's? Recognized by ANPA? Recommended by ABP, and PPA?

14. How many offices do you have?

15. Are these contact and sales branches or complete agency service organizations?

16. How long has your agency been in business?

17. Do your Account Executives do the creative planning and writing on the accounts they serve, or do they handle only contact between client and agency?

18. Will our plans, copy and scripts be written by the men contacting and handling our account, or by a "copy department"?

19. Who will write the trade-paper copy on our account—a trade paper department, a "copy department" or the account men handling our account?

20. Who in your agency would be primarily responsible for servicing our account—and why do you think he is especially well fitted for handling our account?

21. Who else in your agency would work on the account? What would they do? What are their positions in the agency and qualifications in relation to our account?

22. How many members of your staff have been sales, advertising or sales promotion managers?

23. Many agencies regard "space" advertising as their function. What is the policy of your agency with regard to planning, writing and producing direct mail, sales literature, sales manuals, catalogues, merchandising portfolios, dealer ads, retail display material, promotional plans, sales films and all other collateral material needed by many advertisers?

24. For how many of your clients do you now plan, write and produce their promotional display and merchandising materials?

25. Is this work farmed out (planned and created by an outside organization) or completely created by your own men?

26. Do you feel that a substantial proportion of our advertising budget should be earmarked for dealer advertising and collateral materials?

27. Do you invite competitive bids on production of such material?

28. Do you consider market studies and trade surveys an important part of your agency's service to its clients?

Operation:

29. To what extent is your agency departmentalized? Please list departments and outline how their work is coordinated in serving clients.

30. To what extent are principals (partners, executive officers or main stockholders) active in serving clients?

31. Do any of your principals actually handle accounts?

32. Who would be responsible on our account for basic policy, plans and conception of the right appeal in our advertising?

33. How many of your accounts have been with you over five years, over 10 years, over 15 years, over 20 years?

34. If we should select your agency, what people in your company would form the service group? We would like the names, their position or department, and the part of our account service each would be responsible for.

35. On what basis of compensation do you operate? Fee? Percentage of billing? Other?

36. What would be your procedure in handling our account if we appointed you?

The answers to these thirty-six questions by the agency selected, Fuller & Smith & Ross, Inc., covered some forty pages of typewritten data.

COPY TESTING

Advertisers use various methods to test consumers' opinions of the selling power of advertisements, either before or after the advertisements appear.

The wise advertiser does not place his faith in any one method of testing copy. He realizes that each method has its limitations as well as its merits.

For example, the method that tests reader interest —that tells approximately how many readers see, read some, and read most of any given piece of copy —gives no actual index of how good a selling job that piece of copy will do. An advertisement may stop the reader and part of its message may interest him, yet it may completely fail to sell him.

Conversely, while the objective of all advertising is to increase sales, sales records seldom provide a true index of advertising copy. Poorly planned merchandising and sales strategy can defeat the best advertisements that have ever been produced.

Sales to a mass market are always the result of a mixture of causes. It is usually difficult to isolate, even approximately, the effect of any one of these causes, such as an advertisement or a series of advertisements.

Whenever you are considering copy testing, first of all determine what problems you want to answer, then examine all the various ways of testing copy and select the method or methods best suited to your problems. Several authorities have already outlined the best known and most widely understood methods. Some authorities have explained their merits, but few, if any, have analyzed the pitfalls and objectives of the most commonly used methods. Here they are in brief.

The oldest and perhaps the most widely used method of testing the pulling power of an advertisement is to place a coupon in it. For such products as insurance, oil heaters, correspondence schools, business and similar services, this method of testing is particularly useful—largely because an interest in the

Why Pre-test Copy?

"Remember," say Young & Rubicam, Inc., advertising agents, "the *best* advertisement in a magazine is something like five times as effective as the *average* advertisement and fourteen times as effective as the *poorest*."

Carroll Rheinstrom has published a number of case histories of advertising results in "Psyching the Ads." He notes, to cite typical cases, that two advertisements prepared by the same people and used in the same magazines produced such widely varying returns as 205 replies for one advertisement and 11,109 for the other.

In another instance one advertisement produced ten times as many requests for a sample ten-cent offer as did a companion advertisement, identical in size and placed in the same papers.

The Copy Research Council, in announcing its "Appraisal of Copy Research," states: "Before reporting the results, we should like to register with you our attitude toward one *general* phase of the subject. On this phase we see practically eye to eye. Contrary to the wishful thinking of many advertising men, copy research as yet provides no single all-revealing test. In our opinion there is no one test that tells all. No one method, no one technique currently known gives you a complete answer as to which advertisement will create the most customers for your brand of goods, or the most favorable opinion for your institution.

"We look upon copy research in much the same way as we have for a long time looked on market research. In that field the experienced advertising man doesn't consider that a survey has failed because it turns up no revolutionary new use for the product, no important but untouched market, or no entirely new and easy method of distribution. What he wants, and gets, is information. He wants to learn all he can about the people he is selling, or trying to sell. He expects market research to reveal their reactions and behavior on the occasions when they come in contact with his product. We expect copy research to reveal the reactions and behavior of those same people as a result of their contact with our advertisements."

product or service usually exists in the prospective buyer's mind before he sees the advertisement.

On the other hand, the advertiser of products in wide general use, such as food, soap, cigarettes, or clothing, is more likely to attract inquirers without real interest in his product. Also, it is less easy for him to determine whether his inquirers are valid prospects. Successful coupon users among package-goods advertisers take pains to make their coupon offers of a nature to attract the same kind of people as those who buy their products.

When comparing the results of one coupon advertisement with another, recognition should be given to seasonal influences; variations of a magazine's circulation issue by issue; and the cumulative effect of making the same offer in the same publication. The ideal conditions for making such a comparison would include having two advertisements appear in the same magazine in the same position during the same period of time. The coupons should be of identical size and in identical positions. Since these conditions can only be met in publications which offer split runs, comparisons should, as a rule, be made on the basis of at least three insertions for each advertisement.

The same general warnings apply to the "buried offer" type of copy testing as apply to coupons. Usually the quality of responses is higher from buried offers than from coupons but if the offer is more than moderately attractive those who notice it first are apt to tell their friends. Such a development does not invalidate the test but does make the result data somewhat less significant.

The recognition-test method, which was largely developed by Dr. George Gallup, Director of the American Institute of Public Opinion, is based on the theory that an advertisement must be seen and read before it can make a sale. The method, however, does not measure the selling strength of the copy nor does it necessarily predict sales.

The chief difference between Dr. Gallup's method and the usual recognition test is this: Gallup aims to restore the original situation as nearly as possible and so all his interviewers start with the editorial material of a publication, because people buy their newspapers and magazines for their editorial content rather than their advertising announcements.

When consumer juries are used, the advertiser usually depends on the individual opinions of a relatively small number of typical prospects who are shown the advertisements. Two or more advertisements are presented and people are asked which one appeals to them most. Sometimes the question is asked about the headline, sometimes the picture, and sometimes the copy, instead of the advertisement as a whole. When the jury is carefully selected to represent a true cross section, this system eliminates the poorest advertisements and gives an indication of those most likely to appeal to a wider audience.

When advertising aims to *inform* readers rather than influence them to immediate action, results may be measured by aided recall tests. Readers are asked questions to determine whether they have learned the fact the advertiser has been publicizing. The test has no significance, however, without a starting point.

It is a "before and after" comparison. The public's knowledge of the advertiser's proposition must be measured before the campaign begins as well as after it has run.

The sales-test method is probably the ideal test for campaigns that are aimed to produce immediate sales. Yet it is beset with difficulties which are frequently insurmountable, such as the difficulty of selecting test cities that are truly representative of the economic conditions of the country as a whole. If newspapers are used, how can their various amounts of dealer cooperation be equalized? What allowances should be made for the differences in the volume of advertising printed in the test papers? What about competitive activities? These alone may be sufficient to upset a sales test unless they are identical in all test towns; and the difficulties and expense of accurately reporting actual sales must always be overcome.

Sometimes an advertiser makes the mistake of using bigger space in the test than he intends to use nationally, or he may use more frequent insertions to hasten results. Such plans only tend to distort the findings and confuse the returns.

The most successful user of the sales-test method known to the author is one who employs it in conjunction with three other testing methods. This manufacturer of a standard product starts his test in the spring of each year, runs the test for six months, and uses the winning campaign during the following twelve months. However, when such a long interval elapses between the creation of a campaign and its final appearance, the advertiser always risks a change in the competitive situation that might demand entirely new and different strategy on his part.

Certain organizations provide advertisers with a set list of questions, or a predetermined formula. Each question rates a number of points. For example, "Does the headline contain news value?" might score 10 points out of a possible 100. But the answer to the questions and the amount they score are arbitrarily arrived at by the evaluator. Thus this method is, in the last analysis, a matter of an individual's opinion, which all scientific copy testing seeks to avoid.

AN APPRAISAL OF COPY RESEARCH

For a long time, many men interested in using research to make advertising do a better job have felt a need for some effort to define and bound the areas of usefulness of the principal methods of copy research.

To that end, the Copy Research Council set up a Committee on Appraisal of Copy Research under the chairmanship of Sydney H. Giellerup. Under the leadership of that Committee, and with the energetic cooperation of the full membership of the Council, the data and conclusions subsequently reviewed were compiled after eighteen months of study.

There is, of course, considerable literature on how to conduct copy research. In contrast to this, the Council's study is a professional estimate of what various research methods can accomplish, assuming that the technique and methods are sound.

Founded in 1941, the Copy Research Council is an

informal organization, located in New York City, with membership limited to thirty-six research and copy men. Most of them are in advertising-agency work, four being presidents of advertising agencies. The common purpose is to provide an opportunity for the exchange of information and experience among advertising men who are engaged actively in improving advertising copy by testing and other objective procedures.

How can readers, listeners, and viewers indicate how an advertisement affects them? In five ways:

1. By expressing opinions (consumer jury).
2. By reporting or exposing their behavior while reading.
3. By changing their attitudes (comprehension, remembrance, belief, and conviction).
4. By making inquiries.
5. By performing some recommended act— usually that of purchasing the advertiser's product.

When you talk about copy testing, what you mean is the study of one or more of these five actions or reactions of the people your advertising is addressed to. But mark this—no single one of the five tells the whole story. How *much* of it does each one tell? That's what the Council voted on; here is the result.

1. *By expressing Opinions (consumer jury).*

A majority of all Council members believes Opinions are:

    a. Reasonably effective in measuring attention value and interest, and in comparing layouts.

    b. Fairly effective in measuring clarity and in comparing copy themes or appeals, only a few members voting to the contrary.

    c. Not effective in measuring selling power, credibility, conviction, and the extent to which an advertisement will be read and understood, but the vote on each of these points is extremely close.

2. *By reporting or exposing their Behavior while Reading.*

A majority believes Reading Behavior highly useful in showing you whether readers are:

    a. Gaining or losing interest in a campaign.

    b. More interested in some other campaign for a similar product.

    c. More interested in one or another form of text, art, or layout treatment.

A majority believes it moderately useful in showing you how many readers:

    a. Noticed your advertisement.

    b. Associated it with your product or organization.

    c. Read most of it.

Only a few members believe it is any indication of:

    a. How well your advertisement is understood.

    b. How convincing it is.

    c. How many sales it will make.

3. *By changing their Attitudes (comprehension, remembrance, belief, and conviction).*

A majority believes that the measurement of changes in Attitude is highly accurate in determining whether the facts stated in an advertisement are remembered, and that they are moderately accurate in determining whether the facts stated are believed and whether the reader's viewpoint has been changed.

Half the members believe that Attitude measurements are highly accurate in indicating the extent to which the text of an advertisement will be understood. Almost all of the remaining members believe they are at least moderately accurate.

4. *By making Inquiries.*

When advertisements seek to promote sales, either directly or through distributors or retailers, a majority believes that Inquiries when properly used can provide a strong indication of over-all effectiveness.

When advertisements seek to promote an institution, an idea, or a philosophy, almost half of the members believe Inquiries can provide a strong indication, while an equal number believe that they can provide only a slight indication of over-all effectiveness.

5. *By Purchasing the advertiser's product.*

Here the Council felt safe in assuming what the attitude is of most advertising men. Where one advertisement can be shown to result in more Purchases or sales than another, they agree that it is a better advertisement. Consequently, the Committee saw no need for a ballot on the significance of Purchases. But although their significance is incontestable, measurement is extremely difficult and there are many conflicting opinions regarding the technique. No poll was taken on these opinions because the Committee was not engaged in explaining how to measure public reactions, but what the reaction meant after it was properly measured.

One final bit of advice was offered by the Council: "Have your copy research done by those who really know how. When you want advertisements prepared, you assign the job to professional copywriters and art directors. For merchandising plans, or publicity, or radio programs, you turn to people who have been trained in those particular fields. By the same token, a project as important as copy research should be supervised by a person of recognized skill and adequate experience. Technical knowledge is necessary not only in measuring the public's reactions, but in giving them the proper interpretation. So, investigate your copy from all angles just as you investigate your product. But, make sure that the technique is handled on an objective and professional level."

REDUCING THE GAMBLE

Business executives who are called upon to sign the advertising check are frequently in the dark as to why, how, and for what their money is spent. Naturally, as a good businessman, each tries to reduce the gamble in all his operations, including advertising. His desire for light on the subject explains why certain types of systems flourish which promise to tell him before publication just exactly how much sales power his advertising has.

No known system can convert all the phases of successful advertising into standards susceptible to accurate measurements of intangibles as varied as creative genius, artistic ability, and mass human-nature reactions. Many of the attempts to do so simply lead to more confusion and further perplexity in the minds of the business executive.

There are, however, certain common-sense approaches to advertising that will reduce the hazards in advance of its publication. A clear understanding of the technical elements of advertising and their operation in relation to the inspiration behind them and to the resulting advertisement as a whole will help clarify the mystery about this important sales-building tool.

ADVERTISING ANALYSIS

Mark Wiseman, well-known advertising practitioner and author of "Before You Sign the Advertising Check," has translated his experience of many years in practical advertising, followed by more recent work in advertising analysis, into terms directed to the advertiser himself. The basic reasoning of this type of analysis is set forth in this summary:

"When you look at an advertisement for which you are to sign the check, you see

Headline
Pictures
Text

Can you determine, *before* you sign the check and publish the advertisement, whether or not your headline, pictures, and text will do their individual jobs effectively? Yes.

"Behind and underneath these surface factors are the advertisement's 'works':

> Sales idea
> Emotional appeal
> Sales argument
> Vehicle
> Objective

"Can you determine, prior to publication, whether or not the 'works' of your advertisement are effective? You can. A new analytical approach to advertising has proved that a positive answer is possible.

"This approach is not magic. It can't tell you *how many goods* your advertisement will sell, or *how many people* it will sell them to—nothing can do that. But it *can* tell you whether or not each element in your advertisement is *working hard for a sale*.

"This approach separates advertising into its two fundamental aspects—the engineering and the creative—and deals wholly with the engineering aspect. It dismisses from primary consideration the purely creative factors such as beauty, style, taste, and cleverness, because they are matters of personal, individual opinion which cannot be charted or diagramed. It focuses attention entirely upon technical sales factors such as arrangement, organization, readability, and psychological soundness for which simple, well-known, common-sense criteria of judgment exist.

"An advertisement which is properly engineered, and contains a complete set of 'works' that really work, will sell goods, regardless of its purely creative qualities."

The function of advertising analysis is to make certain that your advertisement will work. An understanding of how it will accomplish this purpose may be gained by an examination of the three most important and visible advertising elements: headline, pictures, and text. The material that follows, analyzing headline, picture, and text, is condensed from the book, "Before You Sign the Advertising Check," by Mark Wiseman and is used here with the author's permission.

THE HEADLINE

The engineering job of a headline is to reach out for the reader's attention, capture his interest, and propel his eye into the sales message. Each individual is interested beyond everything else in himself. His first response to every proposal made to him, however he may conceal his motives, is: "What will I get out of it?" Or, in current slang, "So what?"

Read the following headlines taken from actual advertisements and ask yourself after each one, "What will I get out of it?" Or, "So what?"

"Mankind fares as the pioneer dares."
"Every comparison piles up the proof."
"We are lamp specialists."
"America's largest selling gasoline."
"Quality is a great adventure."

If each advertiser had applied the self-interest test, would he have approved his headline? Would he have signed the check? Would *you?*

Next time you are asked to judge a headline, check it by going through the following list of types—to be avoided because they lack self-interest appeal:

1. The product-pushing headline that places your commercial interest ahead of the reader's self-interest ("The better anti-freeze"; "The hallmark of higher quality").

2. The "We are great people" headline ("Genius strikes twice in the same place"; "Through every storm . . . since 1845").

3. The general-proposition headline ("Thirst knows no season"; "Who serves progress serves America").

4. The assumptive headline that unwarrantably takes the reader's opinion for granted ("You'll be amazed"; "You'll *like* a [certain car]").

5. The caption headline that merely describes the picture ("Here is a picture of precision"; "They work in a textile mill").

An effective headline can be *built*—with simple words. There's nothing startling about the wording of the following lines, yet notice how they reach out with a promise:

"What to do when you have a cold."
"I'll do 12 of your dirtiest jobs for a penny."
"Model tells secret of '100-mile' stockings."

> "Look ten years younger."
> "Treat yourself to spectacular Dodge performance—and save money, too!"
> "Cook in clear, clean glass—no pan taste, never grows shabby."
> "No waste! No mess! With the Kleenex Pull-out Package."

Without brilliance of wording, each of these headlines has power—because of its technical form alone—to propel the reader into the text. Directly or indirectly, each promises him definite self-benefits.

A selfish, product-pushing headline can be rebuilt into a reader-interest headline merely by applying engineering technique. Consider the advertiser who wants the reader to know that his product is "America's largest selling gasoline." If used alone as the headline, this phrase *excludes* the reader; he can say, "so what?" And if he is satisfied with the gasoline he is now using, he'll pass on.

Examination of the text of the advertisement in which this headline was used reveals *three reasons why* the reader will benefit from using the gasoline. A soundly engineered headline emerges:

> "3 reasons why you should be using America's largest-selling gasoline."

Or, better:

> "A 3-way profit to you from America's largest-selling gasoline."

No reader can say "So what?" to a line that promises him three profits.

Word brilliance can produce a working headline only when it is based upon sound engineering. For a special, sophisticated audience, Birds Eye Frosted Foods are well warranted in using the clever line:

"How to get more white meat without murdering your brother-in-law."

But, for a mass audience, the following simple line would lure more readers:

"How to get more white meat without spending more per pound."

Here are a few practical engineering questions for your use in judging a headline's ability to work for a sale:

1. Does it offer or suggest benefits to the reader?
2. Can its meaning be grasped at a glance?
3. Is it isolated for attention?
4. Does its typography make reading easy?

THE PICTURE

The basic engineering job of the picture (the illustration used in the advertisement) is to focus the reader's attention definitely and clearly on a situation. For this reason, the pictorial sequence in the advertisement must avoid confusion so that the reader has no difficulty in quickly finding his way.

The second job of the illustration is to present a sympathetic situation in which the reader can quickly imagine himself as taking part. The picture of a man criticizing his wife may be sympathetic to a man reader (if he's a confirmed wife critic), but repellent to a woman reader (if she has been or might be a victim). The picture of a salesman selling a refrigerator to a woman reader is unsympathetic because no woman wants to imagine herself as being *sold*—she prefers to think of herself as *buying*. A picture of the product alone will be unsympathetic unless it is news, or quickly suggests use, or satisfies a latent curiosity.

The third job of the illustration is to create conflict in the reader's emotions. *If there is no such conflict, there can be no sale.* Such conflict is created by pitting the reader's present situation against a more desirable one. The illustration of a Bromo-Seltzer advertisement helps create a conflict between the discomfort caused by hangover and the relief promised by the product. The illustration in a life insurance advertisement creates a conflict between the reader's love and fear for his wife's future, and his desire to protect her from poverty. In both cases, the product or service is the *rescuer* of the reader from the dilemma caused by his emotional conflict.

To make sure your illustration is working for a sale, judge it, not according to your personal likes or dislikes, but as to:

1. Its ability to focus the reader's attention
2. Upon a sympathetic situation,
3. That creates an emotional conflict,
4. From whose dilemma your product can rescue him.

THE TEXT

Writing style alone, however brilliant or charming, sells no goods. Before signing your advertising check, look below the writing, and examine the thought content and organization.

To move the reader to action, your text must do five basic jobs:

1. Win the reader's sympathy and good will and create emotional conflict.
2. Offer satisfaction for his need or desire.
3. Relate the benefits of your product to his need or desire and rescue him from his conflict.
4. Support the claims that you make for your product by evidence that the reader will accept and believe.
5. Justify your product's cost, provide clear directions for purchase, and request some definite action.

Crisco does job No. 1 successfully this way:

"You've probably wondered why children beg for pastries and fried foods. It always hurts to say 'no,' yet you've always felt that you must."

Ingram's does job No. 2 diplomatically and easily, like this:

"What downright comfort—what soothing shaves —economical Ingram's delivers."

Job No. 3 is usually acceptably done, but job No. 4 is often left entirely undone; yet if your claims are supportable, credible evidence should be easy to obtain—from users, from your own research, from your experience or special methods.

Job No. 5 is nothing more than a simple sales "closing," yet it, too, is often left unperformed.

Rules for the Writer of Advertising

Here are a few simple rules which will help make advertisements newsy, cheerful, attractive, and easy to read. They were originated by a master personal salesman, John H. Patterson, founder of the National Cash Register Company:

1. Know your subject.
2. Use short words.
3. Write short sentences.
4. Make paragraphs short.
5. Use big ideas.
6. Put only one thought in each sentence.
7. Write so that a child will understand.
8. Say precisely what you mean
9. Be brief.
10. Be logical.
11. Tell the truth.
12. Never exaggerate.
13. Don't imitate.
14. Be enthusiastic.
15. Write to impress the reader, not to express yourself or impress a competitor.

A good test of advertising text is to ask yourself, "If this were not written about *my* product, would I read it, would my wife read it, would my children read it—and if we should read it, would we be likely to buy?"

The two major points to be remembered in the engineering aspects of the building of the headline, illustration, and text into a selling advertisement are:

1. That advertising engineering must be sound before inspiration can help to sell; and
2. That engineering can be definitely charted before the advertisement is published.

SHOWMANSHIP AND COMMON SENSE

A rational understanding of showmanship in advertising, in the best sense of the word, is illustrated by the case of the young lady from Brooklyn in search of a job.

Miss Ann F., a high-school graduate, took evening college courses. She did quite a lot of good reading and thinking; finally she set out to make a place for herself in the world. But the business world didn't have a place, at least not the kind of a place she could fill. And funds were getting low. At this point, using the brains she had, Miss Ann F. sat down to think the situation over.

Where would you go if you knew for a certainty that you had some thinking power that *somebody* could use if (1) you could present it in the right way and (2) you could present it to the kind of people who would be interested?

Miss F. gave herself a limit of five lines and twenty-five words to say her piece. She knew her first words would have to capture attention. She decided her biggest assets were her youth and her brains, put them first, topped them off with an emotional touch and a fine flair of showmanship, and ran the following advertisement in the classified section of a New York newspaper.

Young lady, intellectually solvent, economically bankrupt and idealistically convinced there must be interesting jobs in this world. Will consider legitimate offer anywhere. Y. 156 *Herald Tribune*

Miss Ann F. received 19 answers, and a position!

Showmanship in advertising has been defined as "tact on a gorgeous scale, tact blown up like a balloon," or, to put it another way, a dramatization of facts, the telling of the truth in an interesting way about your product or service. After all, showmanship is nothing more than the attracting of people's attention and the holding of their interest. It is essentially a preliminary rather than the whole of advertising. It knows no limitations as to space or medium. If the idea is right, an 8½- by 11-inch direct-mail letter can be as good a stage as a 20-foot billboard or a nation-wide radio hookup.

Looked at in this way, showmanship need not be "tricky," a definition some will associate with the word, and it need not be flamboyant, exaggerated, or out of keeping with the dignity that necessarily is inherent in certain types of business.

Advertising and merchandising were not always dramatic and personalized and conscious of the values of good showmanship. Not so long ago advertising placed dignity above drama as a sales appeal and believed pictures of the factory and the founder to be better salesmen in print than pictures depicting human interest.

The important viewpoint to maintain today is that all business, and more especially the merchandising phases, finds it necessary to be interesting. Large masses of our people, and people are markets, can be influenced most effectively by the advertising story presented graphically, dramatically.

The artist, Whistler, once said, "I mix my brains with my colors." In like manner, advertisers must mix common sense with showmanship in advertising, lest they confuse objectives and merely attract interest without following through in the sale of goods.

XIII

Public Relations

IN "The Tyranny of Words," Stuart Chase convincingly reveals that serious confusion arises when words, particularly universals, have a different meaning for different people. This seems especially true in the cases of "public relations" and "publicity," since these terms do not have the same meaning to all who use them.

To many manufacturers and businessmen, "public relations" is regarded as a highly organized and complex activity, frequently selfish and ulterior in its motives, carried on by public utilities and other large corporate bodies. With this fixed viewpoint, they may feel that their concerns are not faced with any problem of public relations; therefore they take little or no interest in this potentially powerful promotional activity.

In reality, public relations means "relations with people," and any business, large or small, has relations with people. In these days of increased competition, the right kind of relationships with customers, prospective customers, employees, stockholders, and the general public are not only highly desirable as a form of business insurance but commercially profitable as well.

"Next to doing the right thing the most important thing is to let the public know you are doing the right thing." A promotional program embodying sound public relations recognizes the basic wisdom of this saying.

WHAT IS PUBLIC RELATIONS?

Public relations is many things to many people. Some think of it as propaganda, others consider it the work of experts who cleverly manipulate facts to favor big corporations, but far and ahead is the notion that it is merely a high-sounding name for free publicity.

So new and unfamiliar, in fact, is the term that it is not even defined in the 1946 edition of Webster's New International Dictionary. Not so inarticulate are public-relations practitioners who, though differing on details, are united on the broad concept back of the name. Here are some of the more familiar definitions:

"Public relations, both in principle and in practice, is the interchange of good will between a private interest and the public interest through which all acts, policies, products, or services of the private interest become reflections of the needs and desires of the public and through which an informed public opinion is enabled to express its understanding, approval, and support."—Robert E. Harper, Advertising and Publicity Director, National Association of Ice Industries; Co-founder of the American Public Relations Association.

"Public relations is . . . a fundamental attitude of mind, a philosophy of management, which deliberately and with enlightened selfishness places the broad interest of the public first in every decision affecting the operation of the business."—Paul Garrett, General Motors Corporation.

And Milton Wright, author of the book, "Public Relations for Business" (Whittlesey House), gets down to bed rock by saying: "Public relations is merely relations with the public. It is the art of getting along with the public."

Beyond that, public relations is frequently thought of as public education, the engineering of consent and the management of opinion. But whether or not (as some would have it) "public relations is the application of the Golden Rule for profit," every business that accepts social responsibility as an integral function of management must establish that position through word and deed.

Public relations is now a "going concern." As a force organized for the betterment of industry is has now become one of the most thought about and talked about subjects in management circles.

Originally this force was employed almost exclusively in the interests of big business; today it is being utilized effectively by many business firms of moderate size.

The unparalleled ability developed in this country to sell goods or services by argument, persuasion, and reiteration does not yet extend to the business of selling ideas. It is in this field that public relations will make its greatest contribution to our social-economic progress.

The true public-relations counselor, and he is relatively rare, might more properly be known as an "economic doctor." He uses publicity, but publicity is only one of his tools; it is to public relations as is the fraction to the whole.

The publicity counselor deals with all functions of a business that require interpretation to avoid public misunderstanding. He is concerned with the effects of a company's policies and actions on the management, stockholders, employees, sources of supply, wholesalers, retailers, salesmen, consumers, legislators, public officials, the press, and the general public. The most efficient publicity counselor believes that the best defense is a good offense; he aggressively presents the truth based on irrefutable facts.

"It is not enough to give employees a square deal," a noted business leader has said. "They must be shown they are getting it."

Public relations is not only the least understood factor in commercial sales promotion but its legitimate values and benefits, both immediate and potential, are more frequently overlooked than is any other phase of sales promotion.

"FREE ADVERTISING"

Another misconception rather widely held is that publicity is nothing more than "free advertising." Nothing could be further from the truth. No businessman can expect to receive much legitimate publicity until he fully appreciates this basic distinction.

The text of the average advertisement is largely a one-way affair. It is prepared primarily in the interest of the advertiser, and, in the majority of cases, it extols the virtues of the advertiser's products. This is altogether fair when the advertiser pays for the space so used; whereas attempts to get free space for such purposes are illegitimate and are resolutely blocked by most reputable publications.

Publicity, on the other hand, is a two-way affair. It must be in the interest of the producer or it would not be produced, but it must also be in the interest of the periodical in which it appears. It must, above all, have reader interest, that is, it must be newsworthy, possessing entertainment or educational value that fits the editorial policy and standards of the magazine to which it is submitted. If an item or article is endowed with these qualities, and otherwise meets editorial requirements, it merits publication.

Many businessmen have the naïve belief that a writer sits down and produces "publicity" and that newspaper and magazine editors eagerly await and print such stories because of the significance attached to them by the concern thus publicized. Such "corporate ego" has slowed up many an otherwise well-directed effort.

Proper publicity consists of commercial literary material of genuine news value, published as the result of an editor's uncontrolled judgment; and all material of this sort that gets into print for any other reason is an imposition on the reader, a liability to the publication, and, usually, worthless to the producer.

BETTER ANNUAL REPORTS

No gesture toward the public which Big Business has made has been so gratefully accepted as the tendency to publish financial statements which can be read and understood without the aid of an expert accountant. The banks began it with statements through which a bright child could figure his way. The great corporations followed with résumés of their business which it was a pleasure rather than a torture to study.

The position generally taken now by the more enlightened corporations is that management is a trustee for the interests of the public as well as of the stockholder and the employee. This results in a simplicity and completeness of statement which make these reports valuable economic and social treatises.

Much credit for the improvement in corporation reports is due to the *Financial World,* which sponsors annual competitions for the best corporation reports and widely publicizes the results. Under the leadership of Weston Smith, this publication focuses management's attention on the desirability of introducing new improvements and appropriate changes—both in supplying statistics and information as well as greater attractiveness of the typographical presentations.

In the past seven of these annual surveys of financial statements, the reports classified by the judges as "Modern" have risen from 6 per cent of the total to 43 per cent; those classified as "Improved" have increased from 16 per cent to 30 per cent; and those indicated as "Unchanged in a Decade" have decreased from 78 per cent to 27 per cent.

It follows, therefore, that although publicity can supplement advertising and do some things advertising cannot do, it is not a substitute for advertising.

USES OF PUBLICITY

Ideally, those directing a publicity program should concern themselves primarily with the manufacture of news; with the organizing of circumstances to cause fortuitous happenings, so that the actual recording or writing of the news is largely handled by the newspapers or publications themselves.

Legitimate publicity can open up new pathways, explore new fields, and give people new ideas. It can bring the name and qualifications of a firm or an individual frequently to the attention of any number of selected groups of people, thereby creating and maintaining prestige and good will. It can announce overnight new products and processes and new applications of old ones on an industry-wide, a nation-wide, or a world-wide scale. It can try out the possibilities of new markets and determine if they are worth serious cultivation. It can promote the sale of old products by educating prospective customers as to their special economies, efficiencies, and applications.

Effective publicity can correct erroneous impressions or misunderstandings that may arise regarding an industry or its products. It can break down barriers of conservatism and prejudice and create new standards of excellence. It can bring to both the trade and the personnel of a firm a larger view of the firm's policies, aims, and accomplishments.

The real test for publicity is the net result on the business publicized. Like all sales-promotion tools, it should make the job of the salesmen easier; sell the company's policies; and build up, over the years, a friendly feeling of good will on the part of the public. Publicity which mounts up in thousands of clippings neatly pasted in voluminous books yet fails to reflect its influence on an ascending sales chart or improved public relations is so much wasted expense and effort. Publicity can and should be measured by the yardstick of demonstrable returns.

PUBLICIZING A PRODUCT

To understand how a publicity campaign is handled, let us consider the simple problem of publicizing a newly developed product.

The objective of our theoretical campaign is to announce the new product as fully as possible so that the maximum number of potential users will be informed about it, some idea of the degree and scope of the demand for the product can be ascertained from the inquiries developed, and salesmen can be assisted in introducing the product to their customers.

The campaign is logically divided into two parts:

1. The selection of the media to which the news releases will be sent.
2. The gathering and studying of all available material and the use of this material in preparing legitimate publicity releases.

Needling a Surgical Market

Surgeons are busy men. They have little time for reading, and what they do read is in the nature of homework, to keep up with professional advancement. They are flooded with wastebasket literature. They detest ordinary advertising methods as the tools of quackery. As a target for advertising, surgeons are almost impregnable.

When America's leading manufacturer of surgical rubber goods decided to appeal directly to surgeons, he knew that here was no ordinary problem; it's a tough job to give surgeons the advertising needle!

Said the manufacturer, "Now what we want is sales literature surgeons will read. It must be ethical, truthful; it must sell our product."

So . . .

Gynecologists, urologists, diagnosticians, surgeons, and specialists all looked a bit puzzled when staff men of a leading printing house asked:

"What can we tell the surgical profession about surgical rubber goods that will be of interest and practical value?"

Gradually a plan began to unfold. In collaboration with surgeons and other medical specialists, a treatise was prepared somewhat lacking, perhaps, in human interest, but packed with professional interest. It contained twenty anatomical drawings. Nine were reproduced in full color.

Subjects illustrated included mastoid, tonsil, empyema, ulcer, cancer, prostate, colostomy, and malformed mouths. On the same page with each anatomical drawing surgical rubber goods were indicated—presented not as advertising, mind you, but as factual, and, to the surgeon, intensely interesting information.

Let the facts speak for themselves:

Two simple letters were sent to each of the 17,400 surgeons on the American Medical Association list—"If you want a copy of the treatise, write for it." Returns equaled 40 per cent!

They respond the right way when given the right stimulant. People whom you wish to reach have wastebaskets, placed handily to receive sales literature of the commonplace, run-of-mine variety. It takes resourceful, pointed, virile stuff to win attention and get action!

Consideration is usually given first to newspapers, which are the most effective molders of public opinion. Everyone reads newspapers; nearly sixty million copies are sold every day. Items seen therein are widely read, hence a product development that can be announced by way of a national news syndicate gets off to a flying start that cannot be equaled in any other way.

Next in importance as a publicity medium is the business press. There are several thousand recognized trade, technical, and professional magazines serving nearly two hundred industries and professions. To select from this total a list of magazines that will be interested in any phase of the subject in hand requires a thoroughgoing knowledge of the individual magazines, their editorial policies, points of view, character of circulation, and use of illustrations and news matter. As a rule, the list has to be hand-picked for each subject, as no existing classification ever exactly fits the case and a list prepared for one purpose is rarely useful for another.

Then come the other channels for reaching the public—local newspapers, the general magazines, photo syndicates, newsreels, industrial house organs, periodicals issued by societies. Any that would be interested in the proposed announcement are listed and the proper method of approach in each case is determined.

With the field of action mapped out, the next step is to determine how the material is to be presented. Sometimes, a brief news item mailed to a selected list of periodicals meets the needs of the situation.

Captioned photos for magazines and illustrated mats for newspapers may be distributed to advantage. Often, extensive articles, prepared after consultation with the editors, can be published in several magazines in different fields.

When the subject is of sufficient importance, it may be announced in an address before a technical, professional, or scientific society; or a formal demonstration of the new development before an invited group of representatives of the newspapers and the business press, writers, departmental editors of magazines, and cameramen may be justified. Usually, except in matters of minor or limited interest, various combinations of these methods of presentation are employed.

The timing of the announcement is of great importance, since there are appropriate and inappropriate times to announce almost any subject.

When the preliminaries are settled, a complete working plan and timetable of the campaign are next drawn up, which, when the zero hour arrives, will be carried out with the precision of a military operation.

WRITING THE STORIES

The careful preparation of the actual copy to be distributed in the form of news releases is the most difficult part of the whole proceeding. Each publicity release will be submitted to the selected media freely and without attached strings. In each case, the editor's decision as to the value of the material as news or educational matter will be final. Hence the whole campaign must stand or fall on the reader interest of the submitted copy, and this interest of various groups of readers in the subject will vary. Newspaper readers will be interested in one phase, readers of a business magazine in another phase, readers of a particular national magazine in still a third phase, and so on down the line. The writer of the publicity releases must have a precise understanding of these varying points of view, if anything he writes is to prove acceptable. He may be called upon to present his material in three, four, or a dozen different ways in order to cover the requirements of a single simple campaign properly.

It may be decided that the newspaper and magazine possibilities of the subject fall logically into three types of publicity releases.

First, The Factual Feature Story. Let us assume, for instance, that the new product to be publicized will be used in the home. Newspaper readers are interested in the living habits and the homes of well-known people. There is a natural desire to emulate outstanding people. Nationally known figures in the fields of politics, stage, screen, or sports, who are users of the product, will be featured in stores, and the news facts about the product interwoven.

Second, The Technical Story. A testing of the new product by an outstanding laboratory, the United States Bureau of Standards, or other well-known institutions, will provide the basis for a story of technical merits presented in everyday language for the average newspaper reader's attention.

Third, The Stunt Feature Story. A beautiful young woman poses with a noted screen star while both examine the new product. A short caption beneath this illustration carries the story that this young woman, a recent bride, was deciding to use the new product in her home.

The campaign, when finally executed, may prove to be anything from a huge success to a complete failure, depending on the intrinsic merits of the subject, the skill of the publicist, and events over which he has no control. In general, the properly prepared publicity campaign based upon a subject of genuine public interest is satisfactorily successful, although it may be weeks or even months before this fact can be ascertained. At the same time, no firm utilizing publicity should restrict itself to a single campaign; it is the net result of a series of campaigns that counts.

KEEPING STOCKHOLDERS INFORMED

While many corporations often overlook the stock-holders in their promotional plans, there has been a tendency on the part of an increasing number of managements in recent years to establish programs of education and information for these actual owners of the body corporate. With the majority of managements the *modernized* annual report, simplifying and interpreting the financial statements for the average investor, has provided an effective vehicle through which to publicize the company's products and thus turn the small or large army of shareholders into a host of enthusiastic boosters. The yearly financial statement can be supplemented by several varieties of stockholder-relations literature to maintain interest and build confidence in the intervening months between annual reports.

Cloaking Annual Reports in Financial Mumbo-jumbo

Many of the nation's leading cost accountants, at a recent annual convention, as reported in the *Journal of Commerce,* indicated that: "Industry is missing a golden opportunity to sell its case to stockholders and the public by cloaking annual reports in financial mumbo-jumbo the average man won't read, and couldn't understand if he did."

The crux of the problem was expressed by Carman G. Blough, director of research of the American Institute of Accountants. He declared, "Concerned over the high cost of living, harreid by fears of the widely proclaimed forthcoming recession, confused by the claims of those engaged in wage negotiations and disturbed by the arguments of those who seek a thoroughgoing revision of American business concepts, people are demanding to be told the facts."

There is no better vehicle for telling them the real facts than through a truly informative, easily understood financial report, he added.

In documenting his criticism of the annual report as it exists today, Mr. Blough called into question the meaning of customary accounting terms—at least as they might be interpreted by the layman.

"Surplus," he suggested, "means something left over and not needed . . . (which) should be distributed in the form of dividends, increased wages, lower prices, or, possibly, as taxes."

"Reserve" carries the implication of "a company holding idle funds which are doing nobody any good," he added. "As though that were not confusing enough, the reader is confronted with 'reserves' for such a mixture of items as bad debts, depreciation, taxes, deferred maintenance and repairs, possible future inventory price declines, contingencies or what have you. They may appear anywhere on the balance sheet and seem to show up frequently on the income statements."

Prior to World War I the corporation annual report was merely a statement to show that the independent auditors had certified the figures as revealed in the more or less condensed balance sheet. Such statements were seldom seen by other than bankers, trust executives, and large investors, who made it their business to keep in close touch with the management throughout the year. In those days most of the big corporations were owned by hundreds of stockholders who held thousands of shares.

Today the big, medium, and small corporations are owned by millions of small investors holding odd lots of fifteen to fifty shares. What has happened in the past quarter century? The answer is "public financing." When Liberty Bonds were redeemed after the First World War, small investors reinvested their savings in the bonds, preferred stocks, and common shares of corporations in many industries as the investment bankers offered these securities for public subscription. Countless others turned to the stock market as speculators, pyramiding their holdings until 1929, when the Wall Street crash either cleaned them out or left them high and dry with substantial losses on the paper they had accumulated in their safe deposit boxes.

The enactment of state blue-sky laws and the establishment of the Securities and Exchange Commission provided safeguards for the small investor. These laws on the statute books drove out the bucket shop and the promoter of worthless stocks, and provided assurance that the speculator would at least have a "run for his money." High margins and heavy taxes have turned the shoestring speculators into small "investors," who have found it more profitable to build their investment portfolios through the accumulation of small lots of stock rather than engaging in in-and-out trading. Meanwhile, all types of investment trusts have enjoyed a tremendous expansion, and these organized funds have had the effect of spreading stock ownership and expanding the number of individual stockholders.

The National City Bank of New York recently reported that stockholders outnumbered workers in seventy-two of the nation's one-hundred largest corporations. These seventy-two corporations had 4,082,805 stockholders in 1945, an increase of 17 per cent in the last ten years, and 2,925,449 employees, the ratio being 1.4 shareholders to each employee. Total pay rolls averaged $2,880 per employee for the year. Dividends paid were less than 12 per cent of wages, and less than half of taxes. For every employee, on the average, there was a capital investment which amounted to $9,300.

The National City found similar relationships in eight large railroad and public-utility companies, with a ratio of 1.2 shareholders to each employee. Wages and salaries were nine times as large as dividends.

Among individual companies, General Motors had 345,940 employees and 425,657 shareholders. The Packard Motor Car Co., at one extreme, had 10.4 shareholders for every employee. The Douglas Aircraft Co., at the other extreme, had only one shareholder for every 3.08 employees.

Thus, the problem of management in handling its sharehold relations has substantially changed from the time when the ownership of their corporations was dominated by a relatively small group of wealthy families, bankers, and financiers. The account of the stewardship of the corporation executive is now addressed to tens or hundreds of thousands of little people in almost every walk of life—more than half of these small investors, on the average, are women, and the large majority of both sexes have had little or no training in corporation finance or even simple bookkeeping.

The formal, or "conservative," annual report, which adequately serves the requirements of the banker or trained investment analyst, is just so much waste paper to the small investor who has not finished high school, or to the widow with a moderate investment portfolio left her by her late husband. But this is the very audience that management should want to reach, if it actually wishes to spread a wholesome understanding of its policies, and win friends and boosters for the products it markets.

The corporation annual reports lend themselves to a wide variety of treatments that provide figures and facts in a form that can be grasped quickly and easily by the readers of the daily tabloid, the popular magazine, or digest publications. The first step in modernizing an annual report is to provide directly comparable figures for two years in the balance sheets and income accounts, but these financial statements also should be interpreted by means of pictorial graphics that show at a glance the trend from the past year.

The second step is to supply a background of comparative operating statistics for ten years or more and these figures likewise can be portrayed by means of charts in many styles of presentation.

With this backlog of simplified statistics, the next step should be to humanize the report: first by writing the "president's letter" and other editorial material in a popular style that is interesting enough to hold the average reader's attention. This section of the annual report can be illustrated by photographs that are both appropriate and dramatic, each with a curiosity-arousing caption to draw the reader into the text. In the editorial section, several of the pictorial graphics can be included to emphasize and clarify the comments on the trend of the business.

Here are the preferences of small investors for photographs and charts in annual reports (in order of their preference), as gathered from an opinion poll of active stockholders:

	PHOTOGRAPHS	GRAPHICS
1.	Products or services	Earnings and dividends
2.	Building and plant facilities	Maps of plants, stores, agencies, etc.
3.	Uses or users of products	Trend of sales, net income, etc.
4.	Processes of manufacturing	Taxes paid to federal, states, etc.
5.	President and officers	Distribution of sales dollar
6.	Outstanding events of year	Organization chart of management
7.	Board of directors	Geographical distribution of stock
8.	Employees in action	Workers' wages and number employed

It is significant that the primary interest of small investors is in the products and services offered, and in "earnings and dividends," and any annual report is remiss if it does not take advantage of this thirst for more information on basic facts. The above lists can be augmented by photographs and charts that are particularly appropriate to the corporation concerned.

Managements that have tested and found effective the "Humanized" treatment of an annual report have taken an additional step by converting these statements into "yearbooks." This is achieved by including a reasonable amount of biographical and historical data, as well as some reference material, which is properly cross-indexed to make it possible to find the required information. A "yearbook" treatment of a corporation annual report encourages the recipient to retain his copy for reference throughout the year. In addition, a yearbook is a more appropriate document for distribution during the year to new stockholders.

Another development in annual reporting is the use of a magazine format to present both factual and statistical data. No annual report should be presented in "catalog" style, where each page has the appearance of all the others with the chart or photograph of the same size spotted in the same corner of the page. By the use of magazine styling every page will have a different and refreshing appearance to renew the interest of the reader, and encourage him to at least start the text.

Corporation financial reports have been utilized effectively to introduce new products and services to the shareholders, and often before such announcements are publicized to all customers. In a number of reports actual samples of products have been "tipped" in the pages or on the covers—such as swatches of fabrics, pieces of ribbon, and miniatures in metal. Other reports have utilized their products as the actual cover, including wallpaper, boxboard, and aluminum ink. Then there have been a few instances where the report has been accompanied with a product, such as a recipe booklet, a dress pattern, or a road map.

The impact of these extracurricular additions to the annual report has usually been reflected in a large increase in the response of stockholders to the annual report. The additional publicity obtained in the financial pages of the newspapers and in the trade journals of the field has generally compensated for the additional expense.

But the annual report should only be the keystone of the program to keep the stockholder informed. The interim or quarterly financial report is the second most important means of presenting management's story to the small investor. An increasing number of companies have converted their stereotyped quarterly earnings statements into attractive bulletins, newsletters, and digest booklets, edited in news style and illustrated with appropriate photographs and charts. One company publishes a quarterly magazine of sixteen pages, published four times a year to supplement the annual report.

One of the most effective forms of stockholder-relations literature is the "dividend stuffer," or the insert mailed with the dividend check as a "free rider" on the same postage. If quarterly dividends are paid, the opportunity is provided to send out four such mailings in addition to the annual and interim reports. These stuffers have been utilized to introduce new products and processes, explain new financing, announce the promotions of executive officers, review past actions of the management, provide biographical material on directors, offer an opportunity to send for a sample of a product, etc. During the war many thousands of dividend inserts recommended the purchase of war bonds and contributions to the Red Cross, U.S.O., and similar organizations, but in peacetime investors are not likely to welcome any suggestion as to how to spend their income, even though the cause may be a worthy one.

Additional mailings to stockholders can include special anniversary booklets that mark the silver, golden, or diamond jubilee of the founding of the corporation. Such information, however, can quite properly be combined with the annual report of the same year, and will likely enjoy a broader reader acceptance. Few investors will spend time to read a "book" or an elaborate historical brochure from cover to cover, and most anniversary editions usually end up unopened in the stockholder's library to gather dust.

One of the most effective means of cultivating the interest of new stockholders is by a letter of welcome from the company's president very soon after the shares have been registered. Accompanying such letters are copies of the latest annual and interim report, and the new shareholder is invited to ask for any additional information he requires, or to offer constructive criticism. Many managements also send a letter of regrets when the shareholder disposes of his shares, and request an explanation for the action. Such letters have revealed some "excellent reasons" for the sale of stock, other than "financial difficulties" on the part of the individual.

The proxy statement has come to the fore as a further method of providing information to stockholders. This is the only vehicle through which the individual investor can voice his opinion to the rest of the owners of the corporation, and an increasing number of investors are taking advantage of this opportunity. Some shareholders will attempt to abuse their privilege by requesting nonessential information in the proxy statement, and management must exercise keen discrimination in the preparation of such documents. This is the place for the listing of executives' salaries and directors' fees, not in the annual report.

The annual meeting of the stockholders is the one function of the corporation during the year where the investor can meet the management face to face and hear the report of stewardship from the lips of the president or board chairman or both. This is the stockholder's forum, but he will not or cannot attend in large numbers if the meeting requires a long journey. Thus, an increasing number of managements are bringing the meeting to the stockholders by conducting regional meetings in large cities across the continent where the largest concentration of shareholders reside. A few corporations have established the policy of providing free bus transportation to meetings held at the "corporate office" when it is located in a small town that is inconvenient to reach.

A modern stockholder meeting is no longer a stuffy affair with hard seats, poor ventilation, and bad lighting. Progressive managements usually conduct both their regular and regional meetings in the small or large ballrooms of the better hotels, and often a luncheon or dinner is provided. A feature of these meetings is the demonstration of a new product, the showing of a movie or slide film, and the distribution of samples and appropriate literature. A question period is provided in which any stockholder can "have the floor" to offer his compliments, suggestions, or criticisms. There is a genuine informality about most of these meetings that make the stockholders "feel at home"—an integral part of the corporation.

Following the annual stockholders meeting the minutes should be sent to all shareholders as a matter of record, and the questions asked from the floor should be included with the answers in this report of the meeting. A few corporations have the minutes of the meeting attractively printed, and some have reproduced pictures of the actual meeting with "flash" photographs of stockholders talking to the officers of the company. This treatment enhances the prestige of the individual shareholder and encourages an increasing number to attend the future meetings.

The newest development in management-stockholder relations is the effort on the part of the corporation executives to encourage shareholders to visit the "home office," the plants, and branches. One company makes it an annual practice to invite stockholders to visit the main plant during their summer-vacation automobile tours, and a special reception program is planned to conduct visiting stockholders on an inspection around the property. Other companies have set aside weeks or days during the year when the branch plants are open to all stockholders who care to see operations, and refreshments and souvenirs are usually distributed to the visitors.

Important among the techniques employed by management in stockholder relations is the use of "opinion surveys" to determine investor interest. Questionnaires are utilized to find out the preferences of a cross section of large and small stockholders on what topics should be covered in annual reports. By this means the management can determine the amount of space that should be devoted to each topic in the annual report. Some corporations employ professional opinion-research agencies to send personal interviewers to a selected list of stockholders in order to obtain an "average" of the stockholder thinking on essential subjects concerning management policies. One company "checked" only its women stockholders, while another covered employee stockholders, and the "results" revealed a high degree of misunderstanding on fundamental conceptions of the corporation's activities.

While the annual report is the keystone of a constructive stockholder-relations program, it is actually only one part of a well-rounded campaign to win and maintain shareholder confidence and support. The bigger the corporation, the greater is the number of techniques that should be employed to keep stockholders informed. And an informed "stockholderate," to coin a term, may prove to be the strongest bulwark that the corporations can develop to assure the continuance of the American economic system.

A PROPHET WITHOUT HONOR

Daily, on every hand, the clear-thinking citizen observes American business at work. So familiar are its accomplishments that they are accepted as commonplace; little thought is given to the connection between the business process and the general well-being of the country. On the other hand, because of the general misunderstanding that has arisen between the desks of management and the work-benches of the country, the purpose and utility of business is regarded with suspicion and distrust.

Business in the United States, partly through its own fault, has been in the doghouse for years. Because of the greed or corrupt practices of a small percentage of businessmen, and because a relatively few corporation executives operated their own companies for their personal benefit rather than in the interest of the stockholders, all business management has suffered criticism.

What is behind this disquieting attitude toward business in a land famed for its supremacy in the production of goods that make life more comfortable, more interesting, and more worth while where business has contributed its share in the best life in recorded history? Why are we part of the bewildering spectacle of a large portion of American citizens literally biting the hand that feeds them?

The basic lack of understanding by labor and management of their mutuality of interests in an expanding economy casts a sobering shadow over a business potential unequaled in peacetime history. And there is more to the American system of free enterprise than material well-being. Closely intertwined with our economic liberties are political liberties, so that the social order itself is dependent on the efficient operation of our productive capacity.

Now we lack neither the dollars, materials, manpower, tools, nor skills to place our economy on a sound basis and enjoy prosperity. If labor, as well as management, exercises restraint and good judgment, if both understand their common interest in a healthy economy, the years ahead will be good ones for all concerned. But the issues involved go far deeper than wages and profits alone and can be solved only when workers and management add to the balance sheet a vital intangible—the spirit of mutual interdependence, trust, and understanding.

To achieve this spirit of mutual interdependence, management must wage an aggressive continuous campaign, not necessarily one to induce employees to act in the interest of management and owners, but instead a sincere straightforward program of objective education in its truest sense—without which employees cannot act intelligently and realistically even in their own interest.

Management must, first of all, realize that unfortunately neither intelligence nor good intentions alone can solve the problem. What is needed, essentially, is a realization that certain readily understood, even obvious, facts to management are completely outside the knowledge, understanding, experience, and imagination of the workers. And, equally important, certain matters that workers consider of vital importance represent points of view that have never occurred to management, no matter how sincere its intentions to see and squarely face the whole problem.

Further, as management attempts to see the problem through the other fellow's eyes, it should remember that statistics show that approximately 50 per cent of the nation's factory workers today are unhappy in their jobs because the jobs are dull and uninteresting. Obviously, attention must be directed to making our system provide the highest possible degree of work satisfaction and the highest standard of living. Psychologically, adjusted and contented egoes and personalities may prove to be coequal in importance with automobiles or air-conditioning units.

UNDERSTANDING PAYS OFF

Perhaps one example will point the moral. The old chestnut, "all the workers are interested in are their paychecks," is still bandied about in the board rooms. And yet, as was so conclusively demonstrated during the war, workers are happier and more productive when they understand the meaning and social-economic usefulness of their jobs and work. A few enlightened managements are proving today that even with the glamor of war eliminated, workers get more satisfaction from their jobs and do them better when they are given a sense of the significance of their work and resultant feeling of accomplishment.

Essentially, then, a basic cornerstone for more harmonious and stable relationships between labor and management is a realization and deeper understanding of the implications involved in the relationships of both workers and employers as human beings, not only in the economic sphere but also in the social and political fields as well.

Such an understanding, coupled with a better interpretation by all our citizens of the Golden Rule as a living creed instead of a forgotten proverb, will help us more nearly attain a permanent solution to economic friction and the full measure of unprecedented prosperity and peace that are within our grasp.

Despite an acceptance of the full implications of the statement that the Golden Rule in operation offers both a satisfactory and lasting solution to labor-management difficulties, it is, realistically speaking, impossible "to love thy neighbor" if you sincerely feel that you are being gouged and not getting your fair share. And that is, essentially, the viewpoint of many in the ranks of labor today. Fundamental, then, to the solution of the difficulty is management's job of explaining how and why profits are distributed and why this distribution is equitable to all concerned— the stockholders, the managers, the employees, the government, and the public—so that the greatest good for the greatest number follows as inevitably as do the seasons of the year.

Many will regard the statement that labor and management don't talk the same language as a play on words, but it is a fact. True enough, they both use the same words but the connotations of these words and their emotional impacts are all too frequently far apart. Not only do the two groups not have a similar understanding of the language they use, but they are also poles apart in their convictions, based on what each believes to be the facts upon which the convictions are founded.

ATTENTION FOCUSED ON "PROFITS"

Dr. Claude E. Robinson, President, Opinion Research Corporation, has frequently emphasized that the public does not appreciate the loss side of the profit and loss ledger; that its attention is focused on the profit side alone. The public, according to studies made by the Opinion Research Corporation, thinks companies made 30 per cent profits in wartime and that they make an average of 25 per cent profits in peacetime on either sales or capital invested—people don't distinguish between the two. Now the public is not against profit; in fact, it believes in making a profit and thinks a profit of about 10 per cent is fair, but it objects to profits of 25 to 30 per cent. Actually, business profits, according to the National City Bank, were 2.9 per cent on sales and 5.9 per cent on investment, during the years 1923 to 1941.

The fantastic public misconception about the profits of enterprise is further described by this fact:

employees think the bosses and owners get 75 cents out of the dollar that is paid out to employees, owners, and managers, and the employees' share is only 25 cents. Actually, the employee gets not 25 cents of this dollar, but approximately 87 cents! And, if all profits were added to wages, the latter would be increased by only 4 per cent, which, obviously, would leave no funds with which to buy additional equipment—and without new tools and machines wages would soon decline. In fact, a company without profits can soon become a company without jobs.

Inevitably, then, a whole chain of human behavior starts with and revolves around this deep-seated misconception as to the profit companies make. It is at the heart of unrealistic wage demands such as: "Companies can grant a 25 per cent wage increase without raising prices because they are making so much money." And it is the kernel of the so-called liberal viewpoint that somehow you can get higher pay by producing less goods per hour of labor.

As a consequence of this lack of understanding about profits, a large majority of the public has fantastic misconceptions that business men are greedy, sitting on moneybags, and taking the shirts off peoples' backs so that they may add to their ill-gotten gains. Equally true is the fact that they have little or no understanding, as Carl Snyder argues in "Capitalism the Creator," that risk takers in the aggregate lose about as much as they gain.

And, as is so well known to businessmen, risk taking in search of profits has been a great dynamic force in American life. Simply stated, the basis of our tremendous industrial strength and our high living standards is the investment of capital, the use of labor-saving machinery, greater output per hour of labor, and lower prices so that the normal comforts of life are attainable by most of our people.

Business has been so preoccupied with its major internal problems that it has grown almost inarticulate. It has been frightened into the notion that it must move through subterfuge, in secrecy, and with doubt as to its approach. It has permitted itself to be pushed and crowded by the "smear" technique of the opposition until it speaks apologetically of efforts to develop good relations with the public.

It is a well-known fact that business, so capable and ingenious in improving and selling its products, has been far less progressive in its human relationships. Much of the time it has been behind public opinion when it should have been ahead. It has been thrown into confusion, not because of any inherent or irremediable weakness within itself, but because it has failed to make clear to the people the philosophy and principles of its existence.

This situation is by no means unique. It is a recurring phenomenon of American life that at varying intervals an administration or public leader launches an attack on certain sectors of business activity or on business generally. This was true in Andrew Jackson's time; it characterized Cleveland's administration; it happened again in the days of Theodore Roosevelt and his "big stick." More recent years have witnessed the re-emergence of similar activities in more vigorous fashion than ever before.

Obviously, large sectors of the American public do not regard these actions as attacks; from their point of view these movements represent proper governmental remedial actions, which cause business to clean house and give the public a square deal.

No responsible leader of this country's business will maintain that all business activities or institutions are perfect and proper or that some activities and certain parts of American business cannot properly undergo a housecleaning. In every group there are good men and evil men, wise men and fools, the just and the unjust, the greedy and the generous. Human nature and human institutions continue under all systems to have their endless variety.

The essential problem of government is to police men's activities so that wrong may not be done and justice may prevail. The politicians and radicals and pseudo economists overlook this. Instead of seeking to reduce and prevent injustice between citizens they blindly attack a system of production and distribution that by its results, as shown in our standard of living, is the best so far devised.

American business should be in a position to refute this malicious, calculated propaganda, even remedy its ill effects so that its policies and purposes may be properly interpreted and, where justified, understood to be right and proper in the eyes of society.

Falsehood and misrepresentation can only be successfully combated by plain unvarnished truth, which in the long run always wins. Unfortunately, the nation's business cannot afford to let "the mills of God grind slowly" for, truly, they grind too slowly to be helpful in the present circumstance. Business cannot proceed too leisurely in making friends, lest the opposing forces completely undermine public confidence in the integrity and usefulness of American business.

A JOB FOR MANAGEMENT

As the *Journal of Commerce* editorializes:

Corporation financial reports are not doing, by and large, the job for which they are designed. They are not being widely read, and too many of the people who read them do not understand or trust them.

This is the discouraging conclusion of a survey carried out by the Opinion Research Corporation for the Controllership Foundation.

Corporation annual reports have become much more attractive typographically. The accounting profession and the Securities and Exchange Commission have worked hard to raise standards in financial reporting. Managements have assiduously tried to make their reports more interesting and more informative.

Unfortunately, these well-meant efforts have had but limited success to date, to judge from the Opinion Research Corporation's survey. For, despite the wider distribution of wealth and security ownership, this survey found that only a third of the adult population of the United States has ever seen a profit and loss statement, and nearly half of these had seen only reports of financial institutions in which they had deposits or insurance policies. Furthermore, two-thirds of those who had ever read a financial statement had not done so in the last six months.

Well over half the adults, according to this survey, regard financial statements as difficult to understand. Nearly half think profits are not accurately stated in financial statements.

Fully 45 per cent think business profits average 25 per cent or more.

Such finding show that management has yet to solve the problem of making corporate financial reports widely read and understood. They lend support to the view that attempts to improve financial reporting have not been in the right direction in too many cases. For the test is not what technicians think about corporate reports, but rather whether the public reads and understands them.

Some managements will throw up their hands at these findings and say by their very nature corporation reports are not popular reading and cannot be made so. But such a view runs away from the problem—it does not solve it.

The root of the difficulty may well be the effort to write reports for too many types of readers. Annual reports are expected to be read by financial analysts, by large and small stockholders, and often by employees and customers as well. They must meet the exacting standards of accountants and the SEC with regard to terminology—yet they are expected to be interesting to laymen, most of whom have no training whatever in bookkeeping and accounting.

If the annual report is to be primarily a vehicle for passing on information to the rank and file of stockholders and the public generally, more radical changes are required in its content and format. Terminology used in income accounts and balance sheets, for example, will have to be modified drastically to become clearly understandable to readers without any technical training in accounting. On the other hand, if the report is to be designed primarily for technicians, many of the recent changes in financial reporting become unnecessary.

More incisive thinking is required about the whole problem. The identity of the desired audience must first be clearly determined. Then, content and format must be modified to attract and convince these readers, whoever they are, even if this means departing entirely from accepted accounting terminology and conventional financial statements. The decision as to which readers are desired for annual reports can be made effectively only at the top level of management.

Who Owns The Flintkote Company?

Let us assume that John Doe has saved $2,000. With it he might conceivably start in business for himself, possibly opening a grocery store or a filling station. If he does, he would naturally devote his time to his grocery store or filling station. He would, therefore, assume all the risks involved and face the long hours of work which are the usual lot of the individual who owns and operates his own business.

However, John Doe may prefer to employ his $2,000 in another way. He may decide to continue to work at his regular job and draw his salary each week. But he wants to put his money, his accumulated savings, to work. So he uses his money to buy common stock of The Flintkote Company and thus becomes a part owner of the business. As a stockholder he acquires the right to share in the company's management and participate in its profits. When he exchanges his money for stock he is combining his funds with those of thousands of other individuals who own the company. His money, paid to the company in exchange for its stock, gives The Flintkote Company additional funds which it can utilize, possibly to buy an electric lift truck to handle materials more easily or, as it has recently, to help finance the erection of a new laboratory, the building of new plants, the completion of additional facilities at its present plants, and to provide additional cash to help operate these increased facilities.

Actually, then, The Flintkote Company is owned not by one man or two; not by any group of bankers or by an individual financier; not by its officers who are employed to manage the company's affairs; but by approximately 11,000 individual holders—enough to form an airborne army division or make a community the size of La Grange, Illinois; Bath, Maine; Fredericksburg, Virginia; or Monterey, California.

The approximately 11,000 owners of The Flintkote Company, the holders of its common and preferred stock, are located in every state of the Union and in the District of Columbia. The average

Who Owns The Flintkote Company?

stockholder presently owns approximately 110 shares of common stock. Some hold less, some more, but no registered holder currently owns as much as 3 per cent of the total share of the outstanding common capital stock of the company.

Thus it is not the investments of a few extremely wealthy individuals but the combined savings of thousands of average citizens that make The Flintkote Company—and most American corporations—possible. Without some such method of providing the necessary money to buy plants, machinery, raw materials, meet pay rolls, and operate the business, American mass production could never have provided jobs for millions of workers or made possible the highest living standards in all recorded history, which we are so fortunate to enjoy in the United States. In the final analysis, it is the investor who is the source of jobs and prosperity.

How did these people in all walks of life in cities, towns, and villages throughout America acquire their ownership of The Flintkote Company and their right to share in its management and profits? Generally speaking, they saved their money and were and are willing to risk their savings, based on their judgment of intrinsic values, by investing in the stock of the company. Basically they believe the company to be well managed and its diversified lines of building materials, products for industry and paperboard products of such merit that profitable sales are the natural result. Actually, each of the approximately 11,000 stockholders of The Flintkote Company is, in a sense, "in business for himself." Combined together this group owns The Flintkote Company and their combined investment makes its operations possible.

(The above statement, which appeared in Flintkote plant magazines, typifies the approach of management to employees in interpreting facts about the company of mutual interest to all concerned.)

BEST DEFENSE A GOOD OFFENSE

Now, perhaps more than at any other time in history, business should raise its sights and present its fundamental case by intelligent, constructive planning in the field of public relations. It must tell its story and win friends as regards "the right further to serve and grow and achieve—the proper relationship with government and government with business —a clear understanding by the people of the functions of business so that business can do more for the people—provide a higher standard of living— better wages—a richer and fuller life."

To do so, business as a whole, individual businesses, and individual businessmen need efficient public-relations counselors, not merely "publicity men." Press clippings will not suffice; there must be competent consulting advice on the proper way to interpret basic economic factors, and the reactions and effects of corporate policies on mass psychology, and, in turn, on society in general.

American business must broaden its views. Business leaders must realize that not every strike is due entirely to the machinations of a labor agitator, or a consumers' boycott to the initiative of a wild-eyed reformer. Many of these costly industrial blunders are caused by the stubborn insistence of a corporation executive who would rather fight than settle and who believes favorable public opinion can be immediately created for his side of the proposition by the running of full-page advertisements expounding his point of view in leading newspapers.

Corporation executives could learn much in the

handling of public relations from the Chinese, who pay the doctor in advance to keep the individual healthy rather than call him in only when the patient is seriously ill or dying.

A few far-sighted business leaders do use this "Chinese doctor" policy. They view good public relations as an important day-by-day activity. They build up an acceptance, over the years, of a justification for their existence; they are consciously alert to interpret their business in terms of human usefulness. In time, the institutions headed by these wise leaders take on a character and a personality that make them appear warm, human, and socially useful in contrast to the ogre-like, cold conceptions of concerns which overlook this highly important duty to themselves, their stockholders, their employees, and the public.

American business, whether large or small, cannot afford to ignore public sentiment. No less an astute judge of human nature than Abraham Lincoln said, "Public sentiment is everything. With public sentiment nothing can fail. Without it, nothing can succeed. Consequently he who molds public sentiment goes deeper than he who enacts statutes or pronounces decisions—he makes statutes and decisions possible or impossible to execute." That statement was true in 1860; it is true as gospel today; and it will be equally true for countless years to come.

THE JOB AHEAD

The great job ahead is the rehabilitation of the American commercial system in the eyes of the American public. This is a difficult task requiring all the ingenuity, sincerity, and vision that our industrial leaders can marshal in its behalf. It may well prove to be the major job ahead for business to tackle and to handle.

It should be clearly understood that circumstances and political propaganda have made it necessary for American business to explain itself to a public that has been taught to be suspicious of explanations that come from business. Thus the influences that have made it necessary to explain business have also made difficult the job of doing so.

The job of preparing explanations of American business is no problem. The facts are available and merely require arrangement. When they are added together and weighed, they are favorable to business. The problem is to find a way to assure the public that the facts are credible.

It is doubtful that the facts about business can be made credible to all segments of the public by any standardized procedure. Facts that are accepted as credible under one condition are rejected as incredible under other conditions. Truths that are self-evident to one group are regarded with skepticism by other groups. Care and great skill will be needed to specialize the story for each group.

Resorting to lobbying bureaus, making heavy campaign contributions, and the lavish wining and dining of the right people are certainly not the proper way to win and build lasting good will. These pressure tactics, the behind-the-scene methods heretofore so frequently used by some sectors of American business, tend only to sour the public and increase its feeling of suspicion.

A more ethical, democratic, and practical procedure must be followed. A disarming frankness and a universal impression of sincerity based on telling the truth in a straightforward manner is essential to success.

OBJECTIVE ECONOMIC EDUCATION

Thus, in the rehabilitation of the American business system in the eyes of the American public, publicity and paid advertising will be of enormous importance. It may be that, whereas these modern promotional tools have heretofore been devoted primarily to selling products or services, they will henceforth be used more for selling ideas. Perhaps the big idea American business will have to sell will be objective economic education, based on seeing the problems through the other fellow's eyes; explaining the facts at issue in language the majority of our people will understand and accept; and honestly interpreting economic laws so that their causes and effects are clearly understood by the masses of our citizens.

Impractical? Too costly? Never done before on a broad scale? Quite true. But remember the wise skipper throws some of his cargo overboard when his ship is threatened in the storm. The amount of sales cargo which may be lost by devoting advertising and publicity to selling the truth about American business will be a drop in the bucket compared with the ultimate good that would come from blotting out the misconceptions about American business that are finding increasing acceptance. The stakes are high; the strategy suggested is at least worth a trial.

XIV

Radio and Television

THE split-second hand of the studio clock nears eight o'clock. An unexpected hush falls over the audience of hundreds of people who have spent many hours to get the coveted passes to the broadcast studio.

The radio announcer begins reading from his script; the orchestra leader raises his baton; the tenor's quavering voice is lifted in a refrain that, carried out over the national hookup, may be heard in ten million or more homes tuned in on the program.

Over in the observation booth, the sponsor settles back contentedly, despite the fact that the next hour's activity will cost his company many thousands of dollars for the production of the program and the time of the stations used.

A big-time radio show is on the air! Eighteen hours or more, each day throughout the year, this same scene is repeated in its essential characteristics so that the radio listeners in the United States may have satisfactory service all day and most of the night over the more than 1,300 United States radio stations, carefully spaced, timed, and powered to assure maximum clarity of reception over the air channels.

How many people are listening to this program? How responsive, from the commercial standpoint, will

Radio Alphabet

From "A Glossary of Radio Terms," Copyright by The Columbia Broadcasting System

Abie—Anyone who is sure fire.

Acetate—The term often erroneously used to describe cellulose-nitrate recording discs.

Adenoid—Any vocalist with a voice that is "tight."

Adjacencies—The programs (on the same station) immediately preceding and following the one under consideration.

Animator—A Goldberg contrivance of lights, mirrors, and other mechanical devices used to animate scenes in television.

Atmospheric—Music or sound used to enhance the mood of the scene being enacted.

Background—A sound effect, musical or otherwise, used behind the dialogue for realistic or emotional effect.

Beard—An error in performance, more often words misread by an actor.

Belcher—A performer with a frog in his throat.

Break—A scheduled or unscheduled interruption of a program, or a recess in rehearsal schedule.

Bye Bye—The script line beginning: "We now leave our studio," or "We take you now to—," or "We return now to—," etc.

Canaries—Singers (often coloratura sopranos).

Clambake—A shapeless program filled with uncertainties; rehearsals marked by errors, changes, and failures, likely to result in a bad performance. Sometimes called Clamaroo.

Cliff Hanger—A serial dramatic program played at a high pitch of excitement on a strong note of suspense.

Crawk—An animal imitator.

Dawn Patrol—The engineers, announcers, and others who open the studio and put on the early-morning programs.

Dead Air—Silence, either deliberate or accidental.

Disc Jockey—The master of ceremonies of a program of transcribed music (records). He turns them over.

Dog House—Early-morning announcing duties. Not disgrace.

Down in the Mud—Music, speech, or sound effect extremely low in volume.

Ethritus—A hardening and inflammation of the ear drums due to continued listening to the loud speaker in the home or station when run at an excessively high level.

Fairy Godmother—An unimaginative musical director.

Fanfare—A few bars of music usually employing plenty of trumpets to herald an entrance or announcement.

Fish Bowl—The clients' observation booth overlooking the acting studio.

Radio Alphabet

From "A Glossary of Radio Terms," Copyright by
The Columbia Broadcasting System
(*Continued*)

Fluff—A mistake in reading.

Full Net—A program fed to all stations of a network.

Gaffoon—A sound man who does two or three effects at the same time.

Gelatine—A tenor with a thin, quavering voice.

Groan Box—An accordion.

Ham Fest—A group of actors discussing a broadcast.

Hold It Down—An order for the studio engineer to reduce the volume of the program.

Hot Canary—A high soprano; an excellent female singer.

In the Beam—Within effective directional range of the microphone or the loudspeaker.

Jam Session—Spirited instrumental ad lib renditions of popular tunes.

Kill the Mike—To disconnect the microphone circuit.

Lady Macbeth—A superannuated tragedienne.

Laugh It Up—An order to the cast to laugh at their own lines.

Leg—A wire circuit which branches off the main line.

Live Mike (also Hot Mike)—A microphone that is connected to the circuit. It transmits what you say, no matter what.

Lock Jaw—The affliction unsympathetically ascribed to a tired or lifeless singer.

Long Underwear—Sheet music.

Madame Cadenza—A flighty female vocalist.

MC—Master of ceremonies. Sometimes written "emcee" and even used as a verb.

Mike Hog—A performer who elbows fellow performers away from the microphone.

Mob Scene—A group of performers serving as a crowd background, to say hobble-gobble or "No, no!" or "Yes, yes!"

Nemo—A broadcast picked up from a point remote from the studio, or from "Nemo," or from "No one."

Neutral—Theme music used under verbal announcements.

Offside—An off-color comedy line. A "blue gag." Tabu on the air.

Old Cow Hand—An experienced staff member called upon to escort important guests about the studios.

On the Nose—The program has concluded exactly on the planned second. (Hurrah!)

Overboard—1. A program which exceeds its allotted time. 2. An excessive characterization; overcut, overacted, or, in music, overintensified; in short, too much.

Pancake Turner—A technician who controls the playing of double-faced records.

Pedal Pusher—The organist who makes incidental music.

Putty Blower—A trombone.

Radio Alphabet

FROM "A GLOSSARY OF RADIO TERMS," COPYRIGHT BY
THE COLUMBIA BROADCASTING SYSTEM
(*Continued*)

Quonking—Disturbing side-line chatter by persons not on the program. It sounds like that.

Rating—The percentage of a statistical sample of radio families interviewed who report hearing a specific program.

Recall—A method of measurement of the number of people who remember listening to a program *after* the broadcast.

Roster Study—A radio-audience survey which helps the interviewed listener's recollection by showing him a list of programs he could have heard at a particular time.

Scan—The television process of changing a light image into an electrical signal, or vice versa—or magic.

Segue (pronounced *seg-way*)—The transition from one musical theme to another without a break or announcements.

Share of Audience—The per cent of listeners tuned to a given station (or program) based on the total of sets in use.

Soap Opera—A patronizing term loosely applied to popular daytime dramatic serial programs because the early sponsors of these programs were soap manufacturers.

Sponsor—One of the 50,000 or more advertisers in America who use radio to sell their products and services.

Stick Waver—An orchestra leader.

Sweep—Curved pieces of television scenery.

Tag Line—The last and most important line of a joke or a scene.

Tear Jerker—A radio script with a sad or pathetic appeal.

Tight Show—A program timed accurately in rehearsal to fit its allotted period like a glove.

Time Buyer—1. The officer of an advertising agency responsible for making the proper selection of radio coverage to meet the requirements of the advertiser. 2. A buyer of radio time.

Under—A program which does not use all its allotted time.

Visual Show—A radio program which is also being presented before an actual audience, called "live."

Volume Indicator—A meter in the control room which registers the program volume, thus enabling the technician to "see" the amount of sound.

Walla Walla—An ad lib mumble in crowd scenes to sound like a mob. Say it several times.

West of Denver—Technical troubles that can't be located.

Zilch—The standard name used to describe anyone who walks into the studio and whose name is not known.

they be? Will the program pay out in increased profitable sales of the sponsor's product? Can the advertiser, one of the 50,000 or more in America who use the radio to sell their products or services, justify a yearly expenditure of $1,500,000 for an hourly program each week over a nation-wide hookup?

The net of these questions is that radio, in its comparatively short span of existence, has demonstrated its commercial utility. In the period from 1931 to 1944, America's 100 leading advertisers have increased both their total budget in network radio and the percentage of total budget earmarked for network radio. In this thirteen-year period this expenditure has risen from $21,285,800 in 1931 to $135,784,910 in 1944, a 585 per cent increase. The share of their total budget spent in network radio has risen from 10 per cent in 1931 to 43 per cent in 1944. It is obvious that radio, properly used, is a modern sales tool of great effectiveness.

HOW BIG IS RADIO?

Radio as an advertising medium began to come into use about 1922. Up to that time nearly all advertising made its appeal through the eye of the reader by way of the printed page.

Today this new form of advertising, which makes appeal through the ear, is as characteristically American as the automobile, the telephone, or the motion picture. Actually, this is a statistical understatement, for if every seat in every motion picture house in the United States were occupied at this moment by radio set owners and their families, only one-tenth of the total potential United States radio audience would be at the movies. There are 35,000,-000 more radios in the United States than passenger automobiles; there are almost twice as many homes in the United States equipped with radios as with telephones. To put it another way, there are more American homes with radio sets than there are with electricity, bathtubs, telephones, or automobiles. Potentially the radio audience in the United States is of almost unlimited size.

Every day new listeners are joining the radio audience, the better to confound those skeptics who have said that the saturation point has been reached. Homes with at least one radio in the United States, as of January 1, 1947, totaled approximately 36,000,000, or 93 per cent of all United States families. In 1936, industry figures showed 22,869,000 radio homes.

In addition there are now about 6,500,000 radios in motorcars and 17,600,000 extra sets in homes. To supply entertainment for the nearly 60,000,000 sets in homes or automobiles, there are over 1,300 broadcasting stations, more than one-half of them linked up with one of the four systems: American Broadcasting Company, with nearly 250 stations; National Broadcasting Company, with nearly 170 stations; Columbia Broadcasting System, with nearly 170 stations; and Mutual, with more than 400 stations. Of the remaining stations, a good handful are linked by smaller networks; the majority are strung over the land to flash out independent broadcasts over local areas.

Careful analysis reveals that the greatest concentration of radio ownership is in areas of densest population. Usually, where there are active markets and economic prosperity, radio ownership is almost universal. New York State, for example, has 97.6 per cent radio ownership; Ohio, 95.4 per cent; Massachusetts, 97.9 per cent; California 96.0 per cent.

The most recent data available indicates that 85 per cent of the farm families had radios, as contrasted with 95 per cent for families in urban areas.

How much money is spent for radio as an advertising medium? In 1946, radio network advertisers paid $133,190,000 for time on the air. In addition, these advertisers spent an estimated $60,000,000 more for production costs of their programs, that is, the cost of the talent used.

Another impressive sum, approximately $190,000,-000, was spent during the same period on nonnetwork radio advertising for time alone, some by national and some by local advertisers.

WHO LISTENS TO RADIO?

Although the figures of radio, reduced to set-ownership figures and time and talent costs, are impressive, they are of secondary importance. The vital question of interest to the merchandiser contemplating the use of radio as a commercial sales aid is: "What is done with all these radios?"

Careful tabulations, based on United States Census figures, reveal that there are 3.17 persons over ten years of age in the average radio-owning family. On such a basis, the potential radio-listening audience might approximate 110 million people.

Of course, everybody knows "everybody" listens

to radio programs. Set-ownership figures and continued annual sales of millions of radio sets are proof of that. But such data are not sufficient for the merchandiser who wants to eliminate or at least reduce the hazards to his marketing success. He must know about listening habits by income levels, by time zones, by size of city, by rural area. He must further know how much time people devote to listening, what their day and night listening habits are, how much they use their sets by days of the week, and how popular his own program is.

Reduced to its simplest form, the answer to this question of listening may be stated somewhat as follows: People in all time zones and of all income levels listen a great deal.

According to the Nielsen Radio Index Average, projected to total United States radio homes by the C.B.S. Research Department:

> The average urban family uses its radio four hours and ten minutes daily.
>
> The average rural family uses its home radio nearly as much; namely, three hours and fifty minutes daily.
>
> The differences in listening time between the highest and lowest income groups is less than half an hour a day.
>
> Upper.................... 3 hours 49 minutes
> Middle................... 4 hours 8 minutes
> Lower.................... 4 hours 10 minutes
>
> 31,987,000 U.S. families use their radios on the average day.

89.8 per cent of all U.S. urban radio families listen every day.

86.8 per cent of all U.S. rural radio families listen every day.

The book publishers, in a special study conducted for them by The Psychological Corporation in 1945, titled "People and Books," by Henry C. Link and Harry A. Hopf, found that the time people devoted to reading, movie going, and radio listening was divided as follows:

Listening to radio...............	49 per cent
Newspapers.....................	21 per cent
Movies.........................	11 per cent
Magazines......................	11 per cent
Books..........................	8 per cent

C.B.S., in the first postwar audit of "Radio Ownership and Total Listening," found that:

The total public outlay for new radios alone in 1946 was $330,000,000. (Additionally, the public spends an annual $200,000,000 a year for electric-power costs of operating the nation's radio sets, plus more millions for repair of radio sets.)

In total family listening hours per day, 1946 was ahead of 1945—the year with the highest previous listening—by 4,600,000 hours. The figures:

January 1, 1944............	120,300,000 hours
January 1, 1945............	129,100,000 hours
January 1, 1946............	146,200,000 hours
January 1, 1947............	150,800,000 hours

Distribution of set ownership currently (including the 8,500,000 sets bought in 1946) is shown below:

ECONOMIC DISTRIBUTION
PER CENT OF ALL FAMILIES IN EACH ECONOMIC LEVEL

	Own Radios	Own 2 or More
Prosperous...................	98	54
Average.....................	97	35
Poor........................	86	16

COMMUNITY SIZE DISTRIBUTION
PER CENT OF ALL FAMILIES IN EACH TYPE OF COMMUNITY

	Own Radios	Own 2 or More
Urban.......................	95	39
Rural Nonfarm...............	93	26
Rural Farm..................	85	20

HOW CHECK RESULTS?

The skeptic may well ask: "How do you know they listen to your radio programs?"

The most satisfactory answer to this question lies in the definite response experienced by advertisers. The results of a radio campaign, whether reported by the advertiser, the agency, or the broadcasters, are obviously the direct results of listening.

The responsiveness of the radio audience manifests itself in many ways. Among them, in direct replies to specific offers made in the broadcast programs.

These "presents with a purpose," these big, free offers, range from booklets and knickknacks that can be had for the asking to more enduring articles given in exchange for labels, wrappers, and box tops. The number of responses to an offer of any given program is one indication of the size of that program's audience. The all-time high is said to be a million replies in forty-eight hours to a single announcement.

Large-scale radio responses, running into hundreds of thousands, and in some cases even into a million or more, are matters of record, known to most advertising men. Yet these are perhaps no more significant than other instances where advertisers with modest programs secure a steady response, year in and year out, thus securing a high return per advertising dollar of expense.

Unsolicited audience mail—fan letters—are another method of revealing facts about a radio program. But it is a well-known fact that fan letters fall short of being a good statistical guide to an audience. The information they contain may not be regarded as a representative opinion of the radio audiences as a whole.

When mail questionnaires are used to determine audience preferences and other factors, the questions asked must be few and worded in such a way that there can be no garbled interpretation of their meaning. There is also the possibility that people who answer questionnaires do so because they are more interested in the subject than those who fail to answer. Information received, therefore, may not be truly representative, even of the sample selected for questioning.

The use of the telephone to determine radio listening habits provides the inquirer with a form of personal interview. Such questioning gives the program sponsor an opportunity to learn what a man or woman is doing about radio at the time the call is made, thus eliminating the errors that are bound to come from a too-confident reliance upon the human memory. It should be noted that telephone calls miss all nontelephone homes, and radio homes today outnumber telephone homes by almost two to one, a condition that becomes increasingly apparent as one gets into smaller communities.

Another method used to check a radio program's responsiveness and depth of penetration is by a series of systematic and personal interviews and by sales returns. Personal interviews can be truly representative of the American radio audience, broken down by size, time zones, and income levels. When conducted periodically, each successive report acts as a check for the others. Thus, over a period of time the broadcaster can develop reliable factual data of value as a measure of comparison.

WHERE GIVE CREDIT?

These efforts to measure the effectiveness and penetration of radio, whether by means of the mechanical recorder, the listener recall, the roster study, the diary, coincidental or other methods, or combinations of one or more of these methods, are laudable. Every businessman wants to reduce the hazards in business, and these activities help him do so. However, it should be clearly understood that the returns from these checks on radio's efficiency as a selling medium are most helpful when they are construed as being indicative rather than conclusive.

In attempting to judge results solely by sales returns and thus allocate credit, the national advertiser faces a perplexing problem in determining what does what to whom. How can the advertiser accurately evaluate the degree of sales effectiveness of his radio program, his magazine and newspaper advertising, his dealer promotion, and his personal selling, particularly in their relation one to another? It simply can't be done; at least not accurately and sensibly enough to make such guesses the basis for sound judgment. Except in the unusual circumstance where radio is used exclusively, all the varying factors just enumerated must be considered.

By the very nature of radio, the physical competition of popular programs, and the size of the expenditures made, it was perhaps inevitable that the advent of radio would focus the attention of advertisers more and more on the desirability of a closer check on the returns from the advertising dollar, not only for radio but for all other media as well. Thus radio has spotlighted the need for a closer check on all advertising's effectiveness; in doing so, radio has made a definite contribution to effective marketing generally.

DOES RADIO REALLY SELL?

In many instances, the relationship between the responsiveness of the audience and the sales of the advertiser's product can be traced with considerable precision. A typical example in illustrating the fact that radio really does sell goods is found in the experience of a large food-product company in the four cases cited:

The Offers Made over the Air	*What Happened to Sales*
1	**1**
A pancake flipper was offered with each large package, or with two small packages, of a product retailing for 34 cents in the large size and for 19 cents in the small size. Sixteen announcements were made, four of which were devoted to explaining the shortage in premiums.	Before the offer was made, average monthly sales were 356,845 lb. During the period of the offer, average monthly sales rose to 770,358 lb., an increase of 116 per cent. One month after the final offer, monthly sales still averaged 610,185 lb., an increase of 71 per cent over the former average.
2	**2**
A spoon was offered as a premium with each 10-lb. or 24½-lb. sack of flour; or one spoon and one fork with each 49-lb sack. Thirteen announcements were made, but four of them had to be given over to explaining the shortage of premiums.	Before this offer was made, monthly sales averaged 28,000 bbl. During the period of the offer, monthly sales rose to 42,734 bbl., an increase of more than 52 per cent.
3	**3**
A cake pan was offered with each two packages of a special type of flour, retailing usually for 29 cents a package. Eleven announcements of this offer were made, of which three were devoted to explaining the shortage in premiums.	During the year preceding the offer, total sales of this product (in the territory affected) amounted to 16,751 cases. During the six *weeks* of the offer, total sales amounted to 23,691 cases, or 41 per cent more than the entire *year* preceding.

4

A cereal bowl was offered with each two packages of a branded cereal product. Sixteen announcements were made, three of which were devoted to explaining the shortage of premiums.

4

Nearly as much business was done in the first 3 weeks of this offer as during the previous 11 months. In 7 weeks, total sales amounted to over 70,000 cases, as much business as was done the previous 15 months.

WHAT MAKES RADIO APPEAL?

The radio medium works. But how does it work? The direct, personal, man-to-man appeal of the radio is the quick answer. The more profound answer is that broadcast advertising, when properly handled, is much more than advertising. It is something to which people turn with pleasure—and for pleasure. It creates, in its audiences, a reaction which is primarily emotional and this emotional reaction makes the audience responsive in a high degree.

In politics, when a candidate is not sure of the outcome of his campaign, he appeals personally to the people, announces his platform, intimately and forcefully, and takes the public pulse. In radio, the advertiser follows much the same course. Over the air, he comes to tell the people what he has to sell. In a friendly, cheerful chat, he, too, is able to discover how the consumer stands.

The response of the radio audience to a personal appeal is surprisingly quick and sure. When severe floods threatened the United States, one of the Rochester stations put on a special program for Red Cross Relief Funds. After five nights on the air, radio listeners from this studio alone contributed almost $30,000 to the fund.

Kate Smith, in a similar emergency, asked for funds over the airways and received cash answers from all over the United States and Canada. Her honest, folksy voice went straight to the hearts— and the purses—of her listeners.

One of the major-network baking-company programs, on offering its child listeners tokens of the program, received requests for a million and a half tokens in less than six weeks.

Modest offers, requiring visits to filling stations, with no prizes, were made over the air by oil refineries. Each offer brought not less than a million answers in visits to the sponsor's filling stations.

Prompt responses are also obtained from single-station offers. A single announcement, made between innings of a baseball game, helped a New York State refrigerator manufacturer to sell a carload shipment. Too many baby chickens with no market for them was the problem of a poultry farmer, who announced his plight over a midwestern radio station. By night he had to order more chickens to fill the calls.

Probably the most famous of all radio yarns is the one about the motor dealer who over the air offered a prize to the first car driver to reach his establishment. Traffic violators filled the courts; the streets were lined with wrecked cars, and the man's business was jammed to the doors.

Another case in which automobiles also figured dramatically was that of the squadron of naval planes lost in a California fog and helped to a landing by the throng of automobiles, which, in answer to a radio plea for help, formed a ring of light around the runway of the landing field.

And so, in commercial advertising, radio establishes the entente cordiale between the manufacturer and the consumer. The air plea seldom goes unanswered.

AMERICAN RADIO'S ROLE IN THE SECOND WORLD WAR

Many of the ways in which American radio assisted in the national war effort cannot be summarized in statistical terms for the industry as a whole. Examples are found, of course, of specific parts played by individual stations, networks, programs, and individuals; and anyone who lived through the war years in this country knows the primary role of radio as a medium of information and morale building.

An industry-wide summary titled "Five Years of Coordinated Public Service Advertising by Business Through Radio," from a report of the Advertising Council for the five years from May 1, 1942, to May 1, 1947, tells the story of how the Advertising Council effectively "coordinated public-service advertising by business through radio" during the war years, and set a pattern for public-service advertising in peacetime that is being actively maintained. Highlights of the report are:

> Radio and radio advertisers have played a major role in public-service advertising and the record for the past five years is outstanding.
> At the outset of the war, the radio committee of The

Advertising Council organized a plan that made it possible, through the solid cooperation of advertisers, advertising agencies, networks, stations, and programs, to utilize the established program structure of radio to reach the largest audiences possible—radio's millions of loyal and regular listeners—quickly and efficiently, day in and day out, with powerful, moving, war-information messages.

This was the Radio Allocation Plan, through which advertisers and networks volunteered to carry war-information topics on a regular schedule on their programs. This plan was placed in the hands of the Office of War Information, and during the week of April 27 to May 3, 1942, programs broadcast their first war-allocation messages.

That first week, radio urged its listeners to buy war bonds, salvage scrap metal, and pool their automobiles. The next week top programs broadcast information announcing and explaining sugar rationing, and later in May these programs took on the job of raising $32,000,000 for the newly formed USO.

Since that beginning, radio, through the allocation plans, has conducted over 175 different major information campaigns in behalf of more than forty public and private agencies. Approximately thirty of these campaigns have been conducted since the war ended.

These 175 campaigns have ranged from the war projects to such vital peacetime campaigns as information on atomic energy, combating the menace of group prejudices, selling savings bonds, finding homes for veterans, safety on the highway, student nurse recruiting, and conservation of our natural resources.

The total radio circulation given these campaigns during the five-year period has been conservatively estimated at more than 130 billion listener impressions. A listener impression is one message heard once by one listener. The very minimum dollar value of this circulation is estimated at well above four hundred million.

These figures represent only the radio messages on which the OWI and the Advertising Council were able to keep records. Radio and radio advertisers carried a tremendous volume of public-service material which went unrecorded. Virtually every program in radio took part in these activities.

Most of these 175 campaigns were repeated several times and had supplementary phases, so that the actual number of information programs conducted runs into the hundreds. The OWI and the Advertising Council issued approximately 450 Radio Fact Sheets.

The organizations receiving the most support through these allocation plans during the five-year period were the War Department, Treasury Department, OPA, Department of Agriculture, American Red Cross, and the Community Chests (National War Fund).

In addition to giving help to these major projects, the Advertising Council, since January 1, 1946, has distributed information on fifty-eight minor public-service activities through its Radio Bulletin. The Bulletin is distributed bimonthly to radio advertisers, advertising agencies, networks, and programs.

For the month of May, 1947, the beginning of the sixth year of this plan for public service by business, radio coverage has been mapped out for such campaigns as Student Nurse Recruiting, Homes for Veterans, Group Prejudice, Prevent Forest Fires, Safety on the Highway, Fat Salvage, and Army Prestige.

At present 181 national and regional radio advertisers are participating in the radio plans. In addition to commercial programs, almost every sustaining program on the four networks also carries messages regularly under the industry's plan. The estimated circulation of the plan is currently running at approximately 300,000,000 listener impressions each week, and the Council estimates that a total of more than 15 million listener impressions will be gained for public-service projects during 1947.

WHY AUDIENCES RESPOND

Granted, then, that a radio call brings an immediate response, just why does this harmony exist, who is behind it, how, in the first place, did it come to be?

Careful investigation of this subject in the field of advertising has shown that there are seven basic factors behind the responsiveness of the radio audience. These may be summarized as:

1. The radio audience is a voluntary audience.
2. It makes a habit of listening to the programs it likes.
3. It listens in groups.
4. It renders appreciation and friendship to the sponsors.
5. Sound makes an intense and enduring impression.
6. The human voice has all the provocative qualities of personal selling.
7. The artistic value of the program entertainment so sways the emotions of the listeners that the sponsor's "sales talk" is accepted in the same spirit.

Before discussing these points in detail, it should be clearly understood that we are not dealing with the listener's reaction to the entertainment side of the program; we are considering solely his reaction to the advertising communication therein.

VOLUNTARY LISTENING

The people who listen to a certain program, day by day, choose that program intentionally and without benefit of outside advice.

In the beginning, picking up a number of stations was the hobby of the radio-set owner. So long did this hit-or-miss station hunting continue that radio as a commercial advertising medium was despaired of. Later, the radio audiences formed the habit of tuning in on a single station—usually the one with the best reception—and leaving it on all day. This helped the advertising aspect, but limited it to the area reached by the most popular and most powerful stations.

In this day of better transmission and better receiving sets, the radio audience is given a wide variety of good stations, and the selective listener now moves from station to station, looking for the program he most enjoys. He listens regularly to the program which gives him the greatest personal pleasure. He is predisposed in favor of that program; he knows what to expect and he likes it in advance; he is prepared to accept the commercial announcement which accompanies it.

LISTENING HABITS

Once the program has achieved the approval of the voluntary listeners, it becomes a habit. Week in and week out, the percentage of radios tuned in on specific programs shows the same trend.

This fact gives the radio advertiser his greatest advantage. He *knows* his listeners. He can plan his radio campaign to fit their needs and preferences. And the radio advertiser can make a safe and sure selection of the editorial frame and mood which will surround his sales message. At least once in every seven days they hear his commercial announcement, and as the sales talk grows in strength, the response becomes stronger. So well known is this that every broadcast advertiser has learned to wait until the listening habit has established itself before he attempts to judge the commercial value of his program.

Families, as a unit, compose the radio audience. The members, from grandfather down to little Bobby, gather around the receiving set, and the listening process becomes a group force rather than a single individual's isolated enjoyment.

We all like to see the other fellow enjoying himself. Our mood of pleasure is accelerated by the pleasure of our companions. The radio, then, has the power to move a group of listeners, a much easier task than that of moving a single person.

Group listening brings on group discussion—another point in the favor of the commercial broadcaster. The more the listeners have to say, in groups, about the merits or weaknesses of the products, the more firmly the name and the product become fixed in the mind of the audience.

AUDIENCE APPRECIATION

In the early days of radio, so spontaneous was the listener's reaction to the entertainment value of the program, be it a favorite dance band or a poignant dramatic skit, that the sponsor, naïvely enough, thought he could depend on audience loyalty to push the sales of his product.

Now, in the light of hard reasoning, the advertiser uses a more scientific and more profitable approach.

He accepts the fact that while the listener does feel a degree of appreciation of the sponsor's effort to entertain him, this appreciation—and the consequent reaction to the commercial message—cannot be achieved until the sponsor shall have learned, with reasonable accuracy, what kind of audience he is reaching and what the audience wants.

In other words, his own subtle appreciation of his radio listeners eventually brings to the sponsor the personal appreciation of that same audience.

Listening is an easy process; it requires no effort. Unlike reading, which requires a certain amount of motion and the use of sensitive eye muscles, listening calls for no exertion or exhaustion. Auditory impressions, therefore, have everything in their favor and nothing against them. When in a let-down and felicitous state, the listener becomes receptive; he is in a mood to believe.

H. V. Kaltenborn, well-known news commentator who for years wrote newspaper editorials, in comparing the power of the spoken and written word admits that there can be no dispute over the superior power of speech. The radio audience's response is more favorable than that of the newspaper audience, he feels, because the listener is relaxed whereas the reader is tense and hurried.

The survey made at Harvard University by

Hadley Cantril and Gordon W. Allport, later published in "The Psychology of Radio" (Harper), brought out the following interesting points concerning the advantages of *listening* to an advertisement:

That straight *facts* are better understood and more interesting when heard over the radio than when read on a printed page.

That *narrative* and *abstract material*, political talks, and expositions are better understood and more interesting when heard over the radio.

That after 24 hours people recalled advertising trade names better when they had been heard over the radio than when read on a printed page.

That numbers and simple words were remembered better when presented over the radio, but that difficult or unusual words were remembered better when presented visually.

That *sentences*, short or long, simple or complex, were recalled better when heard over the radio.

That people remember *directions* better, and understand them more readily, when they heard them than when they read them.

That the human voice tends to make auditory presentations more personal and that more caution was exercised toward printed than toward spoken material.

That material presented over the radio has greater power of suggestion than material read on a printed page.

THE POTENCY OF THE HUMAN VOICE

The strong, rich, provocative appeal of the human voice is the radio advertiser's chief asset. With this, he has an advantage over any other kind of communication. No writer can match a speaker in effect when the very words he has written are spoken, not read. No playwright can hope, through his printed lines, to put forth the same meaning that comes when the lines are spoken across the footlights.

And no salesman has ever succeeded in writing a letter or composing a paper that was half so productive of results as was his own intimate discussion of the same subject when face to face with a prospect.

In radio advertising, the spoken word conveys meanings, delicate nuances, that are lost in cold black type on white paper. In the human voice, we have the benefit of warmth, of spontaneity, of highly personalized contact, aimed, word by word, exclusively at the listener. First the idea is presented, then a suggestion is offered, and finally, with grace and finesse, made possible in talking when it is impossible in writing, the advertiser's message is summed up neatly and brought to a close.

When the advertiser's sales talk reaches the ears of the radio audience, it is, if the sponsor is wise, closely linked to the emotional effect that has been created by the program as a whole. We know that radio listeners are voluntary, and that they are habit listeners, and that when they tune in on a certain program, they are ready to accept its entertainment, because it appeals to them, personally. By the same token, they are ready to accept the commercial announcement, as a part of the program, not as a separate thing. No well-handled announcement is heard by itself; it is shrouded in the magic spell of the entertainment that has preceded it.

Look at a few of the successful programs. A waltz

program soothes its audience into a sense of quiet, dreamy enjoyment. A program of the Bob Hope or Bing Crosby type carries its audience into a mood of robust comradeship with these beloved entertainers. When the commercial comes along on these programs, you do not hear it alone—you hear it against the emotional effect created by the program.

Hearing the announcement is not even remotely comparable to reading the same words on a printed page. In type, the words stand alone, with only the help of layout and illustration. But on the air, they come to the audience against a background of his own emotions, aroused by the appeal of the whole program.

There are many kinds of emotions—the gratitude of the housewife who receives domestic advice on the air; the thrills and chills brought on by the stirring detective drama; the exaltation felt upon hearing a symphony. But whatever the effect, it places the mood of the commercial announcement; and that mood has much to do with the audience reaction.

WHAT MAKES A PROGRAM POPULAR?

There is no sure-fire recipe that will make any one radio program everybody's dish. Popularity doesn't follow a formula. Just as all people cannot eat ham and eggs, so the fancy of the entire radio audience cannot be caught and held by a single type of air entertainment. There is, on the other hand, a steady, normal appetite for radio fare of *all* types, and this appetite does not depend so much on the piquancy of the fare as on its degree of excellence. Here, certainly, quality counts.

Program popularity is not determined by "position" in the schedule of the day, for the radio, from dawn's setting-up exercises to night's slumber music, has its loyal followers, and any canny advertiser thinks twice before he considers changing his location.

Nor is Broadway talent essential to radio popularity or a throng of Hollywood guest stars in a radio revue hour. Nor is top rating the last answer to the question of who ranks first in popularity. As a matter of fact, the hearts of some of the most successful radio advertisers start to sink when their program rating begins to mount. They know all too well that their radio hours are not appealing to the right people, the ones to whom they hope to sell their product. Their best prospects are small-community folk without telephone conveniences, and the new, exciting rating figures come from radio listeners in large cities and in homes with telephones.

Program popularity as it concerns advertising must be considered in terms of audience appeal. When your program appeals to the potential purchaser of your product, you have, for your purpose, a popular program. The "rating" is of minor importance.

If you were selecting space in a magazine, you would consider the editorial content. You would ask yourself: What kind of people read this magazine?

In radio, you are given a chance to determine your own editorial content. You know your product; you know your prospects; you can ask yourself: What kind of program would such a prospect enjoy?

With this question accurately answered, you have the sum and substance of what makes a program popular. From then on, the degree of popularity will follow directly the superiority of its presentation.

The broadcast advertiser will do well to shape his program as much as possible to fit his product or service. A high-quality cosmetic manufacturer will be careful to select "editorial content" that will interest women who like to buy the more expensive face powders and creams and have incomes which enable them to do so. A cigarette manufacturer or a bakery organization would choose entertainment of another nature, because they want programs to go straight to as wide a "base" of radio circulation as possible.

USES OF SPOT BROADCASTING

Commercial use of radio time is divided as to types between national programs, national spot programs, and local spot broadcasts.

National spot broadcasting is really a form of local radio advertising, although there are advertisers who use several hundred stations in a spot campaign. Since spot broadcasting originates from the studios of the stations selected, the use of electrical transcriptions, or recordings, saves both time and money. Entertainment is selected, rehearsed, and recorded, usually in some metropolitan center, and individual disks are shipped to the stations carrying the campaign. Special equipment feeds the record into the station transmitter, and a local announcer handles the commercials.

The use of electrical transcriptions for national spot broadcasting does not mean that the facilities of local-talent shows have been overlooked. The advantages of a locally produced show that features local talent for local audiences are obvious in single-station campaigns; many stations are prepared to work with their local clients in the production of these local spot-broadcasting programs.

Spot broadcasting is for the sponsor who requires special help in the solution of a particular problem. One advertiser has a summer business and a limited distribution that doesn't warrant the use of network radio. Another has an unusual competitive situation. A third has dealers in Oklahoma and Maine who insist on special radio programs of their own. A prominent sponsor sells his nationally advertised product under a different brand name in the southwestern states. All these special situations call for the use of spot radio advertising.

Network and spot broadcasting are complementary, not competitive. Each has its own job. Just as national and local use may be made of other forms of advertising, so radio through spot and network can be made to serve a double purpose. In recent years, several hundred advertisers have learned the value of the "local branch" of radio.

RADIO ON THE FARM

More than thirty million people live on farms and another thirty million reside in small rural communities—a total of sixty million individuals, comprising practically one-half of the nation's consumers.

With returning farm prosperity, extension of power lines, and development of wind charging apparatus, there has been an upsurge in the purchase of radio sets by rural families. The experience of radio advertisers suggests that the rural American is not only being reached to an increasing degree by radio, but also that when reached he is being influenced by radio to possibly an even greater extent than the listener in cities and metropolitan centers.

Competent studies show that the favorite programs of rural listeners include many of the same sponsored network programs that rank highest with the individual and city population—conclusive evidence that the farmer does not belong to a race apart and that his tastes are becoming increasingly similar to those of the city dweller. But the farmer, in addition, has an especially vital interest in radio because it is his only means of close daily contact with authoritative sources of agricultural information. To many farm households, radio is the only source of all outside news, since research shows that a sizeable proportion of farm homes receive no daily newspapers and rely on weeklies for this service.

SUSTAINING PROGRAMS

The radio broadcasting companies and individual radio stations make many contributions to the public welfare and entertainment by annually providing and broadcasting hundreds of programs of infinite variety planned to please the widely divergent tastes of the millions of American radio listeners.

These sustaining programs, financed and sponsored

by the networks and individual radio stations alike as a definitive editorial policy, contribute some of the most important cultural and informative features on the air.

The scope of this activity is possibly not fully realized. Approximately 50 to as high as 70 per cent (varying from time to time) of the total hours of the major-network broadcasts are devoted to sustaining programs in the public interest, containing no advertising.

Broadcasts of this type vary from extensive news coverage and press radio summaries of international news events and nationwide election returns to play-by-play descriptions of sporting events and other outstanding events in the field of sports. Religious programs for members of all denominations; musical appreciation hours for young and old; discussion and forum hours; symphony concerts and broadcasts of operas; ancient and modern classics of the stage; historical and patriotic events; home and farm hours; and other programs too numerous to mention fall under this general classification of noncommercial sustaining radio programs.

BROADCAST MERCHANDISING

Since the pioneer days of 1922, radio advertisers have been asking: "What can we do to better the sales results from our radio programs?" The answer to this question usually is: Merchandise your program in every possible way.

As one advertising expert states, "If your program is to sell your product, you must sell your program. A program is worthless without listeners."

The desirability of telling dealers and salesmen about a program and enlisting their enthusiastic support seems a common-sense objective. The mystery is why so many radio advertisers fail to capitalize on their program potentialities by overlooking the necessity for using additional promotional activities to "merchandise" their program.

There are as many forms of supplementary promotion of radio programs as there are possible appeals to the eyes and ears of salemen and other employees, dealers, and consumers.

GUEST OR SOAP-BOX ORATOR?

Radio, the newest of modern sales tools, has had a phenomenal growth in the brief span of its existence. This growth is due in part to the fact that it has one valuable sales quality that formerly was not obtainable: immediate and personal contact with the prospect.

Radio rings no doorbells; it waits for no opportunities. It carries its sponsor into the privacy of the homes of his prospects at a time when they are in the mood to welcome such a guest. It goes where it goes by invitation only, and it delivers its sales message directly.

Radio advertisers are, in reality, invited guests calling on the homes of America. If they are interesting or entertaining, and if they behave in good taste, they are invited again and again. Some are so well regarded that their weekly calls take precedence over any normal social appointments.

These advertisers, by and large, are the successful radio advertisers because they not only know how

Merchandising Methods

In promoting a radio program N.B.C. reports the following merchandising methods as among those most frequently used. The list, though impressive, does not include by any means all of the ingenious tie-ins employed to make a radio program produce more sales and cash in more completely on its audience appeal.

Artists' photographs
Booklets at dealers
Booklets from sponsor
Bridge score pads
Broadsides to dealers
Broadsides to salesmen
Buttons (dealers' clerks)
Car cards
Club memberships
Contests
Continuities (copies of)
Cook books and recipes
Direct mail for dealers' use
Direct mail to dealers
Direct mail to listeners
Direct mail to employees
Displays
Electrotypes for dealers' use
Envelope stuffers
Exhibits
Handbills
House organs
Invitations to broadcasts
Meetings (sales)
Meetings for dealers

Newspapers for clients
Newspaper mats for dealers' use
Newspaper spotlight ads
Novelty offers
Outdoor advertising
Package stuffers
Poster stamps
Portfolio for salesmen's use
Portable radios for salesmen's use
Printed programs
Publicity, local releases by dealers
Publicity, national releases
Samples
Shows, parades, tours
Slide films
Station and program listings
Telegrams
Tests and surveys
Tie-ins, imprints on stationery
Tie-ins, magazines, newspapers, trade papers

effective radio can be but they also know why radio is effective. They regard their visit with the American consumer as a friendly, neighborly call; they speak as a guest in the home, not as a soap-box orator; and above all, they are sincere in their belief that proper use should be made of the power of radio to influence properly the thoughts and living habits of America.

TELEVISION—A PIONEERING SALES TOOL

The potentialities of television as a medium for selling are being intensively tested by leading advertisers. Currently, more than five hundred national and local advertisers are gathering experience in the use of this new form of radio.

In terms of its cost per thousand, television will probably be a costly medium for a considerable time to come, due to the heavy expenses involved in the use of video equipment and of large staffs of cameramen, monitors, directors, stage hands, and the many others necessary to productions that appeal both to the eye and to the ear. The equipment and personnel requirements needed are comparable to those utilized for making motion pictures.

The advertisers who have already ventured into television have not done so with the cost factor primarily in mind. They have done so largely to acquire ground-floor franchises, either on time or talent or both, which they believe will be of great value in the future; they have also gone into television to acquire experience in the commercial use of the medium. Not to be overlooked, too, is the promotional value, especially with dealers, to the advertiser who is pioneering with a new sales tool and thereby putting his company in a position to share in the expected greater sales returns television may bring in the future.

These advertisers, and among them are some of the country's largest, are experimenting to find the best ways to use television's enormous selling potential. The sales impact possible through this medium may be so great, some believe, that, even in spite of higher comparative costs, it will be eventually widely used as an economical tool of selling.

According to four organizations closely concerned with the development of television—American Broadcasting Company, Inc., Allen B. Du Mont Laboratories, Inc., Columbia Broadcasting System, Inc., and the National Broadcasting Company—as reported in a survey made by Warwick & Legler, Inc., advertising agents, in their house organ, *Ad Quiz*, television today offers advertisers these opportunities:

C.B.S.: (*A*) To acquire essential experience in developing the most effective commercial copy themes and techniques. A number of advertisers feel that they can pick up such skill when needed. But, experience with television indicates that the development of the most appropriate and effective commercials is so intimately woven into the sales techniques of each product that merely adapting skills developed by other advertisers is inadequate. Even such adaptation, if deferred, will require time and work at far greater cost than if done now.

(*B*) To acquire time franchises, both local and network. With a limited number of channels and limited hours of operation, the amount of television time available to advertisers will be quite small, compared to radio. Today's television advertisers are acutely conscious of the franchise value of their time buys.

(*C*) To acquire program franchises. This is most aptly illustrated by exclusive sports franchises, like those of the Ford Motor Company for Madison Square Garden and of Ford and General Foods for the Brooklyn Dodgers' home games. The amount of such top-notch sports entertainment is strictly limited so that such franchises may become extremely valuable as time goes on. Early identification of good program material with good advertisers can pay high dividends.

(*D*) To utilize present television campaigns for dealer promotion. To the retailer, there is magic in the word television and many successful promotions have been based upon current use of television.

A.B.C.: It is our opinion that at the present time there are three important advantages to be gained by an advertiser participating in television today:

(*A*) Experience in a new medium and contribution to the basic fundamentals of the art, which are now being set. The ever-present human element must receive careful consideration, as 88 to 100 persons participate in each complete television production and working procedures must be developed in order to assure future proficiency.

(*B*) Promotion and publicity will result from a coordinated campaign in connection with a client's participation in television, as the word television is very potent today.

(*C*) Great opportunities for the future are available to the television participant in the form of the best time franchises, which are made available on certain television stations.

Du Mont: The opportunities which television offers the advertiser today are limited only by his imagination and the extent of the present audience. To be able to sell by personal demonstration to thousands of people simultaneously has always been the sales and advertising managers' dream. Through television this dream will come true. Today, particularly in the New York market, the television audience is growing by leaps and bounds. The advertiser who learns to use this new medium during this growth period may gain experience at low cost and a valuable time franchise for the future.

N.B.C.: Television is generally recognized as having tremendous potentialities as an advertising medium, perhaps greater than we have ever known. For example, in television is combined the plus qualities of all other recognized successful advertising mediums. Like space advertising, it allows for visual display; like radio, it utilizes the persuasive, dramatic quality of the human voice. In addition, television offers opportunities for animation and motion, and makes it possible, as well, to present the sales message to thousands at the same time and in the space of a few minutes.

Agencies and clients now have an opportunity to experiment and do the necessary research in how to use this new medium to the best advantage.

Of all the mass media, only television provides the advertiser with a chance to show his products in actual use. In every other medium, graphic or verbal, the advertiser can only *talk* or *write* about his product. In television, he can *demonstrate* it. This undoubted advantage for television selling has dictated the direction of most economical message preparation and has led to substantial experience in effective ways to demonstrate products. For example, the ability of television to stimulate appetite—by the attractive display of food—is now well established.

A second selling advantage of television is its ability to foster self-identification by the viewer as he sees an actual demonstration or use of a product.

The most effective commercial use of television poses a great challenge to the creative resourcefulness and ingenuity of the advertising profession. And since the exceptional selling strength of sight plus sound and its powerful and intimate impact upon an audience appears fully established, the nation's advertising agencies will undoubtedly find ways and means to make full use of this great potential sales characteristic. In finding these skills in handling commercial message may lie the answer to the present relatively high cost of television.

It should be noted, as the Columbia Broadcasting System states, that when the first train rushed across the first motion picture screen, the audience knew no standard except a "live" train with which to measure this scientific "miracle." The bare fact that a train was rushing across a screen was novelty enough to be exciting—and to postpone for a long time the question of how a train could be most effectively shown on the screen.

Again, when radio sound was first broadcast into a handful of living rooms, there was no preconceived standard ready to declare that the technique of that sound was good, bad, or indifferent. The fact that wireless sound came in at all was an exciting and satisfactory event.

Neither movies nor radio had to face comparison with other similar arts.

But television—chiefly because the movies and the radio have built popular standards—has a real and unusual problem to face. For it must not only bring in sound and picture, but sound and picture of technical excellence—not only in purity of image and purity of sound, but in programming.

Many questions remain to be solved in creating adequate commercial television techniques. What, for example, is "effective" commercial television: is a question posed by C.B.S. Is it the leading man in a television play offering the sponsor's cigarettes to his leading lady? Is it a demonstration of how easy it is to brush teeth with a new dentifrice? Is it the thirty-second transformation of a package of powder into a tempting dessert? Or is it the satisfaction shown by a family eating the dessert?

Is the most effective commercial isolated or integrated? If integrated into the program, is it apt to lose force? If isolated, can it be a motion-picture film —a sort of "trailer"? And if a trailer, how many times can it be effectively used?

Is it effective if an actor steps out of character after the play and demonstrates or praises the product, as is sometimes done in radio?

Can a slogan be effectively visualized by, say, a shaker of salt in a summer shower? Is a backdrop bearing the sponsor's name throughout the program an adequate commercial in itself? Should a trademark be animated—or not tampered with?

What makes a television commercial "too casual" —or "too dynamic"?

How long need one rehearse a dramatic program? A musical? A news program—if it can be rehearsed at all? Can a television program be all commercial, without the accepted restraint of allotted commercial time common to radio programming? If a fashion show (entirely commercial) is acceptable as well as good looking, is the same thing true of a fifteen-minute cooking school with the sponsor's product as chief ingredient?

Literally hundreds of such urgent questions jostle each other in producers' and clients' minds. They demand answers. Certain tentative conclusions have been formulated. They will remain tentative until audiences have confirmed or changed them.

Whereas two years ago there were only nine television stations, today there are 61. Two years ago the production of television sets approximated 180,000; currently estimates range around 1,600,000 units annually. From a mere handful of manufacturers, the number has now grown to about 90. Several years ago there were only 25 sponsors of television programs; now there are more than 500 sponsors with about 30 per cent of the population, or over 45,000,000 people, living within present television reception areas. And because the stations are in more densely populated metropolitan areas, the audience figures even larger as purchasers of general consumer goods. Within three years, possibly sooner, many authorities believe half or more of our homes will be equipped with television sets.

While much programming and advertising experiment still lie ahead, television has already given convincing demonstrations of its ability in many lines, particularly the covering of sporting events. Prize fights and baseball, including night baseball, are among the sporting events being presented regularly under the sponsorship of advertisers.

In the Warwick & Legler survey previously referred to, this question and these answers were reported:

On the basis of audience reactions, what have proved to be the five most popular types of television programs? List them in order of their preference. Do you think this order will change in the next three years?

A.B.C.: From our experience the five most popular types of programs are.

1. Sports
2. On-the-spot news (live or film)
3. Audience participation
4. Dramatic
5. Variety

The order probably will not change in the next few years—possibly 4 and 5 may be reversed.

Du Mont: According to most surveys the popularity of television programs ranks as follows:

Sports	33 per cent
Live drama	20 per cent
News	19.4 per cent
Musical	7.2 per cent
Movie film	6.1 per cent
Variety	6.1 per cent
Travel	3.8 per cent
Educational	3.0 per cent
New-product demonstrations	1.4 per cent

We would anticipate a decline in the desire for news programs and an increase in the demand for variety shows.

N.B.C.: While practically all television programming has had favorable audience reaction, as proven by the great demand for television receivers, it is felt that there has not been enough experience to 'categorize' television programs in the order of their preference by the audience. It is also likely that program units, as well as the balance between various types of programs as televised today, will not hold for the future. The televiser must always be conscious of the fact that he must appeal to all likes and tastes.

C.B.S.:

(Mean ratings on the scale 0–100 by non-set-owning members of C.B.S. Television Audience Research Institute panels October 5, 1945—January 5, 1947)

There is no present indication of changes in this order.

"Networking" of television stations, that is, linking them together in the same way that radio stations are linked together, is another problem yet to be resolved. Several methods of ultrahigh-frequency transmission have been proposed to form television networks, but the most efficient and economical means has not yet been determined. The attraction of television to national advertisers will, of course, be enhanced when it becomes possible to send a single program simultaneously to a large number of cities throughout the country. Television's attractiveness will also be enhanced, many believe, when natural, full-color pictures can be seen, for a rose is not a rose in black and white. No range of grays can bring to life a slate-blue roadster with red leather seats . . . or the green that went to war . . . or the gold on a jacket, the color and warmth of a face. Much important work on color television has already been demonstrated, particularly by the Columbia Broadcasting System and by the Radio Corporation of America.

❖ ❖ Aɴʏ business, large or small, that undertakes well-organized selling activity uses advertising or publicity. Properly handled, these sales tools are strong commercial factors. Some of these major sales builders are:

1. Newspaper and Magazine Advertising. The primary purpose of these avenues to markets are to assist customers in buying, to influence more people to buy, and to persuade them to buy in greater quantity.

2. Public Relations. The right kind of relationships with customers, prospects, dealers, employees, stockholders, and the general public are not only highly desirable but commercially profitable.

3. Radio. This newest major sales aid is used both nationally and locally to sell goods by ear appeal as contrasted with eye appeal. What makes radio appeal, why audiences respond, listening habits, and the potency of the human voice are questions of intense interest to all merchandisers.

4. Television. This pioneering sales tool enables advertisers to demonstrate their product or services to consumers. Its commercial use poses a great challenge to the creative resourcefulness and ingenuity of advertisers.

❖ ❖ ❖ ❖

A Problem in Public Relations

THE nature of your business brings peaks of sales activity around July and January of each year. Naturally you employ more people to handle orders during these peak periods. Many of these employees are laid off during slack times.

The reasons for this recurring hiring and firing are perfectly clear and understandable to you as the head of the business. You discover, however, that these necessary layoffs cause periodic waves of resentment, not only among the employees actually laid off but also among the employees remaining on your pay roll and the public at large in the cities where your plants are located.

How can you correct this situation?

The way one manufacturer solved this problem of employee and public relations is told on page 481.

XV

Direct Mail Advertising

THIS objective analysis of the uses, potentialities, and limitations of direct mail, aptly termed "the salesmate of all other advertising media," has been prepared by The Direct Mail Advertising Association and is based on numerous studies and years of careful research. Thousands of users of this versatile sales tool make up the membership of this national organization.

When an advertiser distributes his selling massage in print through newspapers, magazines, car cards, and outdoor advertising, or broadcasts it over the air, he can reasonably expect that a certain percentage of his potential audience will read or listen to his sales story. In such circumstances the advertiser knows from experience that it is good business judgment to send his sales message to all the readers of a magazine or newspaper or all listeners to a radio program, and pay for all, even though only some of them are prospects for his product or services.

Obviously, then, if the advertiser chooses to send his sales story by mail, messenger, or salesman, he can exercise greater selection and control. Under such circumstances, if he carefully qualifies his prospects, the advertiser can direct his selling message to specific individuals. This type of promotional activity, commonly called direct advertising, is defined as "a vehicle for transmitting an advertiser's message in permanent written, printed, or processed form, by controlled distribution, direct to selected individuals." A simpler definition might well be that direct advertising messages are the paratroopers of advertising. They can be directed to a specific objective in order to accomplish a specific purpose.

Both definitions are good but bear careful analysis, for direct advertising logically divides itself into three broad classifications, determined by (*a*) what it is used for and (*b*) how it is delivered.

1. *Direct-by-mail Advertising.* The most efficient use of direct-by-mail advertising comes when the user appreciates its limitations. Properly controlled, sent to "prospects" instead of "suspects," direct-by-mail advertising's productivity can be enhanced. Like all advertising, the results, in the final analysis, are largely determined by how many of the right kind of people see it. Furthermore, direct-by-mail has been aptly called the advance agent, the missionary man, "the handshake ahead of the meeting," plus the means whereby post-selling and continuous contacts with customers can be economically maintained. Its chief functions are to arouse interest; to help consumers as an aid to buying; to familiarize prospects with the name of the product, its merits, the name of the local distributor, and remove obstacles to sales; to support the sales activities of retailers; to encourage continued patronage by present and new customers;

and finally to predispose prospects favorably so that the closely geared-in personal selling effort will produce maximum sales returns.

2. *Mail-order Advertising.* This type of direct-by-mail selling promotion includes all methods, other than personal salesmanship and space or radio advertising, for inducing people to send in orders by mail. Promotional pieces of this type—whether sales letters or booklets soliciting orders for one product or a group of closely related products, or the mammoth catalogs of mail-order houses embracing wide ranges of products—are designed as self-sufficient to accomplish the whole selling job without resorting to the help of salesmen and with either little or no support from other advertising media. Mail-order advertising takes the place of the salesman; direct-by-mail advertising helps him sell. Mail-order advertising is reviewed in detail on pages 425 to 433.

3. *Unmailed Direct Advertising.* This classification of direct advertising includes many varied forms of dealer helps such as window, counter, floor, hanging, package, and counter displays, plus printed materials not sent through the mails but distributed from door to door, passed to pedestrians on the street, placed in parked automobiles, handed to customers in retail stores, included in packages and bundles, delivered by salesmen or messengers, or in some other manner conveyed directly to the recipient. Unmailed direct advertising is used for the same broad purposes as direct-by-mail advertising and mail-order advertising.

VERSATILE SALESMATE . . . NOT A COMPETITOR

Direct advertising furnishes manufacturers, wholesalers, retailers, individuals, service organizations, and agencies with an efficient, economical, and effective medium for sales and business promotion. Based on its performance record alone, direct advertising well merits its designation as "a management tool."

Direct advertising widens the influence and increases the power of all other forms of advertising. Properly coordinated with newspaper, magazine, radio, business-paper, outdoor, car-card, window-display, and business-film promotion, direct advertising increases the effectiveness of these powerful media. It is the salesmate and not the competitor of each.

The experienced user of advertising knows that all forms of advertising, when properly used, are good, that each in its place is best, and that the war of counterclaims between advertising media belongs to the horse and buggy era of merchandising. Direct advertising has many uses. For some of these uses there is no satisfactory substitute.

Direct advertising is, in many instances, the most effective, inexpensive, and practical form of business promotion. For a dealer or business man whose advertising funds are limited, it can well be, and frequently is, the major or sole advertising medium. In almost all promotional programs direct advertising is used, irrespective of the size of the advertising budget.

Direct advertising material exhibits great variation as to the design, size, shape, color, and cost of its printed forms, limited only by the ingenuity and budget of the creator. The wise user of direct advertising appreciates both the desirability and the limitations of this inherent characteristic of the medium.

Because of all these possible variations, direct advertising is the most flexible, most selective, most checkable of all the forms of advertising. The student, the practitioner, the user of direct advertising should become familiar with as many of these forms as possible . . . but, more important, he must become thoroughly acquainted with the basic uses of the medium.

These six basic or fundamental objectives follow. They should be kept in the forefront at all times when thinking about and planning direct advertising:

1. Secure contacts for salesmen.
2. Bring persons to you.
3. Influence the thinking of groups.
4. Obtain actual orders through the mail.
5. Stimulate some desired action.
6. Learn facts.

These basic or fundamental objectives have been subdivided and itemized in a chart created by the Direct Mail Advertising Association. This chart, "The Facts and Functions of Direct Advertising," was designed as a checking laboratory for advertising, sales, and publicity departments and for administrative executives and has gained nationwide acceptance and usage by advertisers who are constantly tracking down for themselves the profitable uses of direct mail and printed promotion.

49 WAYS DIRECT MAIL CAN BE PUT TO WORK IN YOUR BUSINESS

Key to symbols:
  M—Manufacturers
  W—Wholesalers
  R—Retailers
  S—Service organizations and associations
  MO—Mail order
  P—Philanthropic and welfare agencies

IN YOUR OWN ORGANIZATION

1. Building Morale of Employees—A bulletin or house magazine, published regularly, carrying announcements of company policy, stimulating ambition, encouraging thrift, and promoting safety and efficiency will make for greater loyalty among employees and better understanding between management and employees. (*M-W-R-S-MO-P*)

2. Securing Data from Employees—Letters or questionnaires occasionally directed to employees help in cementing a common interest in the organization and bring back practical ideas and much useful data. (*M-W-R-S-MO-P*)

3. Stimulating Salesmen to Greater Efforts—Interesting sales magazines, bulletins, or letters help in unifying a scattered selling organization, in speeding up sales, and in making better salesmen, by carrying sound ideas that have made sales, by success stories, etc. (*M-W-S-P*)

4. Paving the Way for Salesmen—Forceful and intelligent direct mail, persistent and continuous, will create a field of prospective buyers. (*M-W-S-P*)

5. Securing Inquiries for Salesmen—Direct mail can bring back actual inquiries from interested prospective customers—inquiries salesmen can call upon and sell. (*M-W-S-P*)

397

6. Teaching Salesmen "How to Sell"—A sales manual sent to salesmen at one time or in the form of a series of messages will educate them on "bagging more and bigger" orders. (*M-W-R-S*)

7. Selling Stockholders and Others Interested in Your Company—Enclosures with dividend checks, with pay envelopes, or direct messages will sell stockholders and employees on making a greater use of products or services and in suggesting their use to others. (*M-W-R-S-MO-P*)

8. Keeping Contact with Customers between Salesmen's Calls—To assure your firm of receiving all the customer's business you should send messages to customers between salesmen's visits. (*M-W-S*)

9. Further Selling Prospective Customers after a Demonstration or Salesman's Call—Direct mail emphasizing the superiorities of your product or service will help in "clinching" sales. It will make it difficult for competition to gain a foothold. (*M-W-R-S-P*)

10. Acknowledging Orders or Payments—An interesting letter, folder, or mailing card is a simple gesture that will cement a closer relationship between you and your customers. (*M-W-R-S-MO-P*)

11. Welcoming New Customers—A letter welcoming new customers can go a long way toward keeping them sold on your company. (*M-W-R-S-MO-P*)

12. Collecting Accounts—A series of diplomatic collection letters will not only bring in cash and keep accounts up to date but will leave the recipients in a friendly frame of mind and hold them as customers. (*M-W-R-S-MO-P*)

BUILDING NEW BUSINESS

13. Securing New Dealers—Direct mail offers any concern unlimited possibilities in lining up new dealers.(*M-W-S*)

14. Securing Direct Orders—Many organizations have built extremely profitable business through orders secured only with the help of direct mail. Many concerns not now selling direct by mail can, in like manner, accomplish the same results. (*M-W-R-S-MO-P*)

15. Building Weak Territories—Direct mail will provide intensified local sales stimulation wherever you may wish to apply it. (*M-W-S*)

16. Winning Back Inactive Customers—A series of direct mail messages to "lost" customers will revive a large number of them. (*M-W-R-S-MO-P*)

17. Developing Sales in Territories Not Covered by Salesmen —Communities unapproachable because of distance, bad train schedules, or poor automobile roads offer the alert organization vast possibilities to increase its direct sales by direct mail. (*M-W-S*)

18. Developing Sales among Specified Groups—With direct mail you can direct your selling messages to those you wish to sell and talk with them in the language they will understand . . . and act upon. (*M-W-R-S-MO-P*)

19. Following Inquiries Received from Direct Mail or Other Forms of Advertising—A series of messages sent to those who have expressed their interest in your product or service, outlining the "reasons why" your product or service should be bought, will increase the number of sales. (*M-W-R-S-MO-P*)

20. Driving Home Sales Arguments—Several mailings, each planned to lay stress on one or more selling points, will, point by point, educate your prospective customer on the many reasons why he should buy your product or service . . . and from you. (*M-W-R-S-P*)

21. Selling Other Items in Line—Mailing pieces, package inserts, or handout folders will educate your customers on products and services other than those they are buying. (*M-W-R-S-MO*)

22. Getting Product Prescribed or Specified—Professional men, such as physicians and dentists, will prescribe a product for their patients if they are correctly educated on its merits and what it will accomplish. Likewise, consumers and dealers will ask for a certain product by name if they are thoroughly familiar with it. Direct mail can be profitably used for this purpose. (*M-S*)

23. Selling New Type of Buyer—Perhaps there are new outlets through which your product or service might be sold. Direct mail is a powerful selling tool in the development of them. (*M-W-R-S*)

24. Bringing Buyer to Showroom—Invitation through letter or printed announcements will create the desire for prospective customers to visit your showroom or factory. (*M-R-W-S*)

ASSISTING PRESENT DEALERS

25. Helping Present Dealer Sell More—Assistance given your dealers through the mails and through the use of point-of-purchase helps will receive the dealer's hearty cooperation, for it will sell your product or service faster. (*M-W-S*)

26. Merchandising Your Plans to Dealer—You want as many of your dealers as possible to use your material, for the more of it used the more sales you make. Use direct mail to sell the use of this material to your dealers. (*M-W-S*)

27. Educating Dealers on Superiorities of Your Product or Service—All our memories are short when it comes to remembering the other fellow's product or service and its superiorities. It will pay you to keep telling your dealers the features of your product or service. (*M-W-S*)

28. Educating Retail Clerks in the Selling of a Product—Clerks are the neck of the retail selling bottle. If they believe in a company and a product their influence is a powerful aid to sales. If they are indifferent the manufacturer is losing an effective helper. Direct mail, addressed to the clerks, will bring you their cooperation and more sales. (*M-W*)

29. Securing Information from Dealers or Dealers' Clerks—Letters, printed messages, a bulletin, or a house magazine will bring back helpful data from the individuals who actually sell your product or your service—information you can use to your profit in passing on to other dealers or sales clerks to help them sell more. (*M-W-S*)

30. Referring Inquiries from Consumer Advertising to Local Dealers—Direct mail should be used to refer quickly any

inquirer to your dealer in his territory, and to inform the dealer about the inquiring prospect. Not to do so is to pass up many sales. (*M-W-S*)

THE CONSUMER

31. Creating a Need or a Demand for a Product—Direct mail, consistently used, will stimulate the demand for your product or service and will remind the customer to ask for it by name. (*M-S*)

32. Increasing Consumption of a Product among Present Users—Are your consumer customers putting your product to all the uses they might? If not it is probably because they do not know how else they might. Package inserts, booklets, etc., should be used to educate them on all uses. (*M-R-S-MO*)

33. Bringing Customers into a Store to Buy—Personal, friendly, and cordial direct-mail messages from retailers, telling customers and prospects about merchandise and creating the desire to own that merchandise, will bring a large number to their store to buy. (*R*)

34. Opening New Charge Accounts—This also applies to retailers. There are many people in every community who pay their bills promptly and will do the bulk of their buying where they have accounts. A careful compilation of such a list with a well-planned direct-mail program directed to them, inviting them to open charge accounts, will bring considerable new business. (*R*)

35. Capitalizing on Special Events—Retailers in particular can make capital, through direct mail, of such consumer events as marriages, births, graduations, promotions, etc., to help them sell more. Likewise, letters should be sent to select lists featuring private sales and to other groups to feature general sales. (*R*)

GENERAL

36. Building Good Will—The possibilities of building good will and friendship through direct mail are unlimited. It's the little handshake through the mail that cements busi-

ness relationships and holds the business of your customers even though your salesmen leave you to go with a competitor . . . or your competitors are aggressive in trying to wean your good customers away from you. (*M-W-R-S-MO-P*)

37. Capitalizing on Other Advertising—Direct mail will permit you to capitalize on your other advertising investments and bring back more in sales for each dollar spent. (*M-W-R-S-MO-P*)

38. As a "Leader" in Other Forms of Advertising—To make the ultimate sale of a product or service, more words are oftentimes necessary than publication space or time on the radio will permit. A booklet or attractive folder can be featured in this other advertising, which when sent to prospects who ask for it will help to make more sales. (*M-W-R-S-MO-P*)

39. Breaking down Resistance to a Product or a Service— Often sales are hindered due to resistances in the minds of prospective customers. Direct mail will help to overcome these resistances. (*M-W-R-S-MO-P*)

40. Stimulating Interest in Forthcoming Events—Such an event might be a special week or day devoted to a greater use of a product, an anniversary, the taking on of a line by a new dealer, an "opening" . . . or scores of other happenings. Direct mail, built around such an event, can help greatly to increase sales. (*M-W-R-S-MO-P*)

41. Distribution of Samples—There are thousands of logical prospects who could be converted into users of your product if you proved its merits to them. There is no better way to do this than by letting the prospects convince themselves by actual test . . . provided your product lends itself to sampling. (*M-S*)

42. Announcing a New Product, New Policy, or New Addition —There is no quicker way to make such announcements to create more sales or stimulate greater interest in a concern and what it is doing than through the personal, action-producing medium of direct mail. (*M-W-R-S-MO-P*)

43. Announcing a New Address or Change in Telephone Number—When such important changes are made a letter or printed announcement sent through the mail has a personal appeal that will register your message better than any other form of advertising possibly could. (*M-W-R-S-MO-P*)

44. Keeping a Concern or Product "In Mind"—Blotters, calendars, monthly mailings will all assist in doing this . . . a most vital problem with any concern faced with the keen competition of others who are trying their hardest to take customers away from you. (*M-W-R-S-MO-P*)

45. Research for New Ideas and Suggestions—Direct advertising research is a powerful force in building sales. Direct mail can be used to find market facts, to eliminate sales fumbling, and to charter direct, profitable trails to sales. It furnishes all the important tools for sales research, to discover what to sell, how to sell it, and to whom to sell. (*M-W-R-S-MO-P*)

46. Correcting Present Mailing Lists—Householders have an average annual change of 22 per cent . . . merchants of 23 per cent . . . agents of 29 per cent . . . advertising men of 37 per cent. Keeping a mailing list up to date is a most important detail. Direct mail can be employed to keep your list accurate by occasionally asking your customer if you have his correct name and address . . . or if there are others within an organization whom you should be reaching. (*M-W-R-S-MO-P*)

47. Securing Names for Permanent Lists—Direct mail can be used to secure lists of prospects from dealers, to write municipal clerks or other influential people in a community for names of a certain type, to secure names of friends of customers who might be prospects for you . . . and in many other ways. (*M-W-R-S-MO-P*)

48. Protecting Patents or Special Processes—Shouting forth the ownership of such patents or processes by direct mail can leave no question in the minds of your customers, present or prospective, as to whom they must come for

such a product or process. At the same time it gives you greater protection from possible infringers. (*M-S*)

49. Raising Funds—For directing appeals to a selective list of prospective contributors, direct advertising affords an effective economical methods of raising funds for worthy causes. (*P*)

FORMS OF DIRECT ADVERTISING

The forms of direct advertising are limited only by the ingenuity (or lack of ingenuity) of the creator. Direct advertising is cut to fit the pattern of the user's problem. Size, shape, pictures, type, and colors are not limited as they are in other mediums of advertising where specifications are definitely predetermined.

The following information and explanations give a general picture of the elements that affect the selection of the physical form.

First to consider is the purpose for which the printed piece is designed, for example, whether it is a calling card for a salesman or a catalog for the consumer. Almost all direct advertising could be classified into four groups: informative, persuasive, reminder, and utility. Of course some pieces have a dual or multiple function and would fall in more than one of these groups, broken down as follows:

Informative:

Catalogs	Charts
Price lists	Menus
Sales manual	Package enclosures
Instruction books	Package labels and stickers
Counter, store, and window displays	Invitations
	Programs

Streamers, pennants, and banners

House organs

Reminder:

Calendars

Blotters

Printed novelties

Persuasive:

Printed letters

Illustrated letters

Folders

Booklets

Giant letters

Miniature newspapers

Die-out action pieces

Business-reply action forms

Utility:

Letterheads

Envelopes

Business cards

Business-reply cards and envelopes

Survey, research, and informative bulletins and forms

Posters

Reprints

Memorandums

Note books, diaries, and pads

Postal cards

Mailing cards

Broadsides

Brochures

Blow-ups

Premiums

Coupons

Labels

Printed packages and cartons

Tickets

Order blanks

WHAT SIZE AND STYLE

In deciding on size and style of the physical presentation of a message, it is wise to check the facts of the problem against the following:

1. In which classification, as to purpose, does the single piece belong?

2. What format within that classification would be best, based on the answers to the following questions:

   a. How long is the story to be told and how much of it will be told by pictures?

   b. How much space will illustration require for reasonable display impression?

c. At whom is the piece directed? Should it be for filing size, smash impression, or a quick selling flash? Simple or elaborate?

d. Limitations of price? Number of pieces needed within what price?

e. Methods of distribution—should it be a self-mailer? Fit a mailing device, package, or rack space? Meet point-of-sale or other distribution requirements?

f. Does it fully meet postal requirements?

GUIDE FOR DETERMINING FORMAT

A study of the most widely used forms of printed advertising makes an excellent guide for selecting the physical form. Often there is choice of form. Your understanding of the better functions of each form will make it easier for you to make a recommendation when such situations as a choice of forms arise.

When to Use Folders. Folders are the most commonly used of all printed advertising forms because they are comparatively inexpensive and most flexible. Size, shape, and style are unlimited. In format, folders bridge the gap between personal letters and the booklet, a good rule to remember when considering the use of folders. Use them to precede and follow the more elaborate forms, books, and presentations. Use them for the short, direct printed messages that hammer home selling points in a quick concise manner. Use them for single shots or for a series. Use them when the sales message should have a compact form that the reader can grasp quickly. Inject them with novelty and color, but never at the expense or interruption of the natural flow of the advertiser's story to the prospect. Folders can be used to inform, instruct, persuade, remind, or bring home the order.

When to Use Broadsides. Broadsides are large folders, used advantageously when the average folder is not adequate to convey the story and a booklet is not the form needed or wanted; when a smash effect is sought, particularly at the beginning of a campaign, or for a special announcement, or for a special emphasis of certain appeals; when a large surface is required for pictorial and bold copy expression; when the psychology of bigness is desired.

In designing broadsides, capture interest right at the beginning and make sure that the interest is continued throughout, without confusion. Although large, a broadside should be designed for easy handling by the reader, with a physical makeup and layout that will lead the reader through in definite sequence quickly and impressively. Avoid smashing effects that confuse. They don't sell the reader.

When to Use Booklets. From the brief explanations covering when to use folders and broadsides, it is quite evident that booklets should be used when these two mediums are not adequate to convey the longer story, or lack sufficient prestige value or appropriateness for certain printed-advertising selling jobs.

The use of booklets is almost as wide and flexible as are the functions of its smaller brother, the folder. Usually designed for thorough reading and study rather than "flash" sales presentations, booklets must be attractive, interesting, and easy to read.

Booklets have a multiplicity of purposes. Booklets are to be used when the story is lengthy; when it cannot be accomplished by a folder or other lesser presentation; when dignity of approach is desired; when desired elaborateness does not reach the "brochure" classification.

Catalogs, house organs, sales booklets, instruction books, directories, price lists, etc., are some of the functional purposes of booklets (and books).

When to Use Mailing Cards. Mailing cards are usually the least expensive of all forms of printed advertising, yet they have great utility value. You can logically use mailing cards when brief announcements (not confidential) are desired; when budgets do not allow for more expensive format; when a teaser idea is used to introduce a campaign; when single messages or thoughts are desirable to influence prospects or obtain leads; when quick reminders are effective; when the element of time is most important; when notices, announcements, instructions, invitations, and other short direct messages lend themselves to this inexpensive, open, quick-reading format.

It is wise to check with your local post office for rulings on limitations of size, style, forms, folding sealing, and postal regulations and requirements.

When to Use Brochures. Brochures are for the glamorous phases of printed advertising and should be used when an elaborate presentation of company, product, or service is desired; when there is a need or desire to go beyond the booklet and broadside format for richness, power, and impressiveness in size, illustration, color, materials, bindings, etc.; when the presentation of a story must match the bigness of the selling job, must reflect the stature and dignity of the company responsible for its production.

When to Use Unusual Forms. Cutouts, pop-ups, novelties, and sample pieces can be used when realism is desired; when it is important to make a fast single impression on the mind of the prospect to gain immediate interest; when you want to show things that cannot be done by other forms of advertising; when original, individual, and effective presentations of products and services, or their features, can be achieved through forms that are different and unusual, but extremely appropriate and forceful.

MAILING LISTS

Although the advertiser is familiar with the uses and forms of direct advertising, the ultimate success or failure of his own advertising will largely depend on the choice of the mailing list.

Most experts agree that the list represents at least 60 per cent of the chances for successful direct mail . . . and is definitely the largest single factor in the planning and preparation of any campaign.

A basic factor about lists, and the one that always seems to get lost in the shuffle of collecting names and putting them together, is: Mailing lists are not made up of mere names—they're made up of people. It may sound silly to repeat it here but never forget that the Browns, Jones, Smiths, et al., who finally find a place on your cards or stencils are just like you.

They have the same feelings, emotions, senses,

likes, dislikes, problems, joys, sadnesses—and yes, even the same hangover. Remember then, build your "list," keep it up to date, and use it as you will . . . but if you're going to get any real value out of it, don't think of it as a thousand or a million stencils ready to be run through a machine at your slightest whim. Think of it rather as a group of people who will do your bidding only if you treat them as people and appeal to their emotions and senses only as you would have someone else appeal to yours.

Potentially, direct mail is the only perfect form of advertising. If we could look forward to the millennium we could conceive of a list of prospects who would all want to buy your product or service at the exact moment you told them you have it ready to sell. But it seems possible that that state of utopian bliss will never arrive nor will any such list ever be built. However, if you make certain you choose only prospects instead of suspects for your list, you may still approach that state of perfection.

It's almost impossible to define a true prospect for your own product or service without knowing as much or more about your business than you do now. Nevertheless, a prospect may be said to be a man, woman, company, or institution who under normal conditions will have a definite use for, sufficient money to pay for, and in whom a desire can be created for your product or services.

Once you have defined the group who make up your true prospects, only your own ingenuity limits the sources of your mailing list.

One famous list story concerns a man who was

called on to build a list of fat ladies whose husbands' had incomes of $10,000 or more a year. A manufacturer of foundation garments, with retail shops in Chicago and New York, had something special to offer these fat ladies. First he studied the real-estate records of both cities and picked out neighborhoods that had rental values necessitating $10,000 annual incomes. Then he hired some high-school girls and boys and placed them at strategic corners between four and six o'clock in the evening. The girls and boys were taught to follow fat ladies to their homes. If they entered private homes and there was no apparent party in progress, they merely took down the address, which was later checked against city records; if, however, they walked into an apartment building, they asked the doorman, "Wasn't that Mrs. Smith who just went in?" and the doorman would usually answer, "No, that was Mrs. DePuyster."

That's a special case and one that may never be of any value to you in solving your own problem, but you can check your own list or build a new one by using some of the following sources:

1. *Commercial list houses.* There are many that compile local or national lists, some who specialize in lists of doctors, dentists, nurses, etc., others who handle only lists of teachers, lawyers, automobile owners, or other groups. Most, if not all, are thoroughly reliable and can be depended on to furnish the best available list to suit your own particular

specifications. If however, you want to build your own list, the field is almost unlimited.

2. *Trade directories.* Practically every trade or industry has a directory published once a year or more frequently that you can buy for only a few dollars. These directories, to a varying degree, contain full information about every organization in the industry and in most cases include a list of the top personnel of each company.

3. *City directories.* Many cities issue annual or semiannual lists of all residents and business organizations. In some cases the information goes so far as to list the occupation and employer of the individual, making it possible to compile company-employee lists.

4. *Credit-rating books.* Dun & Bradstreet, etc., contain lists of practically the entire business community of the country. Most of them do not list local addresses but they can be checked against telephone directories for this information.

5. *Telephone directories.* Practically every telephone book published in the entire country is available (for a ridiculously small fee) through your own local telephone company.

6. *Membership lists.* Fraternities, sororities, chambers of commerce, Rotary, Ki-

wanis, Lions, professional and technical societies, religious, labor, and political organizations, trade associations, social and golf clubs, all have membership lists—some of which are for sale or may be procured free of charge. *Note:* Although many such lists are available for the asking, many others are carefully guarded. Lists are private property and you'd better check before you buy. Be certain you're not paying for a piece of stolen property.

7. *Voting lists, etc.* State, city, county, and village clerks or other representatives frequently have lists or will compile them for you from voting, tax, license-permit, or even real-estate or building records.

8. *Trade and consumer magazines.* The advertisers in various magazines will make either an industry or general list which may suit your needs.

9. *Clipping bureaus.* A good news-clipping bureau can give you, particularly from small city or suburban newspapers, lists of engagements, marriages, births, deaths, new businesses or organization changes, fire damages, building permits, moving notices, etc.

10. *Government lists.* The United States Government publishes more directories than any other known source. A list of these

directories will be mailed to you free of charge by the Superintendent of Documents, Government Printing Office, Washington 25, D. C.

11. *List brokers.* Many organizations rent their lists to noncompeting organizations through brokers, who have recently organized into the National Council of Mailing List Brokers.

12. *Subscription and circulation lists.* Many publishers, particularly in trade lines, rent or sell whole or part of their lists. In other cases they will only allow their lists to be used by advertisers in their own publications. It may be worth while to advertise in order to secure the use of a particular list otherwise unavailable.

13. *Company records and personnel.* Ledger records, sales slips, C.O.D. orders of your own company are profitable mailing-list sources. Remember your customers, past and present, are your competitors' best prospects. Your own salesmen and service representatives can, if properly trained in the job, add the best possible prospects to your list.

14. *Enclosures in your mailings.* Many a good prospect has been added to a list by leaving space on order blanks, etc., for your customers to list the names of friends or business associates.

15. *Contests, coupons, fan mail.* All too many times these names are not checked and added to lists. By the same token names on the stubs of admission tickets to conventions and exhibits are overlooked, as are the names in the guest books at booths and in reception rooms.

All of the sources listed above can be extremely valuable in building lists, but the best system for building lists on a national scale calls for cooperation between the home office, the dealer and the company salesman. The big difference, though, is how the cooperation is developed. Long, bitter, and expensive experience has proven the following method the best one to follow:

First, compile or buy the best list you can at the home office. Second, break it down into dealers or sales territories. Third, send the list for each territory to the interested salesman or dealer with a letter telling him it's the best list that has ever been built. Be sure you lay it on thick. You might even go so far as to infer that it's much better than he could do even though he's right on the spot.

Maybe it's the vanity of the being, but whatever the reason, the more you pour it on in your letter, the better will be your final list. The very fact that you tell the man in the field that you've done a superb job seems to guarantee that your original list will be torn apart, and in its place (usually quicker than you dare hope) will come what will probably be the best list ever compiled for the territory.

Remember—send the salesman or dealer a list (almost any list will do), but don't expect him to build one for you. He'll tear apart what you think is good but (usually) he'll do no good compiling one on his own hook.

INDIVIDUALITY OF DIRECT MAIL

Perhaps the users and promoters of all the different media of advertising would profit by adopting the "platform" as outlined by the Direct Mail Advertising Association on its chart of function and facts, which reads, "Direct advertising furnishes the advertiser with an efficient, economical, and effective medium for sales and business promotion. It subscribes to the platform that all forms of advertising when properly used are good, and that each in its place is best. Direct advertising has many uses. For some of these uses, there are no satisfactory substitutes."

The representatives and advocates of each medium of advertising would do well to recognize the advantages of each of the others, particularly with respect to that last phrase of the D.M.A.A. platform: "For some of these uses, there are no satisfactory substitutes."

Direct advertising can be employed to good advantage in many instances where other media are being used; in other cases it would be foolish to consider direct mail as the major medium. But there are many jobs for which direct advertising must be the logical choice. These cases can be viewed only in the light of instances where other mediums do not provide a satisfactory substitute. The following outline of the individuality of direct mail illustrates the point.

There are ten distinct differences between direct advertising and other media—ten reasons why it is truly the salesmate of all advertising media.

1. Direct advertising can be directed to specific individuals or markets with greater control than any other medium. An appeal can be directed to 100 hand-picked millionaires just as rapidly as to a very selected professional list of 100,000 book buyers. These lists can be obtained in many cases, with postage guaranteed, up to 98 per cent accuracy. How else or how better could a promotion be limited, yet assure absolute coverage, than through a direct approach by mail to present customers, or past customers, or recommended customers?

2. Direct advertising can be made personal to the point of being absolutely confidential. Whether a letter, order blank, confidential price list, or product information—regardless of the appeal or number of people to be reached—a first-class mailing can do it. All direct mail is not of a confidential nature, but when such an approach is needed, only this medium can provide the means.

3. Direct advertising is a single advertiser's individual message and is not in com-

petition with other advertising or editorial matter or both. At the moment of reception, or when a piece of direct advertising reaches the reader, it has his complete attention without any distracting elements. It will stand or fall on its appeal just as will any other advertisement—but at least it will have a better chance because there is no competition for the reader's attention, even if only momentarily.

4. Direct advertising does not have the limitations on space and format as do other mediums of advertising. Almost no limit exists as to the size, shape, style, number of colors, and all of the other elements that enter into the makeup of direct mail and printed promotion. Format ranges from the small poster stamp and miniatures to booklets, brochures, and broadsides as big as the top of a desk, to accommodate any length of message or size of illustration. The piece can be made to fit the story, and the possibilities are as boundless as the ingenuity of the designer.

5. Direct advertising permits greater flexibility in materials and processes of production than any other medium of advertising. Production of direct advertising includes every phase of reproduction known to the graphic arts—print-

ing, lithography, photo offset, roto-
gravure, steel engraving, silk screen,
multigraph, mimeograph, multilith, etc.
Added to these are the processes of die
cutting, scoring, punching, tabbing,
swatching, varnishing, laminating,
mounting, all kinds of binding and folding. Because of these facilities, and because each piece is individually produced, greater latitude exists in the use
of materials—all kinds of papers, inks,
plastics, etc. These are the reasons why
direct advertising can be custom made
and can fit any pattern.

6. Direct advertising provides a means for
introducing novelty and realism into the
interpretation of the advertiser's story.
Cutouts, pop-ups, odd shapes and patterns are employed to good advantage
by users of direct mail. If a folder or
booklet is wanted in the shape of a
bottle, box, or barrel, the effect is easy to
obtain. Even invisible colors and invisible writing are used in some printed
pieces for novelty and as powerful
attention getters. Odd folds and tricky
pieces are used daily to sell the reader on
paying more attention to a piece of
literature.

7. Direct advertising can be produced according to the needs of the advertiser's
own immediate schedule. For a quick

promotion, or an emergency mailing to take advantage of a situation, the production of direct mail can be geared to meet the need without waiting for a publication date or for some other medium of advertising to do the job.

8. Direct advertising can be controlled for specific jobs of research, reaching small groups, testing ideas, appeals, reactions. Before the big campaigns in which other media may be employed, confidential questionnaires can be used for research —ideas, appeals, and reactions can be tested. Next to personal contact, direct mail affords the best medium for research and individual contact.

9. Direct advertising can be dispatched for accurate and in some cases exact timing, both as to departure of the pieces as well as to their receipt. Material can be mailed according to set plan. Even departure schedules are available at the post office to help achieve good timing. Dealer material can be scheduled to reach dealer counters according to plan. Sales, holiday promotions, stockholders' meetings—distributor, dealer, jobber, and consumer promotions can be timed for maximum results.

10. Direct advertising provides thorough means for the reader to act or buy through action devices not possible of

employment by other media. The business reply card and envelope make it possible and easier for the recipient of direct advertising to take action. Complete order blanks and other action enclosures can also be used.

LESSONS FROM THE THEATER

Users of direct-mail advertising can learn much by observing the technique followed by the modern theater. Aside from its recognition of the importance of good showmanship, there is another factor inherent in every stage success. Helen Hayes has stated this principle clearly:

"Being brought up in the theatre, I have grown accustomed to directness and conciseness, and I am uncomfortable with verbosity. In the case of my play, 'Victoria Regina,' the original thirty-two scenes were compressed into nine, and Laurence Housman retained all that was most interesting and significant in Queen Victoria's life. To read any one of the biographies of the great Queen would take three or four times as long as we took to act the play. A lifetime has been condensed to an evening. In the theatre one must deal only with the essential—everything else is ruthlessly stripped away. And we employ suggestion skillfully, so that imagination can fill in the spaces.

"Succinctness is an indispensable attribute of everything we deal with, because it has been trained into us. I want to get right to the heart of the matter in whatever I read. And the less leading-up-to-it there is, the better."

Showmanship, the dramatic presentation of sales facts, is indispensable in the success of any direct-mail activity. But the showmanship by itself is not enough to keep the cash register ringing.

The side-show barker at the county fair uses lots of showmanship and gets plenty of customers too. But don't forget, he plans to move on to a new and equally fertile field next week. He's not interested in repeat business. He's strictly a one-time, high-pressure salesman. Most businesses are deeply rooted in their respective markets. Unlike nomadic barkers, they have to keep plugging in the same place to essentially the same people. They must deliver the goods over and over and over again. Therefore, showmanship must not be extreme; it should not promise more than the product can deliver lest it act as a boomerang in the face of the merchandiser who expects to get repeat business from satisfied customers.

DIRECT-MAIL LEADERS

Every user of direct-mail advertising should inspect, each year, the "Fifty Direct Mail Leader" campaigns selected by the Direct Mail Advertising Association.

These campaigns are featured at numerous meetings held by advertising clubs in the United States and Canada. They are also widely used as case examples for study groups in many leading colleges and universities.

In selecting the winning campaigns the judges are guided by the following rule of the association:

"In picking winners for the exhibit the judges shall

allow not to exceed 25 points for results from the campaign; not to exceed 25 points for continuity, or cohesion, plan, etc.; not to exceed 25 points to copy; and not to exceed 25 points for design, layout, and appearance; 100 points shall be the highest number any campaign shall receive.

"Each contestant shall submit a signed statement on his own letterhead as to costs, quantities, methods of distribution of the campaign, results, and any other information that may assist the Committee in judging the entry. In cases requiring confidential treatment—supplementary information may be given to the judges—and this data will be kept confidential."

These annual contests are open to all users of direct-mail advertising—provided the campaign does not advertise supplies, equipment, or service used in the production of direct mail. The contest entries usually close in September or early in October each year and are not limited to members of the association.

Generally, hundreds of leading advertisers submit their campaigns for these coveted awards. The campaign submitted may consist of any number of pieces or parts, three pieces or fifty pieces, just as long as the campaign as a whole produced results.

A campaign may have been planned to help dealers sell more, to secure more dealers, to secure more consumer customers, to regain lost customers, to get direct orders, to help salesmen sell more, to produce better results during a special season, or for any of the forty-nine divisions of direct mail. Or it may be just a year-round merchandising campaign. Its purposes may have been many, including coordination with other media, but the most important point considered by the board of judges is—Did it bring the desired results? In some types of campaigns, results cannot be determined in percentages or dollars. The word "results" in such cases is defined as "accomplishment of objectives."

XVI

Mail Order Selling[1]

ANOTHER powerful arm of the selling forces is mail order. Very few products and services can be marketed by mail-order methods alone, but mail order can be an aid in marketing most things. If you want to wring the last dollar's worth of profit out of a space or radio advertising program, support that program with mail order.

Perhaps the most starkly difficult task to assign to any piece of advertising is the task of securing alone and unaided a direct order. This is the task of mail-order selling. Your mail-order campaign comes to an absolutely cold prospect. It must stand entirely on its own feet. You have first to get your prospect to be interested enough to open your envelope. Then immediately you have to get his complete attention and interest. You have at once to make him want violently what you have to sell. You have to convince him that your product offers him overwhelmingly good value and that what you say about it is utterly dependable and provable. You have to answer all his possible questions about it. You have to show him clearly all its uses and benefits to him.

[1] The realistic résumé on mail-order selling that follows is the contribution of a nationally recognized authority in this specialized field, Mr. Frank Egner, President, Funk & Wagnall's Company; formerly Vice-President, in charge of Mail Order, McGraw-Hill Book Company, Inc.

This is such a stupendous endeavor that the mail-order campaign can waste no word or any second in getting right down to action. Starting even with the envelope, it must smash home its story starkly, bluntly, in a minimum of time. It has to be quick acting because it must achieve quick action.

Consequently mail order needs a quick-action formula. The most important elements in this formula are the following:

1. Headlines must instantly not only win attention but evoke desire.
2. The lead-in following the headline must be inspirational; it must picture dramatically to the prospect what he can get out of the product or service; it must justify the headline.
3. The lead-in should be followed by a concise definition of what the product specifically offers.
4. A success story should be included.
5. Testimonials should be used to aid the success story in building conviction.
6. Conviction should be further built up if possible with statements of guaranties or official endorsements.
7. A specific statement of the potential value of the product to the prospect in relation to the price asked for it.
8. Action must be hastened by special inducement.

This formula applies completely to both the sales letter and the circular used in mail-order selling. Experienced mail-order men have proved conclusively that a sales letter is almost indispensable in a mail campaign. The preferable format of a mail campaign is the sales letter, the circular, and the order card. The sales letter and the order card, mailed alone, all things being equal, will outpull the circular and the order card, mailed alone. But the three elements together will bring the greatest results. As has been said, the formula applies to both the sales letter and the circular. This does not mean that the circular is a simple duplicate of the letter; while the pattern for both should be the same, the phrasing of the copy for the circular should be different and indeed the circular should adduce additional points, arguments, etc. Further, the circular provides opportunity for effective illustration of the product or service in use.

In writing mail-order copy for either a sales letter or a circular, the experienced copy writer just writes a concise definition of the product or service, especially from its points of difference. What will this product do for the prospect that products of a similar type cannot do? What is it that makes this product unique? What are its competitive advantages?

Harper and Brothers, in describing a book on sales letters, says:

"This book first presents 27 practical devices for increasing the pulling power of sales letters, and then shows in detail how to use each one. With simplicity and directness it gives definite means and methods for putting into sales letters the specific appeals that psychology and salesmanship demand."

Examples of perfect sales definitions of products are afforded by the small-item descriptions in mail-order catalogs.

The second step in the writing of mail-order copy is the writing of the headline. This headline must tell the prospect as dramatically as possible what the product will do for him.

Examples:

> How to make your next cocktail party sparkle (Glassware)
> *Now*—you can un-dye color (Rit)
> To a $5,000 man who would like to make $10,000 (Alexander Hamilton Institute)
> How to provide a retirement income for yourself (Phoenix Mutual Life Insurance Co.)

It has been found that there are certain key forms of headlines that invariably prove effective. The most widely used of these key forms are the following:

Announcing	*Wanted*	*When*
At last!	*Why*	*Have you*
Free	*Because*	*Write us*
How to	*These*	*Report on*
If	*What*	*News about*
New	*This*	*Suppose*
Now	*Advice*	*Bringing you*
To	*Can you*	*Easy*

As an example of adaptation of a headline to these key forms let us take the glassware headline given above.

> Announcing a new idea for making your next cocktail party sparkle
> At last!—a new idea in cocktail glasses
> Free—a booklet showing you how to make your next cocktail party sparkle
> If you want to make your next cocktail party sparkle, etc.

Naturally there can be no absolute form for a headline. Many a successful headline has been written that is far from these key forms, but these key forms have been proved effective over and over again, so that the copy writer is well advised to heed them unless he is convinced that his nonconforming headline is really an inspiration.

The lead-in following the headline should develop, should elaborate upon, the promise of the headline. It should explain why the promise of the headline is possible and plausible as regards this product. This, with the headline, is the inspirational part of the message. It is possibly the most important part of the mail-order piece. Most human decisions are made emotionally and then rationalized. The lead-in must evoke emotional response—desire. The remainder of the mail-order selling piece is simply to help the prospect rationalize his emotional acceptance and to move him to act upon his emotional response.

Here is an example of an excellent lead-in:

You make up only once a day—yet are exquisitely made up all day long. In Paris women have found a new way in make-up. A cheek rouge that stays on beautifully all day long so that you can go through the day with the assurance that you'll have a bewitching color at the end of it. And you don't have to fuss or primp with your make-up to keep yourself appealingly attactive all day long.

You apply it in the morning, under the familiar lights of your own dressing table, where you can see that it's on properly, evenly—and in just the right tone to bring out your best points.

The following example illustrates clearly how the lead-in supports and elaborates the headline appeal:

Are you fed up with life on Monday mornings?
If so, there's a remedy that doesn't come in bottles— a fortnight's stay at the Spa Hotel.

You know how much an increase of vitality and vigor means at the end of a long, hard siege of nose-to-the-grindstone activity. A stay at the Spa Hotel will give you that added gusto for living fully again.

No need to tell you about the restorative qualities of these world-famous springs. Your doctor can tell you more convincingly.

Now comes the success story. This may sometimes be almost a slogan. Packard used to say, "Ask the man who owns one!" and surely that implies success beyond doubt. A clothier says: "For more than a quarter of a century we have been fashioning clothes for gentlemen." The publisher of a course in practical electricity says: "More than 10,000 electricians have trained themselves for better jobs with these books." A hardware manufacturer says: "Last year 40 dealers in your state increased their profits 20 per cent through handling our line."

Genuine, specific testimonials are always most convincing proof material. Other valuable conviction-building elements are official endorsements of the product or service, or laboratory-test results, or guaranties of various kinds. Sometimes a special patented method of manufacture may be described in such a way as to be excellent conviction-building copy.

The mail-order circular may use as conviction-building material lists of special advantages of the product, lists of ways of using the product, questions and answers on proper use of the product.

Many salesmen as well as many advertising copy writers are price cowards. If a product has value to the prospect, it is worth its price. The mail-order campaign must convince the prospect that he has far more to gain from use of the product than by retention of the amount of money asked for it in price. A book publisher usually uses the line, "One idea from this helpful book may be worth more to you than many times its cost." Such a specific statement of the relation between potential value to the prospect and actual money cost may be emphasized in every good mail campaign.

Possibly the copy element of a mail campaign that is most important next to the headline is the action inducement. Action copy must explicitly outline what you want the prospect to do and if possible must give him a plausible reason for doing it promptly. A definite offer must be made and a definite time limit set for acceptance of the offer. The threat of a rise in price, the lure of a limited supply, the offer of a premium are all helpful devices for stimulating quick action. The on-approval offer, the money-back guarantee, the blanket guarantee of satisfaction are also effective aids.

The whole quick-action formula boils down to three points:

1. *Give the prospect a personal reason for buying.*
2. *Give him a reason for buying now.*
3. *Convince him that the benefits he will secure from possession and use of your product are worth more to him than possession and retention of the money the product costs.*

Suppose you tell your prospect that you have just published the most perfect book in the world on electronic engineering. What does he care? He probably doesn't know anything about electronic engineering and isn't interested in how perfect the book is. But suppose you tell him that just as radio opened a whole new field of opportunity for thousands of alert young men who have made fortunes out of it, so today electronic engineering offers him a great new rapidly growing field of opportunity. Suppose you tell him right now an electronic engineer who knows his job is easily able to demand, not ask for, twice as much money as he now earns. Suppose you tell him that this new book gives him understandably a thorough, step-by-step training that will enable him to take advantage of the golden opportunities in this new field. You have given him a personal motive for buying.

A folder is generally more effective in a mail-order campaign than a booklet because the prospect must turn almost every page of a booklet to the last page before he gets the complete story, whereas a well-displayed folder with good subheadings gives the prospect the whole story almost at a single glance.

In sales letters and in mail-order circulars a second color will usually pay for itself. Be careful in mail-order work not to overdress your campaign. The prospect senses something awry in a fancy campaign on a low-priced product.

Long letters are not to be too severely frowned upon. It is very difficult to tell a real sales story on almost any product or service in just a few lines. Furthermore length frequently suggests importance. The essential point is to hold your prospect's interest.

Next to the opening space of a letter, a postscript has the most eye appeal. The postscript offers an effective means of restating and rephrasing the essential appeal of the headline.

Two great obstacles must be overcome in every mail-order campaign. These two obstacles are (1) human inertia and (2) competition for the prospect's dollar. The whole weight of average human nature is on the side of doing nothing, of letting things be, of not making a decision. Advertising folks are effective goads that sting human beings into enjoying more things. And the mail campaign is one of advertising's most effective weapons of attack on human inertia.

XVII

Visual Sales Aids

O<small>NE</small> of the first and most outstanding of the modern marketers to recognize the value of the use of the picture screen as a form of effective communication was that many-sided genius John H. Patterson, founder of the National Cash Register Company. In the late nineties, Patterson was using hundreds of thousands of stereopticon slides and glass painted pictures annually at sales conventions, in dealers' showrooms, and in his own model plant at Dayton, Ohio. These slides, arranged in hundreds of sets, were used to sell the idea of cash registers to his salesmen, the consuming public, and distributors, and also for the purpose of training employees in their duties.

Later, about 1910, in the early days of the movies, this pioneer salesman moved equipment in his plant onto the roof to permit the filming of plant operations, which at that time could not be satisfactorily done indoors.

The use of commercial moving pictures and slide films is a relatively recent development. The first corporation formed to offer moving pictures to merchandisers was organized in 1911, while slide films first appeared on the market in 1924. Great progress has been made since then both in production technique and in the development of projection equipment, a progress greatly accelerated by the suddenly multiplied usage in World War II, and today motion pictures and slide films are firmly established as one of the modern merchandisers' most effective weapons for management and sales training, dealer stimulation, and consumer-selling activities.

The business film, it should be clearly understood, is a medium of business communication rather than a form of entertainment. It belongs, in the merchandiser's thinking, at the top of the list of communication methods rather than at the bottom of the list of novelties. This distinction is basic, and those businessmen who fully appreciate its implications will gain many more times the return per film dollar than do those who use films as an afterthought in their merchandising plans.

Business pictures may be divided, as to purpose, into two broad classifications: (1) *management* and (2) *marketing*.

The management type of business picture uses a method of communication whereby a train of thought of a qualified individual, in the form of a series of ideas, is presented so that the listener or observer may grasp the meaning with the least possible misinterpretation and the least possible original mental effort.

Thus the "agony of thinking" is reduced to the minimum for the person seeing the business picture, and the mind, eye, and ear of both the originator of the film and the observer are in harmony. By using this management type of business picture, a well-qualified sales manager may present the most effective version of the sales story about a new product which, in the film presentation, receives the uninterrupted eye and ear attention of his salesmen and automatically does their thinking for them.

The marketing type of business picture is primarily concerned with the presentation of a form of word-of-mouth advertising at a uniform rate of delivery, set against a well-staged emotional background. All merchandisers realize that unsolicited word-of-mouth advertising is the most effective form of all promotional activity. A marketing type of business picture simulates this activity to a high degree and possesses the added psychological advantage of encouraging self-participation by the audience. Thus a picture of this type may show an admiring visitor inspecting the new refrigerator in the pantry of her hostess. The audience, psychologically, joins with the visitor on the screen in the praise and admiration shown for the refrigerator, thereby registering the sales impressions desired by the film's sponsor.

Business pictures also divide into two major groups as to kinds:

1. Motion pictures.
2. Slide films.

Motion pictures are used most effectively when the basic objective is telling a whole story to a new or uninformed audience. They are capable of telling a fast-moving story and can present business information in whatever detail the sponsor desires.

Slide films can tell a more comprehensive story and

cover more material in the same length of time than is possible with a moving picture. This type of business picture may be compared to the Rocky Mountain goat who jumps from precipice to precipice in that it presents, pictorially, the high spots of the story. Therefore, slide films can be used most effectively if the sponsor has an informed audience that does not require minute or detailed information to make the story intelligible.

The sound slide film combines the pictorial presentation with the story always told the way the sponsor wishes and presumably in its most effective version. The silent slide film permits the telling of whatever localized story the user of the film desires.

The commercial field may be further divided into four classifications as to kinds of films, as follows:

1. Employee-relations Films. Covering the specialized methods of the manufacturing of a product for the information of the consuming public.

2. Sales and Dealer-training Films. Planned specially for the instruction of the sales staff, factory representatives, distributors, dealers, and service men, for the more efficient marketing of an individual product.

3. Public-relations Films. These are divided into two distinct types. First, straight entertainment, with the sponsor's name on the main title; second, an obviously entertainment film that carries only a

subtle reference to the sponsor's product in the subject matter of the film.

4. Short-length Ad Films. These carry a short, terse message concerning the manufacturer's product direct to the audience, and shown in usually a minute's time.

The style of the commercial picture may include any of the following or a combination of two or more of these types of visual and vocal items:

Cartoon	Newsreel
Photoplay	Travelogue
Musical	Tour of inspection
Vaudeville	Offstage voice
Dialogue	Color

What kind of business picture should be used for what? Needless time and effort have been spent in attempting to answer a question that cannot be answered intelligently. All types of business pictures have their place and proper uses and are not competitive, one with the other, in any sense of the word. In principle they are different forms of communication and the same considerations govern their selection as determine the handling of your everyday correspondence. You dictate some letters; you multigraph others; some letters you mimeograph; and some of your business correspondence is handled by telegraph, telephone, or word of mouth.

FIELDS OF USE

Business pictures, according to a listing prepared by Francis Lawton, Jr., president of General Business

Films, Inc., of New York, are used for the following purposes:

Teaching workers	Consumer selling
Instructing clerks	Demonstrating goods or
Training salesmen	services
Stimulating dealers	Consumer advertising
Educating students	General publicity
Coordinating executives and employee relations	Public relations

Few business organizations today have a complete program embodying all the purposes listed above. The Chevrolet Motor Car Company, which has been unusually successful in its use of business pictures, is the rare exception. Increased activity is being evidenced in the use of business pictures for public-relations purposes, that is, the showing of pictures that will tend to clear a public misunderstanding or misinterpretation of facts harmful to commercial progress, presented to both employee groups and the general public. Pictures are also being widely used for "general-publicity" purposes when the primary objective is to make the name, background, commercial contributions, and products of the sponsor better and more widely known.

THE AUDIENCE

To whom will your business picture be shown? The answer is that no sponsor has ever failed to get all the circulation (audience) he was willing to pay for, either theatrical or nontheatrical.

The audiences of business films, like charity, begin at home, with the sponsor's own employees. The next group is the "trade" or wholesale and retail connections. Films are shown to these groups, from audiences of one at a silent pocket-slide film presentation to conventions of thousands at which full-fledged talking motion pictures are presented. Small, economical, and convenient portable projectors of many kinds now make sound pictures possible anywhere electricity is obtainable from an adequate source.

Public or consumer circulation is of three kinds: nontheatrical, theatrical, and small family audiences reached via television. The first is secured through commercial, civic, social, educational, and religious organizations or institutions, among which the unstimulated demand for nontheatrical pictures is far beyond the existing supply. The second is obtained among the theaters which see fit to book sponsored pictures, while the third is invited into the home by television owners.

People do not resent well-prepared commercial pictures; most audiences and many motion-picture exhibitors welcome good ones. There is no known record where any major proportion of theaters, for any period of time, have excluded commercial pictures from their programs.

Many business pictures are not intended to be shown to the general public. That is not their purpose. They are prepared for special groups and are expected to do a specialized job.

Listed below are some of the kinds of groups of people to whom your business picture may be shown:

Manufacturing force
Clerical staff
Executive officials
Sales representatives
Distributors
Wholesalers
Branch representatives

Retailers
Inside salespeople
Outside salespeople
Customers
Selected prospects
Students

Your nontheatrical business picture will actually be shown to individuals, informal groups, meetings, or conventions. Actual showings will take place in a variety of places: in offices, stores, factories, homes, clubs, theaters, schools, colleges, churches, ballyhoo trucks, on ships and planes, at exhibit booths in home and trade shows, conventions, and county, state, and world fairs, and by television in homes and public places.

AMATEUR MOVIE MAGNATES

The utility and effectiveness of many business pictures are frequently seriously impaired because business executives attempt to step out of their accustomed roles and serve as self-appointed moving-picture experts.

In doing so businessmen mislead themselves because all they know about business pictures finds its origin in two sources:

1. Existing business pictures.
2. Theatrical entertainment.

Existing business pictures, whether sponsored by competitors or firms in other industries, are not to be relied upon as sound signposts, because the businessman is at the obvious disadvantage of not knowing the details of the business sponsoring the picture, the "reasons why" the picture was created, and what its intended purpose is.

Far more important, however, is the fact that businessmen are misled because of their misplaced faith in the moving-picture theater as a source of experience. The film seen and enjoyed at the movies is made by experts in the entertainment field with the primary objective of selling tickets to movie-goers.

The legitimate movie has literally the whole surface of the earth to draw from for its effects, and production expense is secondary if the film's backers believe they have a smash hit with box-office appeal. Furthermore, most theater pictures, for mass-audience effect, are addressed to the lowest possible norm of intelligence, and their producers have no concern with all the varied interpretations the audience may place on the story presented.

Contrast these characteristics with those of the business picture and the fact that the former is no criterion for success in the field of business pictures is readily apparent.

The basic objectives of the business picture are to sell goods or services and to guide, conduct, and influence thought. The business picture is limited in its story material to the confines of an industry, even to a particular firm's part in an industry. The control of expense is properly uppermost in the minds of those producing a business picture. When a business picture starts out for its showings, further expenses are immediately encountered before direct or indirect sales returns or managerial improvements may be anticipated. A business picture appeals to and is aimed at a high level of intelligence—its prospects are usually found among those grouped in the average or above-average brackets of intelligence. Above all, the business picture, as previously stated, is not a form of entertainment but is, instead, a medium of business communication faced with the problem of getting a clean-cut story or impression across to its observers and listeners for a predetermined purpose.

Experience proves that the best business pictures are produced when there is a three-way meeting of minds between the sponsor, the sponsor's advertising agency, and the film-producing firm, with each sticking to its own knitting. In such a combination, the sponsor supplies an expert's knowledge of the product to be visualized; the advertising agency contributes its specialized knowledge about the public in relation to the product; and the producing film company supplies the knowledge of how best to use the moving-picture medium with its highly specialized functions of film technique to accomplish the desired objective.

The well-equipped commercial film-producing company is usually capable of giving expert services and counsel on all phases of plan, production, exhibition, and projection service. On their staffs or at their command are expert authors, animators, directors, performers, cameramen, orchestras, sound crews, and costume designers. All these varied and specialized skills are needed to produce a business picture that will return maximum results to the commercial sponsor.

XVIII

Buying Promotion

No merchandiser will disagree that the most powerful form of sales promotion is, and always has been, the display of goods, preferably in use, so that prospects may inspect and compare values.

From the earliest times the makers of pottery and the weavers of cloth displayed and sold their products by the roadside, in the market place, at the guild fairs, or in the baronial halls of their wealthy prospects.

The display of goods enters into the sale of nearly every product sold, from chewing gum to houses. More and more skill is being exercised to display goods effectively—in store windows, in automobile salons, at world's fairs and home shows, by traveling trucks and demonstration cars, by house-to-house canvassers, at roadside fruit and vegetable stands, by free samples given away at exhibits or sent in response to coupon inquiries. The suave salesman in the Fifth Avenue store who thrills you with the racks of expensive pipes and individually blends your own tobacco and the machine which makes pancakes in the restaurant window are doing exactly the same thing—they are displaying goods.

However, not all goods can be actually displayed in the market place. Some, like yachts, locomotives, and other bulky products too numerous to be listed, cannot be carried economically about the country. Others, like movie stars, cannot show their smiles and lovely figures everywhere "in person." And in many instances it is either too costly or physically impossible for the manufacturer to attempt to have his own sales representatives actually show his products to all the prospective buyers.

Where producers cannot give prospects a chance to see and examine products by direct display many resort to pictures and descriptions; in short, to marketing in print by the use of catalogs. Unfortunately, too many merchandisers overlook the sales importance of a well-prepared catalog; the necessity for its proper distribution; and the desirability of its accessibility as an ever-present, currently accurate piece of buying promotion in the hands of prospective buyers.

MARKETING IN PRINT

The technique of preparing catalogs and the principles of their effective distribution and use may be made clear by a résumé of years of research by a group of experts of the F. W. Dodge Corporation. Arthur G. Elkington and L. W. Brooks, of Sweet's Catalog Service, a division of the F. W. Dodge Corporation, give the following account of the experience gained by their company in dealing with this problem.

❖ ❖ ❖ ❖ ❖

"If you want to sell 'em, show 'em the goods." The fundamental truth of that old selling adage is so obvious as to be axiomatic. Its corollary is, "If you

445

want to make your products easier to sell, make them easier to buy."

For the retail merchant, coming in direct contact with his customers, this requirement is met by the physical display of goods and the presence of competent sales personnel. But where there are wider gaps in the distribution line, or if the product is one that requires a considerable amount of detailed study before selection and purchase, other means must be used to accomplish the purpose. It is at this point that the catalog takes its unique place in effective marketing procedure.

The term *catalog*, as it is generally understood and used today, goes far beyond the limitations implied by the narrow dictionary definition, "a complete enumeration of items." Catalogs are capable of so many different treatments, each according to the specific job it is to do, that a functional definition will serve better as a starting point for effective catalog planning. To a greater extent than in any other form of printed information, the function of a catalog is to help buyers buy. This distinction becomes clearer by contrast with other information forms.

ARE CATALOGS ADVERTISING?

Advertising in its various forms—publication, direct mail, etc.—is used mainly by sellers looking for buyers. To succeed, it must interrupt, direct the reader's attention to something he probably was not thinking about, hold his attention by offering him advantages along with enough information on the product to get him to consider the idea of buying and, where necessary, to request further buying information.

A *catalog*, on the other hand, is used mainly by buyers looking for sellers. Nearly always, it has the voluntary attention of the reader. Its chief purpose is to answer questions asked by people who intend to buy but who have not decided from whom to buy.

There are exceptional cases, of course, in which the advertising function and the catalog function overlap. Nevertheless, the principal job of a catalog is to present organized buying information on a product to people who *want* to study it. And the selling power of a catalog lies in its ability to facilitate buying.

So in organizing the material for a catalog, it is most important to keep in mind the information needs of the buyer. Also, in deciding on how a catalog is to be designed and distributed, the objective will be to get it used by the greatest possible number of prospective buyers.

One of the first questions the catalog planner should consider is, *"What kinds of buyers constitute my market?"*

Perhaps your prospects fall into groups, determined by common interest in certain of your products, or by interest in different applications of the same products. In that case, you probably will find it advantageous to design special catalogs—one for each group. There has lately been a trend away from general catalogs, containing information on every item made by a manufacturer, except as they are needed by certain trade factors. This type of catalog, having an excess of irrelevant information from the viewpoint of any one buyer, has been found wasteful and inefficient from the viewpoint of the seller. The specialized catalog can be produced and distributed without waste and at lower cost. Also, it can be replaced more economically when its information becomes obsolete.

Another basic consideration will be, *"What kind of buying action do I want this catalog to produce?"* What is the typical buying procedure of the prospects to whom you will send it, and what do you want them to do after they have studied it? Do you want them to call in your local sales representative? write your product into a specification? visit a dealer? place an order direct? Whatever it is, the information in your catalog should be directed to that end.

CATALOG DESIGN

Catalog design has three main objectives—to make the information easy to *find*, easy to *read*, and easy to *comprehend*. If these seem too obvious, let it be remembered that finding is not easy when a needed item of information is hidden in a solid block of type, with no sign to indicate its presence, nor when products are grouped according to manufacturing departments rather than according to use. Reading is not easy when type is too small to satisfy average conditions of vision and lighting, nor when, in order to follow a certain line of inquiry, the eye must travel an erratic course between text, illustration, and tabular matter—frequently, not even on the same page. Also, comprehending is not easy when exact meaning is obscured by generalities; when illustrations, whether photographic or diagrammatic, are sized to fit available space rather than to take the prospect close enough to see what he needs to see.

The index of a catalog often can be made more useful than a mere table of contents. With a little skill, this sometimes commonplace item can be designed to function as an important guide to the selection of the right type or grade of product as well as to the location of the information wanted.

The "visual unit" represented by any two facing pages of the open catalog should be planned to embrace a self-contained unit of information. The resulting orderliness contributes greatly to ease of finding.

Headings and subheadings should be used generously to point up the subject matter in each unit. This is a matter of judgment rather than of rule, but generally there is less danger of using too many than too few.

That a catalog should be easy to read is probably the most obvious requirement of any, but easy reading can and should be the result of design and not left to accident or hunch. Our habitual reading direction is from left to right and from top to bottom. The visual emphasis should follow this pattern, not only in the text but over the entire visual unit. Poor eyesight and inadequate lighting are prevalent conditions in which your catalog will be read. Therefore type faces and sizes would be chosen for legibility rather than for individuality, and length of lines and leading between lines should be carefully considered for the same purpose. Contrast between text and background also should be preserved.

With the possible exception of the "glamour" product, descriptive text should consist of concise factual statements, especially where frequent cross reference is likely to be required. Words are often subject to various interpretations and therefore they should be selected critically. Precise technical description favors "325 lb. per sq. in." to "stronger," or "800 sq. ft. per gal." to "good coverage." Charts and tables are more effective for presenting or summarizing comparative information than quantities of text and should be used wherever possible.

In planning illustrative matter that is to help prospects visualize your products and their uses, it should be remembered that the efficient photograph brings the reader as close to the object as he himself would come in order to examine and understand, also that it places him in position to observe from the most informative angle. Drawings are often more useful in clarifying details of construction and operation. In drawings not made to scale, all principal dimensions should be given.

Color, usefully employed, helps comprehension in many ways. It is obviously desirable in illustrating products of which color is an inherent feature. Complicated diagrams can be simplified by reproducing certain parts in color. Also, color can be used effectively to emphasize or to segregate items of information.

Here is a six-point check list for testing catalog design:

1. *Identification.* Does the front cover identify the products and the manufacturer or

vendor? Does it tell at a glance—by use of illustration, manufacturer's name, product name, trade-mark, or by other means—what the catalog describes?

2. *Index.* If the catalog covers various products, are they easy to find? Does the index also help the user to find his way through the catalog by indicating the organization of the contents?

3. *Organization.* Is the catalog arranged in clearly defined sections and visual units? Are the products grouped according to specific uses and do various types of information appear in the most logical sequence?

4. *Visual Flow.* Is the catalog visually interesting? Does it make use, wherever possible, of pictures, diagrams, charts, and tables in place of wordy texts? Is color employed usefully, and not merely ornamentally?

5. *Content.* Is there sufficient information on product features, range of performance, applications, etc., to facilitate comparison? Is it so developed that it prompts selection of the product and the intended buying action?

6. *Action.* Does the catalog suggest the next buying step? Does it tell the prospect what to do and how to do it? Does the back cover list the names, addresses and telephone numbers of branch offices and sales representatives?

CATALOG DISTRIBUTION

Design is but one characteristic of a good catalog. As with advertising, where the payoff comes after people read and act, so with catalogs. The best catalog is just paper and printing until the information it contains is studied and acted on by prospective buyers. So methods of catalog distribution should receive careful study.

Some efforts to get catalogs used frequently defeat themselves—one in particular. This one is based on the reasonable assumption that if a prospect takes the trouble to write for a catalog, he probably will pay more attention to it when it arrives than he would if it were sent to him without his request. The method is to require all recipients of the catalog to declare their interest through a request for further information. The low percentage of response which is considered good by those who use this technique indicates how few of those who could reasonably be expected to write actually make the effort. So, in getting the catalog before the attention of relatively few inquirers, this procedure results in many prospects going uninformed and undeveloped.

In well-defined markets where buying is relatively continuous, it is better to send catalogs to all qualified prospects, even considering that a large number might subsequently be lost, than to risk loss of potential business through inadequate coverage. Obviously, a basic requirement of this method is the compilation and maintenance of accurate lists.

Several industrial fields are now served with catalog

services that distribute catalogs in bound collections, or files, which have done much to get manufacturers' catalogs into the hands of important prospects and to overcome the problem of keeping catalogs accessible for use on the receiving end. These systems are based on a simple reversal in procedure, namely, the filing of catalogs in advance of their basic distribution.

In the catalog, the printed word reaches the limit of its capacity to influence buying. Outside of the mail-order field, in which the catalog assumes the entire marketing burden, it occupies a distinct place between advertising and personal selling and it should be closely coordinated with each. These three constitute the production line for the economical production of orders. Planning the design and distribution of a catalog will assume new importance when it is remembered that as long as a prospect is studying your catalog, you still have a chance to get his order.

XIX

Billboards, Car Cards, and Displays

OUTDOOR-SIGN advertising traces its known history back to the earliest days of recorded history. In the ruins of Pompeii and Herculaneum were found signs of Roman shoemakers and public housekeepers who used this medium to keep alive in the memories of their Roman customers the wares and services they had to sell.

During the eighteenth and nineteenth centuries sign advertising became almost a public nuisance through the general practice of the indiscriminate posting of printed bills on the walls of both occupied and vacant buildings. In this country from the time of the Civil War to the beginning of the twentieth century, painted signs were used widely, and these advertisements, principally of patent-medicine makers, defaced the barns and fences of the countryside with little regard for property rights.

Gradually the pressure of outraged public opinion brought about needed improvement in both methods and standards of sign advertising. Associations of billposters and sign painters, utilizing leased or owner sites, were formed, and the standard sizes were established for the more widely used sizes of sign advertising. Today the outdoor-advertising industry is well organized. In approximately 1,800 towns and cities in the United States and Canada a systematized posting service is available. Most of the estimated seventy-five million dollars expended annually for sign advertising is made through these regulated channels.

CHARACTER OF BILLBOARDS

Outdoor advertising is of two main types: (1) painted signs and (2) posters.

Painted signs are, in most cases, prepared individually by artists who paint directly on the display panels. Contracts for painted display signs are customarily on a yearly basis, with repainting two or three times a year. The sale of space on walls and bulletin boards is by individual advertisement unit; the advertiser may buy one such sign or many. These painted signs are to be found in cities and suburbs, along highways, and adjacent to railroad rights of way.

Poster signs, the commonly used type, are printed, lithographed, or painted on paper and then pasted in place on the display panels. Posters eight feet eight inches in height and nineteen feet six inches in length, called "twenty-four-sheet posters," are most generally used, displayed on boards twelve feet in height and twenty-five feet in length.

Showings of poster signs are by groups of panels so located throughout a city as to provide what is considered to be proper coverage of the area. These showings are further designated as *full* or *representa-*

455

tive. A full showing provides enough panel displays to cover a city area evenly and thoroughly; a representative showing provides the same general coverage of the area but with only half, or a lesser number, of billboards. Showings are usually booked on a calendar-month basis.

ADVANTAGE OF OUTDOOR ADVERTISING

In discussing the advantages of outdoor advertising it is imperative that the merchandiser clearly understand one basic factor.

Sign advertising stays in one spot. Its utility depends upon whether or not it will be seen by the flow of traffic (pedestrian, automobile, trolley car) past that spot. Therefore, a well-prepared, attention-getting display poster is only part of the job. To pay out, the poster must be placed where it will be seen by the kind of people who will and can buy the product it advertises.

Outdoor advertising appeals to an audience on the move. It must present the sales story quickly, graphically. Pictures should be large, copy short. The appeal is primarily to suggestion, seldom if ever to argument.

Outdoor advertising awakens the response of a wide audience, of large numbers of people of varied tastes, pocketbooks, and needs. Logically, then, it is most effectively used by advertisers promoting products of wide appeal and established acceptance. It may be used near the point of purchase, to serve as a reminder to prospective purchasers, and, since it is a flexible type of advertising, it may be concentrated in market areas where distribution has already been secured or in markets needing promotional efforts.

CAR-CARD ADVERTISING

Car cards, another form of sign advertising, carry an advertiser's message to a relatively unselected group of prospects, who average 39 million rides a day on the subways, street railways, busses, and elevated cars of the country.

Car cards, from the standpoint of picture and story, are very similar to billboard posters; they should appeal primarily to suggestion rather than to argument and tell the sales story speedily and pictorially.

Many users of car cards believe that this medium receives a considerable degree of attention on the theory that the passenger has ample leisure time to devote to the study of the advertisements. Studies made of subways contrasted with surface cars seem to substantiate this reasoning, since it was found that the presence of outside distractions considerably decreased the attention given to the car cards.

Car cards are used most widely to advertise soaps, dentrifices, chewing gum, foods, and popular medical remedies such as cough drops and headache powders; in other words, mass appeal products of the repeat-sale and low-unit-cost type.

For these products, car-card advertising is usually a supplementary rather than a major medium; it aids in establishing the brand names in memory and in reminding the prospect about the product while en route to the place of purchase.

WINDOW AND STORE DISPLAY

Modern merchandising leaves nothing to chance. The most successful marketers do not overlook the truth of the saying, "A chain is as strong as its weakest link." Therefore, the sellers of nationally advertised products are not satisfied that their newspaper, magazine, radio, direct-mail, outdoor, or car-card advertising serve to complete their impersonal selling to consumers or their dealer good-will building activities.

They know that sales are made in stores and showrooms, not in the home, streetcars, or busses. They take pains to repeat their advertising message at or near the point of sale, realizing that when the prospect reaches the buying place he steps from the role of consumer to that of shopper.

They meet the shopper at the point of purchase with a "silent salesman" in the form of a window, counter, floor, "serve-yourself," package, or hanging display, either inside or outside the retail outlet, which psychologically greets the prospect as an old friend and then, often subconsciously, gets in the last licks of the selling story before the shopper actually makes his purchases.

Displays are not expected to perform the missionary or educational selling functions. They are primarily the clincher medium, the sales aid that combines the effects of all the other promotional efforts at the retail outlet where this added help can be most influential in making actual sales. In the well-conceived sales plan, displays perform a deservedly important part; they are far more than just another dealer help—they figure as a major selling medium.

These display media afford the manufacturer his last chance to be of real help to the retailer in inciting purchases, influencing buying decisions, and building sales. In many instances they move the product down from the shelves, take it out of the category of a "shelf-warmer," and get it out in the open where customers may see, inspect, compare, and serve themselves.

Displays may be classified by types as follows:

Window displays
Counter displays
Floor displays
Hanging displays
Package displays
Container displays

WINDOW-DISPLAY CHARACTERISTICS

If the window display is to approach maximum effectiveness, it is essential that the factors incident to its planning, development, and distribution be studied and weighed. In doing so the merchandiser will find this review of the characteristics of display advertising helpful.

Minimum of Waste Circulation. Displays in a store window are directed to the people who travel on the sidewalk in front of that store, the majority of whom live in that neighborhood and are most likely to be potential customers of that store.

Selectivity of Coverage. Window displays provide the means for a very selective type of coverage, both geographically and by classes of consumers. Displays can be directed to specific areas:

1. To stimulate sales in a lagging sales area.
2. To promote a specific product in certain class areas.
3. To make or supplement a new product sales test, and for any other special purpose, as well as provide a more general sectional or national coverage.

Winning Dealer Good Will. It would be impossible for dealers, individually or in groups, to provide themselves with the wide variety of high-grade lithographed window-display material that is so universally employed in present-day merchandising. The unit cost would be prohibitive. The manufacturer, however, is able to supply these displays to dealers, thereby affording each dealer an opportunity to dress his window in keeping with neighboring retail outlets, identify his store as a source of supply, and thus build profits for dealer and manufacturer alike.

FUNCTION OF WINDOW DISPLAY

The ways in which displays can and must serve both the manufacturer and the retailer may be grouped under two fundamental functions.

First, the display must sell the storekeeper or dealer on the idea of making proper use of the display. To accomplish this the display should be sufficiently attractive, outstanding, and forceful to win a showing in his valuable window space in competition with displays promoting other products.

It must be of such nature that it will stimulate the interest of the retailer and his clerks in that product during the time the display appears, fostering their good will and cooperation.

It must win a place on a top shelf or back bar after use in the window, or on the counter, as a further influence on buying action.

It must provide a cooperative means whereby retailers can sell more of their complete line by embracing the "companion-sales" idea. When good group-item window displays of this type are developed, the final results are most gratifying to manufacturer and retailer alike, in that they sell the advertiser's product, sell other allied merchandise in the dealer's stock, and sell the dealer's store or service to the public.

Second, the display must prove its worth by influencing shoppers to purchase the product. In order to accomplish this, it should command the attention of the passing shopper by means of size, comprehensiveness, attractiveness, domination, unusual design, motion, or novelty of display effect.

It should develop features that will hold the attention long enough to invite a favorable product interest and exert an influence on buying action.

It should act as a stopgap by reminding of the product during the interval that elapses between the time the advertising message is seen in other media and the time the purchaser stands in the store asking for the product—a period during which many factors may influence a change of mind.

It should impress the observers with the quality and desirability of the product, and remind them of forgotten needs or intended and desirable purchases.

It should tie in with advertising in other media, supplementing such advertising by emphasizing the high spots and illustrating the message in an attractive and colorful manner.

It should introduce new products quickly and economically, when other media do not seem to provide the same selective type of promotion that is inherent in window-display advertising.

PITFALLS TO BE AVOIDED

There are six common pitfalls that have prevented advertisers from achieving the best results from window displays. They may be avoided by recourse to organized thinking and applied common sense.

Ask yourself:

1. Does the idea have a hook that will draw them in? Not a special merchandise offer, such as a free deal, but a basic appeal

that selects prospects from among the passers-by.

2. Is the display simple in design? And fast? Will people who cannot read the language know what the display is selling? Do the added niceties of design detract from the essential sales idea?

3. Is the display easily set up and sturdily built? Call in your office porter. Ask him to open up the package and set up the display. Then try an elevator runner in his half-hour off. If they can do it, you are safe.

4. Does the art technique successfully convey the idea? Some advertisers produce mediocre displays because they start with a piece of art work instead of an idea.

5. Are the name plate and copy well placed? Can the passer-by identify the sponsor? Does the copy get the idea across rapidly and dramatically? Can it be read ten feet away?

6. Is the display equally adapted for open-back or closed-back windows?

DISTRIBUTION OF DISPLAYS

The throes of creating and developing a window display of the type and adaptability that will successfully perform a specific merchandising job only mark the beginning of the work. No marketer can afford to scatter these displays indiscriminately throughout the trade in the smug, self-satisfied conviction that *his* display—his baby, as it were—is the one display of importance in the lives of his retail distributors.

Retailers receive hundreds of unsolicited displays each year, many so poorly conceived and badly executed that after a cursory glance they are consigned unused to the cellar or the rubbish barrel. The presence of these poor displays should but emphasize the importance of making *your* display a selling tool, deliberately planned to sell merchandise which the retailer will welcome and use to your mutual satisfaction and profit.

The type of product, the extent of territorial coverage, the size and comprehensiveness of the displays, the quantity, the retail problems in that industry—all these should enter into a consideration of the proper method of display distribution.

Distribution can be accomplished by shipping the displays in the same container with the goods; or through installation by professional display service organizations. Better still, a large corps of retail salesmen is a "natural" for proper and effective distribution. The salesman not only can see personally that his display is used and used properly; he can also watch and check the results.

Another method of window display distribution is by means of thoughtfully planned trade-paper advertising to the retailers, showing what material is available, its nature, what it is designed to accomplish, and how to get it. Retailers may also be reached by direct mail and furnished with return post cards on which they can request the display material.

Offering window display with deals is another

method, one that should be pursued with caution and good judgment. Many retailers are bitterly opposed to some particular manufacturer who, through an attractive-appearing deal, has loaded them with slow-moving merchandise, which the most attractive displays could not dispose of.

Informing the retailer just how to set up the display and what to include in the window with the display can be accomplished by an instruction sheet tipped on the back of the display, carrying an illustration of an interesting window arrangement with the display in place and an actual listing of suggested products to include with the display. This may also be done by pasting one of the instruction sheets on the outside of the window-display container, indicating to the retailer just what is in the container and the desirability of making a place for that display in his window.

EVALUATION OF DISPLAY ADVERTISING

A comprehensive field study, conducted for the Advertising Research Foundation, supplies a positive method of evaluation of window displays on a circulation basis. This scientific research was made in nineteen different cities and communities whose population ranged from 15,000 to 300,000; the windows of more than 16,000 retail stores were analyzed, and the individual movements of 2,000,-000 persons were observed and recorded. Merchandisers interested in effective advertising should familiarize themselves with the results of this research.

Window displays, like other profitable advertising

media, require careful thought and study. No specific rules can be laid down that will fit each individual display program. No one display ever can fulfill all the functions of display advertising. However, window displays built to meet the needs of the retailer are succeeding and producing results that justify the budget allotment set aside for this merchandising vehicle.

COUNTER, FLOOR, AND HANGING DISPLAYS

The merchandiser must take a realistic attitude toward his product in relation to displays. Certain products, by their nature, depend entirely on other media of advertising to send buyers into the retail outlet. Still others will not be featured in the dealers' windows because they do not pay the dealer a large enough profit to warrant the use of his valuable window space; others turn over too slowly or appeal to small groups of people; still others are kept out of windows because they are used as footballs in price-cutting activities.

What is the merchandiser to do if his product falls into these classifications? He can either let his product remain on the shelves or behind the counters, and be sold only when people ask for it, or he can bring it into the light of day and the consciousness of potential buyers by means of various types of counter or wall displays.

A "counter merchandiser," designed to carry one, two, or a dozen units in the smallest possible space, together with the price, sales message, dramatized illustration, and consumer give-away literature, is usually the answer for the marketer of shaving creams, dentifrices, and other small unit products who desires to speed sales. Display baskets, metal racks, a novelty counter display that invites self-participation by the consumer are other types of this medium successfully used for the same purpose.

Island displays, counter-end demonstrators, open displays, "serve-yourself" floor units, and aisle merchandisers offer another means of getting products out in the open where customers may see, inspect, compare, and serve themselves. The makers of soaps, cleansing powders, canned goods, inexpensive cosmetics, to mention only a few, have long known the value of these "silent salesmen." They frequently sell five, ten, even up to twenty times as much as when the commodity is left on the shelf and brought forward only on the request of shoppers.

Hanging displays placed above the counter or soda fountain provide another means of calling attention to the product. Corner hanging displays placed diagonally across the end of a room and suspended from the ceiling are another kind of silent salesman that recognizes the physical limitations of store layout by utilizing unused space to place sales messages before customers.

The open-end display, or self-service type, is based on the chain-store principle: "Get the merchandise into their hands and it is more than three-fourths sold." Such displays eliminate the elaborate pyramids of canned goods that no customer dares touch lest they topple over, and they provide customers a freedom of selection with no interference from salesclerks.

The self-service display is typified by these variations:

1. The assortment or selection display presents an assortment of merchandise for the customer's selection.
2. The bargain display. People have the impression that merchandise thrown into one pile represents a bargain. This form of display, popularly called the "jumble-tray" stand, is so built that the goods keep the jumbled bargain effect, which is a potent stimulator of pick-up sales.
3. The family-group display. Such displays present an assortment of the same kind of merchandise. For example, three coffees of one manufacturer are displayed for the consumer to choose from, with a brief characterization of each.

USING PACKAGES AS DISPLAYS

Packages themselves are being used with increasing effectiveness as display media. One arrangement which makes use of an automatic snap-up construction converts the package holding a bottle into a highly effective display, making the bottle and label and sales message printed on the inside flap of the package a carefully coordinated sales message. Other packages are designed so that various combinations on the dealers' shelves either spell out the name of the product, present its humanized trade-mark in various scenes, or tie in with the current advertising or broadcasting activity by the use of copy messages or pictorial material.

Containers and cartons, too, are used widely for display purposes. In some instances, they are designed to serve as display baskets or tray displays. Others act as bases for the display of the product. Still others, with pop-up sections carrying the sales messages, are effectively used as counter displays, notably in cigarette merchandising.

NO "ORPHAN ANNIES"

Merchandisers using displays get best results when they keep these three facts in mind:

1. Displays are not "Orphan Annies." That is to say, they are not just another form of dealer-help material. They are a major selling medium and, as such, are part of a coordinated sales plan.

2. The average small-town dealer receives, on the average, over 100 display pieces a year. Most dealers change displays not more frequently than once a week.

3. Display material should be aimed at the dealer, not through him. Its primary purpose is to help the dealer move his goods, not to glorify the manufacturer. The more subtly unselfish the display appears to be, the more it suggests a "dealer help" rather than a "manufacturer help," the greater are its chances of being used.

❖ ❖ SALES helps help sales. Many and varied are the promotional activities of the modern marketer. In your aggressive sales campaign, you may use one, several, or all sales aids. The more important are:

1. Direct mail

2. Motion pictures and slide films

3. Catalogs

4. Billboards and car cards

5. Window and store displays

Before you make your choice of sales tools, determine carefully which best fits your personal needs in relation to your immediate and long-range objectives, your actual and potential profits, and the amount of money you can afford to invest in such an activity.

❖ ❖ ❖ ❖

$\mathcal{A}$ Direct-mail Problem

You are the seller of a specialty product in a city of 250,000. You are convinced you can sell more of this product if you promote it more aggressively. The manufacturer of the product provides effective direct-mail material which you can purchase at reasonable cost.

You employ four salesmen and have a carefully selected list of 1,250 prospects in your file.

The sales representative of the manufacturer urges you to send a direct-mail campaign consisting of four mailings, at ten-day intervals, to each of your 1,250 prospects. The cost to you, including the postage, will be 24 cents per name, a total of $300.

Are you using the best business judgment if you accept the suggestion of the manufacturer's sales representative and send out these mailings as he proposes?

The seller of a specialty product, known to the author, facing the same situation, made his $300 investment produce profitable sales results by following the procedure reviewed on page 482.

Appendix

The Solutions to Marketing Problems

The Solution to a Product Problem

The president of the rubber footwear concern decided that his company was not yet ready to manufacture the new line of galoshes recommended by the style and color experts and endorsed by his own sales and manufacturing departments.

More facts were needed from people *outside* the business—from dealers expected to promote the sale of the galoshes and from the women expected to buy them.

His salesmen were supplied with sample galoshes and a questionnaire. The opinions of shoe dealers and managers of shoe departments in dry-goods stores, large and small, were secured as to the price to be charged. Color and style preferences were itemized in detail.

Approximately one thousand women, in selected market centers, were shown the new galoshes and asked if they would pay the proposed price for them. Their opinions and preferences, as to style and color, were recorded.

After these dealer and consumer opinions had been correlated and carefully studied the manufacturer found that both groups were in agreement in believing two of the colors would find little, if any, acceptance. A third color found such slight acceptance that it was also eliminated.

The line of new galoshes, made in the four colors dealers and consumers liked, was introduced that fall and found general acceptance. Dealers were well pleased because none of the colors became a burden on their shelves; also their stock inventories were less than if a wider line had been introduced. The manufacturer's production problem was simplified and his profits greater than they would have been had he manufactured several items that either did not move at all or, at best, moved slowly.

Thus possession of all the market facts proved profitable and paid many times for the expense and trouble expended in their collection.

The Solution to an Organization Problem

The cement manufacturer, with the cooperation of his advertising agency, decided to stop national advertising activity and use the money formerly spent for this purpose in a program designed to help the individual dealer make the conduct of his business more profitable.

The manufacturer announced his conviction that in his industry the interests of one were the interests of all—that anything detrimental to the dealer was detrimental to the manufacturer—anything helpful was advantageous to both.

Therefore, the manufacturer proposed a program based on teamwork between dealers and himself for their common good.

A series of books on subjects most important to the dealer were prepared, based on an interchange of dealer experiences and the most constructive ideas of dealers and other authorities. These books were distributed by the manufacturer's salesmen to his dealers, free of charge.

Members of the manufacturer's sales force were carefully trained so that they could properly interpret the contents of each book to their customers, thereby qualifying to serve as business counselors to their trade.

Much good will and attendant favorable publicity were created. The manufacturer's dealers, being human, expressed their gratitude by placing orders for increased tonnage with his sales representatives. New dealers, anxious to gain the benefit of this merchandising help, were more easily secured. Since no other manufacturer in this field had a similar service for the trade, nor cared to imitate his program, the sponsor of this dealer-help activity enjoyed a distinct advantage over competitors.

A Market Research Solution

The XYZ Company conducted the following investigations before attempting to formulate a sales policy for the possible sale of its product to the poultry trade.

1. Leading physicians and hospital authorities were interviewed to determine whether the possible sale of the product to poultry raisers would have an adverse effect on the product's established standing in the medical field.

2. County agents and poultry raisers were interviewed to determine the extent of the losses incurred by chicken mortality and lessened egg production by hens.

3. Experimental brooder and hen houses, equipped with the cellulose-acetate product, were installed at the poultry farms conducted by leading agricultural colleges and state universities. Comparative tests were run with similar batches of chicks and hens and the results were recorded and studied.

4. Leading manufacturers of brooder and hen houses were interviewed and arrangements completed for the use of the cellulose-acetate product in place of ordinary window glass.

5. Hardware and other dealers were interviewed and their opinions asked as to the salability of the product to poultry raisers. Data were also secured about the proposed price for the product.

When these studies were completed and the composite answers weighed, the XYZ Company decided a real market existed for their product. Sales plans were accordingly formulated and a profitable business developed in the poultry field.

A Consumer Problem Solution

It is the intent of this report to indicate why past consumer advertising has not been more productive and to outline the changes required in the basic policy so that greater returns per advertising dollar may be realized in the future.

We must realize that our customers—home owners—are human beings and that every human being is interested, beyond everything else, in himself. Our customer's reaction, your reaction, my reaction, to any proposal made to us, no matter how each of us attempts to conceal our motives, is, "What will I get out of it? What will this product do for me?"

Our advertising copy has been entirely lacking in this fundamental self-interest appeal. We have talked, rooster-like, about our product, our leadership in the industry, our skill in making good paint. In other words, our advertising message has wasted costly space to say, "We are great people."

The illustrations used have been entirely lacking in ability to focus the reader's attention on our advertising. The pictures of a can of paint, so prominently used, have aroused no sympathetic situation nor created an emotional conflict from whose dilemma our product can rescue the reader.

The text of our advertisements have not been built on a psychological platform that moves the reader to action. We have not won his sympathy, offered a satisfaction for his needs or desires, related the benefits of our product to his needs. And we have not supported the claims made for the product by understandable evidence the layman will accept and believe nor have we justified its cost in a dramatic manner.

It is proposed to base our future advertising on a humanized friendly appeal, written around the theme that home is the castle of everyone's dream and that home deserves the best possible paint protection. More space will be devoted to illustrations showing our product in use on beautiful homes, both large and small. Technical data will be subordinated: if used at all, they will be presented in popular form. Every effort will be made to shift the emphasis from what the product is to what it will do for the purchaser.

In these sample layouts you will see a visualization of how this will be accomplished.

The Solution to an Exhibit Problem

An exhibit booth, in the form of a simple English thatched cottage, was erected. Inside the cottage a life-sized diorama of Sir Luke Fildes's famous picture "The Doctor" was staged before a black velvet background.

Appropriate musical effects were softly played on a recording machine behind the velvet curtain. An announcer's voice recalled the importance of the doctors' services to humanity and the value of the company's laxative product.

The complicated emotional reactions so evidently stirred in the great majority of the visitors by the appealing sight of the deathly sick innocent child, the anguished mother, the brave father, the kindly doctor proved to be an effective vehicle for the sales story on laxatives.

As visitors, and they came by the hundreds of thousands, left the exhibit booth each received a post card reproduction of "The Doctor" with a brief product sales message on the reverse side.

The Solution to a Problem of Changed Market Conditions

The ABC Company cannot continue to compete profitably with others selling their products through the same channels of distribution that this company uses until it further diversifies and broadens its line of products.

Diversification of the line means the addition of new products which can be profitably sold through our existing dealers, thereby further cementing these dealers to the ABC Company and fully utilizing the dealer good will so carefully nurtured over a period of years.

It is recommended that the board of directors of the ABC Company give careful consideration to a policy of conservative capital expansion so that new products may be added to the line, thereby equipping the company to continue its aggressive sales-building policy.

Outlined in the accompanying report is a proposed product-expansion policy to be undertaken during the next five years. Details as to financing requirements are summarized in a separate report prepared jointly by the chairman of the finance committee and the treasurer.

The Solution to a Planning Problem

I would be less than candid and failing in my obligations to serve this company to the fullest extent of my abilities as advertising manager if I did not strongly advise that *no* national advertising campaign "be given a try for the first six months of next year."

National advertising, as pointed out in my original memorandum proposing its limited use in those markets we are agreed are most susceptible of profitable cultivation, is not and never will be a panacea for our sales problems. Of and by itself, national advertising cannot be expected to sell directly any real volume of our products. That is not its purpose, and to expect it to do so merely builds false hopes.

The primary purposes of national advertising are fourfold:

1. To help consumers as an aid to buying.
2. To influence more people to buy our product or use it more widely.
3. To prepare the way for sales by educating potential prospects on the merits of our product and removing obstacles to sales.
4. To encourage continued patronage by present and new customers.

None of these objectives can possibly be attained in the short period of six months' time. Continuous telling of our story over a much longer period of time is necessary before we might hope to begin to reap the benefits of our expenditures in national advertising.

Until such time as we are in agreement that national advertising is a daily, continuing part of our required activity to produce sales at a profit, until such time as we can agree on the wisdom of a capital investment in this form of business insurance over an initial period of several years, it would be fallacious to start a program possibly foredoomed to a brief six months' trial existence. Money spent in such a trial effort can more profitably be spent in other ways or not spent at all.

A Promotion Problem Solution

The association of lumber manufacturers, working closely with governmental housing agencies and leading building-materials concerns, prepared a series of plans and elevation sketches for eight low-priced homes costing between $1,750 and $3,400 to erect, exclusive of lots.

A series of direct-mail letters, newspaper electros, and publicity releases announcing the availability of these low-cost home plans were assembled in packet form and released to lumber and building materials dealers. Complete instructions were included explaining the market possibilities for homes in this price range and telling how the promotional material could be most effectively used. Dealers were urged to erect demonstration homes in their communities so that prospects could actually see and inspect the kind of home they could purchase for a relatively small sum of money.

Speakers featured the story of this activity and its profit possibilities for dealers at the annual lumber-dealer conventions. Effective publicity stories were published in the leading trade papers urging dealers to take advantage of this market opportunity.

The amount of money spent on this joint promotional effort was relatively small in comparison with the results achieved.

The Solution to a Public-relations Problem

The solution of this problem in employee and public relations became possible when the manufacturer realized that he had never taken the time to tell his employees and the public enough about the nature of his business to enable them to know why the periodic hiring and discharging of people twice a year was necessary.

He discovered, too, that a majority of those laid off naturally assumed they had been discharged because their work was unsatisfactory or because the boss had it in for them. Many of the permanent employees shared this point of view and were resentful and in sympathy with the discharged employees.

To correct this situation the manufacturer supplied all his employees with the facts, assured the competent that their work had been appreciated, and expressed the sincere hope of rehiring them as soon as increased business made this possible.

This, of course, did not obviate the serious fact that many were out of jobs, but it did change their attitude toward the company. Those dissatisfied with conditions as they were went elsewhere to seek more stable employment. They did so, however, because they understood the nature of this manufacturer's business and not because they held a grouch against the manufacturer.

As a result of this experience the manufacturer adopted the permanent policy of issuing bulletins at each plant, over the name of the plant superintendent, explaining the policies of the company. These bulletins were mailed to the workers' homes. Periodically, the manufacturer tells his people the company's attitude on labor, unionism, hours, wages, and other questions directly affecting the workers. An annual report is sent each employee, telling in A-B-C language what the company does with each dollar it receives; how much goes to stockholders, to wage earners, to executives, to reserves, to profits.

In those communities where the company's plants are located newspaper advertising is used to inform the public about the company's policies, particularly with regard to its attitude toward its employees.

The Solution to a Direct-mail Problem

You would be using poor business judgment if you followed the suggestion of the manufacturer's sales representative and issued a direct-mail campaign of four mailings, at ten-day intervals, to your 1,250 prospects.

Your four salesmen could not follow these mailings to so large a list of prospects soon enough to enable you to get maximum sales returns from your advertising expenditure.

A more logical and sensible controlled plan of gearing personal selling with promotional effort would be:

1. Divide your prospects into four groups by neighborhoods, one for each salesman.

482

2. Each Saturday send out fifty direct-mail pieces per salesman. On the following Monday or Tuesday each salesman calls on as many of these fifty prospects as is possible. On Tuesday evening a report is made on these calls and that same evening ten, twenty, or thirty more direct-mail letters are sent out per salesman.

3. Thursday and Saturday evenings this same procedure is repeated.

Thus a continuous direct-mail activity is carried on. Every recipient of a direct-mail piece receives a personal sales call within a few days after the receipt of a mailing piece. Careful sales records are kept and each salesman has an active list of prospects to work on every day.

The sales results obtained by the seller of the specialty product were far greater than if mailings had been made in one job lot at ten-day intervals and in such quantities that prompt personal sales calls, except on a minority of prospects, were physically impossible. This merchandiser recognized that, like good food, prospects are not much good when they have been allowed to cool off.

INDEX